SAGE was founded in 1965 by Sara Miller McCune to support
the dissemination of usable knowledge by publishing innovative
and high-quality research and teaching content. Today, we
publish over 900 journals, including those of more than 400
learned societies, more than 800 new books per year, and a
growing range of library products including archives, data, case
studies, reports, and video. SAGE remains majority-owned by
our founder, and after Sara's lifetime will become owned by
a charitable trust that secures our continued independence.

Los Angeles | London | New Delhi | Singapore | Washington DC | Melbourne

Praise for the Book

Coal is the main energy source for India. While it would undoubtedly have economic and environmental dimensions anywhere in the world, in India it has overarching political concerns due to the rent-seeking that goes with a virtual state monopoly on mining of coal. In his clinical style, Subhomoy Bhattacharjee gives a rounded view of the coal economy and the critical place that it enjoys in the energy security of India.

—**Ashok Chawla**
Chairman, The Energy and Resources Institute (TERI), and former Finance Secretary

Coal, often referred to as black gold or black diamond by some, is an important sector in a developing country such as India. There are so many issues related to the coal sector—energy issues, environmental issues, labour issues, social issues, economic issues, trade union issues and the issues around coal mafia.

Subhomoy, in his book *India's Coal Story*, has not only tried to flag the various issues but has also brought historical as well as recent perspectives to these issues. The history of coal is almost parallel to the history of India since the days of the British rule. The book is well researched, providing wonderful insights into the troughs and crests that the coal industry has undergone.

Coal not only has been a key mover in India's energy sector but also seems to have moved politics. There are various instances of this in the book. Having earlier worked in a coal-producing district in erstwhile Bihar (now Jharkhand), I can correlate my own experiences with what Subhomoy has presented succinctly in his book.

Over the nine chapters in the book, he has captured the vicissitudes in the emergence of the coal industry, with vivid description of the events that unfolded in the journey, bringing to the attention of the reader the facts and events, as well as the stories behind such facts and events.

On the whole, the book, I am sure, will attract not only economists but also historians, political commentators, industry onlookers and anyone who wants to know anything and everything about coal in India.

—**UK Sinha**
Chairman, Securities and Exchange Board of India

The convoluted evolution of India's energy policies is difficult to unravel, and this is particularly the case with respect to coal, which remains the primary source of power in the country. Subhomoy has done an admirable job in bringing alive the politics of coal in India, the main dramatis personae in its unfolding saga and the outlook for the future as the international energy environment undergoes significant changes, given the growing concerns over climate change. This is an extremely useful reference for all who may be interested in understanding how India will meet its daunting energy security challenge and the role coal will play in this regard.

—**Shyam Saran**
Former Foreign Secretary (served as Prime Minister's
Special Envoy for Climate Change)

INDIA'S
COAL
STORY

With compliments

Subhoy

INDIA'S COAL STORY

From Damodar to Zambezi

SUBHOMOY BHATTACHARJEE

Los Angeles | London | New Delhi
Singapore | Washington DC | Melbourne

First published in 2017 by

 SAGE Publications India Pvt Ltd
B1/I-1 Mohan Cooperative Industrial Area
Mathura Road, New Delhi 110 044, India
www.sagepub.in

SAGE Publications Inc
2455 Teller Road
Thousand Oaks, California 91320, USA

SAGE Publications Ltd
1 Oliver's Yard, 55 City Road
London EC1Y 1SP, United Kingdom

SAGE Publications Asia-Pacific Pte Ltd
3 Church Street
#10-04 Samsung Hub
Singapore 049483

Published by Vivek Mehra for SAGE Publications India Pvt Ltd, typeset in 10/12 pt Palatino by Zaza Eunice, Hosur, Tamil Nadu, India and printed at Saurabh Printers Pvt Ltd, Greater Noida.

Library of Congress Cataloging-in-Publication Data Available

ISBN: 978-93-864-4600-8 (PB)

SAGE Team: Rajesh Dey, Sandhya Gola, Syeda Aina Rahat Ali and Kapil Gulati

To my daughter Debolina, who'd much rather I had written a fiction

To my wife Neeta, who thinks I have

Thank you for choosing a SAGE product!
If you have any comment, observation or feedback,
I would like to personally hear from you.
Please write to me at **contactceo@sagepub.in**

Vivek Mehra, Managing Director and CEO, SAGE India.

Bulk Sales

SAGE India offers special discounts
for purchase of books in bulk.
We also make available special imprints
and excerpts from our books on demand.

For orders and enquiries, write to us at

Marketing Department
SAGE Publications India Pvt Ltd
B1/I-1, Mohan Cooperative Industrial Area
Mathura Road, Post Bag 7
New Delhi 110044, India

E-mail us at **marketing@sagepub.in**

Get to know more about SAGE

Be invited to SAGE events, get on our mailing list.
Write today to **marketing@sagepub.in**

This book is also available as an e-book.

Contents

Foreword

Coal has continued to fire the imagination of the country. It is vital to the energy needs of the nation. Mother India has enough and more coal in her bowels to meet the requirements of the nation. However, over the years, we have imported coal from all parts of the globe, and when the opportunity came to systematically exploit our own extractable reserves, we decided to have the government and people plunder the wealth for narrow personal gains rather than scientifically use it as fuel for captive power plants. The question that needs to be answered is this: Why can we not formulate a transparent, equitable and commercially viable policy to extract coal, which provides reasonable revenue to government and also permits power plants to generate power and earn normal profits? Attempts to extract coal have seen people and agencies try insidious means to gain undue profit from the policy. Thus, whether it is the person getting the coal mining block or the person in authority doling it out, both collude to deprive the state coffers. That has been the history of this non-renewable energy source of India.

Subhomoy Bhattacharjee has done intensive research to trace the history of our attempts to exploit this critical resource. The dependence on imports has in fact very severely dented our energy security. Yet, we do not seem to learn from past experiences. The author concludes that due to our avowed belief in the socialistic approach in the early post-Independence years, the nation appeared to place too much trust on our public sector enterprises. The nation continued to labour in the belief that energy security, whether it be from petroleum products, gas, coal or hydrocarbons, will be better served if we restrict their exploitation to state-owned enterprises. This philosophy does not appear to have worked out to the nation's advantage. Besides the usual inefficiencies of the public sector, it set up a paradigm which was opaque in addressing the activities of exploitation, pricing and allocation.

It was only when it was realised that the inadequacy of power was constricting the growth of the economy that the Narasimha Rao government decided to permit power generation to be undertaken in the private sector and to allocate coal blocks to ensure captive fuel linkage to plants that had been given licences for generating power. However, until the turn of the millennium, mining of indigenous coal was not lucrative. It was only when the international prices of coal turned buoyant that covetous eyes were cast on Indian coal mining blocks. This unleashed a whole pack of entrepreneurs with no genuine interest in power generation to start lobbying for allotment of coal blocks. The interest generated was from newspaper owners, garment dealers, truckers and so on. There was a willing dispensation in the government that was ever willing to oblige at the slightest persuasion. Despite policy decisions having been taken by the then prime minister, every trick in the political armoury was employed to ensure that a transparent allocation policy is not permitted to be operationalised. The dispensation was incapable of enforcing its will and lobbyists continued to corner coal blocks. There was a particular entrepreneur who was influential enough to get six coal blocks allotted to himself—all these to provide coal to only one power plant! Such was the extent of influence they could exercise and the limit to which the administration was willing to acquiesce that blocks continued to be allotted with no mining activity being undertaken in them. Those very people who had been mandated, in fact had taken an oath of allegiance to the Constitution to protect the interests of the nation, appeared to collude in its plunder. Was it a case of the fence eating the crop? The jury is out. The courts are engaged in establishing mens rea. We eagerly await the verdict.

The author has very vividly brought out the different turns and twists that played out in the allotment process. He has marshalled his facts well and succeeded in drawing attention to all that should not have been done. The attempt is wonderful as an alert media and a citizenry that seek more accountability from those in authority make it imperative that we are enlightened about the wrongdoings of those who represent us. Time has come when the citizenry will ensure that those in power play the game by the rules of the game—that the trust reposed by people in their representatives vindicates the faith of those people. India still has to go a long way in scripting its energy path. Unless we have the means to generate enough power, transmit it to the distribution agencies and have the power supplied at rates which are self-financing, the country will not be able to enthuse enough credible promoters to take up the challenge of setting up the required projects.

Subhomoy has done a tremendous job in collating facts and putting them together to weave a very credible and readable narrative. He needs to be complimented on the effort. I am sure the book will be an excellent contribution to the campaign for educating the public and thereby ensuring that people's vigilance on their government ensures good governance.

Vinod Rai
Chairman, Bank Boards Bureau, and
former Comptroller and Auditor General of India

Preface and Acknowledgements

Newsrooms are untidy places. No night's collection of news ever ends the way you plan for it from the morning—a new development or a new story sweeps away all of it. It is unusual then that from 2010 onwards, one theme kept recurring, infrequently at first and then almost every week: 'the business of coal'! It would not go away.

Every day, in my conversations with colleagues in the business bureaus of *The Financial Express* and later in *The Indian Express*, aspects of coal business would spring up, demanding attention. Frankly, I confess that I had not paid too much attention to it until then. Like most analysts, we agreed that the pressure points of India's energy business and policy lie in the oil fields. Until the coal story exploded! I found myself drawn to the study of the ramifications of this industry, supposedly nationalised yet with an omnibus reach among all industrial groups. It seemed to be a metaphor for plenty that was mismanaged in the Indian economy.

I realised that to provide justice to the theme, I needed the support of a library and the time and space to read up in detail. The generous offer for both at this juncture came from Professor Rajesh Chakrabarti, who was then the executive director at Bharti Institute of Public Policy (BIPP) at the Indian School of Business (ISB), Mohali. Rajesh has the fantastic ability to get a project off the ground, and he generously took over the responsibility to organise my floating ideas into a rigorous structure. The work on this book would not have progressed at all without the financial support he made available from BIPP, where I spent a remarkable number of weeks. In this connection, I must record the concomitant assurance provided by Pradeep Singh, deputy dean of ISB, Mohali, at every stage.

The work got even better with the amazing group of men and women BIPP had assembled under one roof during this period. Vikram Jain, now an entrepreneur in his own right, did the massive job of classifying my research data on coal; it finally shaped the nature of my investigation. Abhishek Das was my sounding board and a hard critic for my draft chapters, as well as a great ally. Mandar Kagade and Gaurav Dubey's enthusiasm for analysing all public policy issues from first principles was masterful. At each stage, Rinki Chopra was a pillar of strength in getting me support from ISB, and I can never thank her enough. Divya Nair took over many of those roles later.

A book of this sort demands long hours of interviews which must have tired my interlocutors as I went back to them repeatedly. The former chairman of Coal India, Partha Bhattacharya, was always keen to share his vast experience in the industry with me; so did Narsing Rao, now principal secretary to chief minister, Telangana, about his coal days. Subrata Chakrabarty, then executive director at Eastern Coalfields Limited (ECL), organised my visits to underground mines, which were powerful learning experiences. Tapas Kumar Lahiry, chairman of Bharat Coking Coal Limited, was a treasure trove of information on coal policies. Rajiv Ranjan Mishra, chairman of Western Coalfields Limited (WCL), filled me up on the challenges of coal mining in the politically charged Nagpur belt, as did U Kumar, former chairman of South Eastern Coalfields, and, of course, Suthirtha Bhattacharya, the present chairman of Coal India.

In Delhi and elsewhere, the successive coal secretaries were generous with their insights. Leading them will be Prakash Chandra Parakh, who formidably presented the lay of the land for me at his home in Secunderabad; so did Alok Perti, who analysed the threadbare audit reports that changed the Indian public policy so much, and his successor, Sanjay Srivastava. Anil Swarup brought me up to speed on how the sector and the ministry have changed since then. Lucid perspective on industry came from Anil Sardana, CEO and MD, Tata Power; Ujjwal Chatterjee, then chief operating officer of Tata Sponge; Sanjiv Goenka, chairman of RP–Sanjiv Goenka Group; Sajjan Jindal, chairman and MD of JSW Group; and, of course, Vinayak Chatterjee, co-founder and chairman of Feedback Infra Private Limited, who dissected India's infrastructure policies for me to understand. Others from the coal industry were Ashish Kumar, CEO, Jindal Africa, and Vishambhar Saran, chairman, Visa Steel.

Former coal minister Sriprakash Jaiswal, former environment minister Jairam Ramesh, current railway minister Suresh Prabhu and current power, coal and mines and renewable energy minister Piyush Goyal were happy to share their perspectives at short notices.

Valuable discussions took place with Vinayak Mavinkurve, group head, Project Finance, IDFC; Rajiv Behal, president director of PT Amiraj Energy Indonesia; and Ajay Dua, former industry secretary, with Bibek Debroy, member, Niti Aayog, who made possibly the most famous comment on the coal cases, and Vivek Bhardwaj, the nominated authority for coal auctions at the coal ministry. Nitin Zamre, managing director, and his deputy, Gurpreet Chugh, head—energy (ICF International), and from BCCL, the team of DC Jha, director (technical), BK Panda, director (personnel), and the deeply committed Dr Raju Evr, deputy GM (environment), took me to see from up close the dousing operations of a coal mine on fire.

From the industry chambers, Vikas Pandit, FICCI; Soma Banerjee, CII; Subhasri Chaudhuri, Coal Consumers Association, Kolkata; and SK Chowdhary, president, Indian Coal Forum, offered valuable insights. Arunabha Ghosh, CEO, Council on Energy, Environment and Water; Kaushik Ranjan Bandyopadhyay, associate professor, TERI University; Partha Mukhopadhyay, senior fellow, Centre for Policy Research; Rajiv Kumar, director, Pahle India Foundation; and Sachin Chaturvedi, director general, along with SK Mohanty, professor, RIS, offered me deep insights. On the same note, I must thank Shruti Sharma and Vibhuti Garg of the International Institute for Sustainable Development for their excellent insights. Deep Mukherjee, visiting faculty at IIM Kolkata; Atanu Chakraborty, director general, Hydrocarbons; and Ashok Lavasa, expenditure secretary, provided important contexts.

I owe a lot to the following people within media: Shishir Arya, *The Times of India*, and Vivek Deshpande, *The Indian Express*—both based in Nagpur; Priyadarshi Sidhantha, *The Indian Express*, Delhi; and Indronil Roychoudhury, *The Financial Express*, Kolkata, who is too modest about his abilities.

I thank Padmesh Gupta, CMD, Gupta Corporation; S Chandrasekhar, GM, Singareni Collieries Co. Ltd; Ashish Tayal, deputy manager, WCL; Abhijit Mallick, GM, ECL; and Tanmay Maitra, assistant vice president, Birla Corporation. Thanks are also due to a legion of volunteers in Dhanbad who, led by SH Tahseen Ahmad, principal of the Surya Deo Singh Smriti Gurukulam School, recounted the coal stories.

Creating space to write a book means offloading my share of work to willing colleagues and making the editors agree to it too. Ashok Kumar Bhattacharya, editorial director at *Business Standard*, was willing to give me the space to complete my manuscript for which I am so beholden; so did Shyamal Majumdar, who succeeded him as editor. It would have not been possible at all to get this book through without their good-humoured support.

On the publication front, Chandra Sekhar, formerly with SAGE, has been a bulwark of support, and so has been Joseph Mathai of ActionAid, friend and critic, who guided me through very difficult phases of writing the book.

I began with a Rajesh and I have to end with another Rajesh—Rajesh Dey, commissioning editor at SAGE. He has shown far more faith in this book than I would have myself. Thanks to his meticulous attention for detail and penchant for asking inconvenient questions. A big thanks to Sharmila Abraham and the team at SAGE, especially Sandhya Gola, for sticking to my eccentric demands with extremely good humour.

I count it as my rare privilege that Ashok Chawla, former chairman, Competition Commission of India; my mentor in a long journalistic journey, UK Sinha, chairman, SEBI; and Shyam Saran, former Foreign Secretary and now *Business Standard* columnist, agreed without any ado to endorse my manuscript. Each has put his stamp on India's key economic policies; I just hope this book has done justice to the faith they have shown in me.

Finally, the man who rewrote the face of coal economy and the role of probity in public policy in India, Vinod Rai—he not only graciously agreed to write the foreword for this book but also made it more than the sum of the chapters, adding his deep insights. Few individuals change a country's public policy as resolutely as he did. It needs immense belief in the country to make such a call; hopefully, this book was not as difficult for him to take a call on.

To my readers: I have retained the original spellings of names of places and people. Original documents would have read funny otherwise. Also, the first chapter 'Ole King Coal' is my condensed tour of the entire landscape of coal and mismatched energy politics of India. We walk into the mines thereafter.

1

Ole King Coal

Prelude

Water began rushing out from the Damodar River on the night of 13 July 1943, sweeping over the Grand Trunk Road within an hour. It soon breached the sole rail line connecting Bengal with Assam as the waters rapidly loosened the soil from under the rail tracks. Sir George Giffard, general officer commanding, Eastern Army in India, had just heard a week earlier that Subhas Chandra Bose had assumed the command of Azad Hind Fauj at Singapore. A combined attack on India's northeast by Bose's units and Japanese divisions was possibly just days away. Without the road and rail links to replenish supplies, the isolated Allied army units in the dense jungles around Kohima and Imphal would be butchered. Worse, the waters were pouring into the coal mines that ran parallel to the road and rail lines, cutting off supplies of fuel to run the trains. The monsoon rains were likely to prove fatal to the Allied war effort on the Eastern Front.

Giffard gave orders for mobilising every resource to tame the worst floods in the river seen in the last twenty years. A massive engineering effort was launched before the dawn broke. 'Tens of thousands of labourers', including women and even children forcibly drafted from the nearby Santhal tribes, were put on the job to get at least some of the mines back into action with the rail link restored. 'It was like the D-day operation' was how one of the eyewitnesses to the giant exercise described it. Despite everything that the British Army threw at it, Calcutta remained isolated from the rest of the country throughout July, while all communications between Giffard's headquarters and the Assam units remained suspended until the end of September 1943. Coal supplies from the inundated mines on the right flank of Damodar remained patchy throughout the year.

The risk of Damodar, India's 'river of sorrow', breaching the embankments had been raised several times since the last mega flood happened in 1913. Proposals were placed on the table of vice-roy's executive council in every decade to dam the river at several places to cut the risks to the coal mines and the rail lines. But as the costs were always going to be higher than the possible benefits, an expenditure-conscious colonial government shot those down. And then came the floods to stall the forward march of the Allied troop. The General Headquarters was infinitely lucky. The Japanese government too made no moves until the waters receded. Had they been aware of the logistical nightmare in the coalfields of Bengal the British were caught in, history would have altered!

India's coal reserves have always proved to be too hot to handle for its governments. It owns the fourth largest reserves in the world. It should have provided a first-class opportunity to keep the economy driving ahead at full speed; it has instead been its first-class curse.

Disasters, natural or man-made, have always been just a step away from the coal economy of India ever since large reserves of the mineral were discovered in the late eighteenth century in the area. Coal has etched a crazy motif on the Indian economy.

The devastating Damodar floods in the Second World War were just one mighty example of those myriad disasters. Indian governments, colonial or post-Independence, failed to make the connection between assuring themselves of a safe line of energy and securing a sizable growth rate for the economy. More often, unlike the natural ones, the disasters have been of political economy.

It has at times helped a motley crew to stake out a political career, but has otherwise made a mess of plenty of business reputations, and in the bargain starved the Indian people of an opportunity to tap into the potential riches despite being the owner of this vast energy resource.

Post Independence, the man-made disasters began with a zeal for a socialistic approach to keep the control of energy sources under the state power. Each government assumed that simply keeping control over production would cancel out the need to provide a transparent, rule-based access to those sources—not just coal but even oil and gas—to industries, private and public.

For seventy years after Independence, successive governments failed to set these rules. The neglect allowed industrial magnates to attempt to get close with the political powers of the day. Some succeeded, some failed.

The first of those episodes flared up within a year after Independence when the first industrial policy was being written; it resumed in the 1950s when the Congress government despite protests from the industry wrote in an explicit socialistic goal for the economy. The clash became intense in the 1970s in the course of the all-embracing drive for the nationalisation of coal and oil companies. Even as these policies failed to set transparent rules, they made the private sector learn how to game the system. As the political establishment refused to learn the right lessons from each episode, howbeit the private sector learned those, the risk of a bigger crisis became all too possible. It arrived through an audit report.

As these machinations continued, some larger questions on the country's energy challenges were left gaping open. Every Indian government was convinced that coal belonged to the past but never came up with any viable alternative to replace it with. Critical investments in the sector consequently suffered. The second Five-Year Plan formulated in 1956 mentioned that it makes no sense to carry coal across the country on coal-powered railways. Yet in 2016, coal is the largest freight revenue earner for the Indian Railways, eclipsing its total earnings from passenger traffic.

As the state repeatedly failed to develop the coal mines adequately to provide for the fuel needs of companies, Indian industry was gradually forced to look abroad to source coal on the banks of another river, this time in Africa, Zambezi in Mozambique to the deposits of Australia and Indonesia. It is possible that by 2018, every third tonne of coal used in India could come from across the seas. That creates a mighty challenge for the energy security of the nation.

For instance, most of the imports will be hauled on ships across the Indian Ocean. But which country will work as the policeman on these waters? Can an unfriendly island in the Ocean propped by a powerful country create an energy crisis for India? And does India have the ports with the deep draught necessary to berth the coal vessels?

Interlude

India's coal challenge mirrors similar questions the British wrestled with when they discovered oil in Persia in the early twentieth century and decided to build their navy on it. They were immediately forced to patrol the Atlantic to ensure peace for the British shipping. From there to the two World Wars, the subsequent Cold War, the search for energy security by the Asian Tigers and the bloody trail of coups and counter-coups through most of Africa and even the rise of militant Islam trace themselves to this energy put.

Coincidentally, it was the Somali pirates in 2008 that made the Indian political establishment aware of the same risk of unpatrolled sea lanes a hundred years later. As the US Fifth Fleet winded down its operations from the Indian Ocean moving to the Pacific theatre instead, New Delhi realised that it had a task on its hand. For the first time, the Indian Navy ventured into blue ocean patrol duty in 2011 to chase these pirates from out of the sea near Aden, an area through which most of India-bound coal ships were sailing from Africa. The scale of engagement in the Ocean since then to neutralise other and stronger threats has been mostly a response to the coal question.

The timeline of the history of India's energy politics can be almost neatly divided into two halves. The first half began when coal deposits were discovered by British geologists along the right bank of Damodar River in Bengal almost at the same time as similar discoveries were made elsewhere in Europe at the crack of the Industrial Revolution. It would be another fifty years when the mineral would begin to be heavily exploited in India and a lively flourishing history of entrepreneurship would grow up around Damodar and the river it fed its water to, the Hooghly near Calcutta, the second city of the British Empire.

The entrepreneurship was led by Dwarkanath Tagore, the grandfather of Rabindranath Tagore. The elder Tagore positioned himself neatly in the East Asian opium triangle that the British built. The opium was manufactured at Ghazipur in Uttar Pradesh, transported by Ganga to the ships from Calcutta from where it was shipped to China. The cargo was opium, the fuel was coal and Tagore ran the largest coal business in the country. It came asunder as the company fell through the crack of insufficient finance and interests of the adventurers in the East India Company who were keen to cut themselves a share of the lucrative trade. As the opium trade fizzled out, the demand for coal slumped.

Decades later, as the theatre turned to West Asia, interest in coal revived. In the late nineteenth century, Britain and Russia began a fight to control the oil wells of Asia, including Persia. The Indian colony of Britain stepped in to play a crucial supporting hand in this game. The viceroy of India, Lord Curzon, raced to build a pan-Indian network of railways to transport troops and supplies to the possible war fields of Asia. The railways needed coal to run and so begun the second phase of interest in India's energy game. British managing agencies Shaw Wallace, Andrew Yule and the Bird Brothers competed with erstwhile railway contractors from Gujarat such as Ramji Chawda in the rush for coal. The business exploded as a new industrial group from Bombay stepped into the cocktail. It was led by Sir Jamsetji Tata's son, Sir Dorabji Tata, with an extensive interest in the business of steel and consequently of coal to smelt that steel. The ones whom no one bothered about were the coal miners.

Those miners would, however, provide the impetus for the first industry and supply minister of India, Shyama Prasad Mookerjee, to write India's first industrial policy advocating state intervention in the mining of coal and oil. Although he was not a Congress man, he was backed up by Prime Minister Jawaharlal Nehru who was convinced that India's road to prosperity would be built by steel and the steel would be smelted by domestically sourced coal mined in government-run coal mines. Indian industrialists were too few and cowered at that stage to suggest anything else.

It was just one step short of takeover of the domestic industry by the government of independent India. India had chosen a model for its industrial growth which took it a long way away from the course of global energy politics of the past hundred years. Coal mining like that of oil will be progressively a government monopoly in the new order. The iron curtain was coming down on the Indian industrial sector and would remain fixated inward for the next sixty years because of the sharp suspicion the Indian political class harboured about the economic policies of the imperialist nations, especially their chase for energy security. Nandan Nilekani writes, 'India's energy strategy post 1947, was ... complicated by the Indian government linking energy independence with independence from foreign influence'. Yet the inward-looking policy could not keep India secure from the maelstrom of global energy headwinds.

The first of those arrived soon. One evening in 1954, in response to a particularly harsh Parliament debate, Finance Minister Chintaman Deshmukh and Nehru scribbled the word 'socialistic pattern of society' into the next industrial policy. The only sector where there was an easy entry for the implementation of this policy was coal. Financial centres of the world exploded in anger in response. The anger found support among the resurgent Indian industrial leaders too. The British and US energy companies, including Burmah Shell and Esso who were at that point exploring the possibility of tapping into Indian reserves of oil, were convinced that India's coal policy was a harbinger of expropriation ahead for them too. Egypt, under Nasser, had begun to nationalise its oil wells. Nehru's friendship with Nasser was the stuff of new world order.

A livid World Bank severely ticked off Deshmukh's successor TT Krishnamachari at the finance ministry. Nehru's second government which had meanwhile lined up mega industrial parks like Durgapur, on the banks of Damodar and at Rourkela in Orissa, got into a terrific jam. These parks were supposed to be based on use of coal as the source of energy and would be financed through foreign technology, the planners had estimated. But as the autarkic model of development was talked about derisively in the world financial capital, the investment promised by the Western nations ran dry. Finding itself in a mess, the Indian government reached out to the most trusted industrialist ally it had, Ghanshyam Das Birla, to sue for peace. The old industrial order took up the slack to re-establish its primacy in the political space.

It was however a temporary truce. It was watched closely by Nehru's chosen successor, his daughter Indira Gandhi! She also noticed that the same industry leaders from Bombay and Calcutta who fought against her father had cosied up with her bête noire Morarji Desai. She had found her reason to be distrustful of the private sector. The distrust provided the rationale for her political plans that veered to an extreme left of centre position. It was now just a matter of time when she would attempt to completely take over the energy sector.

The trigger was provided by the first energy shock of 1973. India had not anticipated the scale at which the oil crisis would impact the economy. Throughout the 1960s, it had let its coal reserves go dry due to lack of investments. As Prime Minister Indira Gandhi had found the perfect storm to nationalise coal and oil production in the country, she had cut them to size with the nationalisation of the banking sector, the soft energy sector was putty in her hands. The political environment to support the measures was created by her politically astute coal and industry minister Mohan

Kumaramangalam, whom Gandhi had snatched away from the communist camp a few years ago. The minister ran a high-decibel public campaign to make media aggressively support coal nationalisation. Later, the same template was used to takeover oil production from the American and British firms too. It was to be the last business of the fiery minister—he died in an air crash the day after the president signed the overarching coal nationalisation bill into a law.

The law pulled private sector out of the business of coal production but solved a few problems in its stead. Instead, a huge illegal market in coal sprang up on the banks of the Ganga at Varanasi. How this city of temples and *pandas* got into coal trade is amazing. It has a lot to do with geography. Varanasi is located on the obverse side of the coal-laden mountains across the Ganga. As the trucks with illegal consignments came down from the Mirzapur hills, the city lay tantalisingly close to do a roaring business. It also had a lot to do with transport. India's largest rail network of yards and junctions lie sprawled next to the city of Mughalsarai; it also had plenty to do with money. The holy city was populated with local financiers who could lubricate the trade in sale and purchase of illegal coal.

At a stroke, nationalisation of coal mines in India had reduced authorised coal trading companies like those of former Indian Davis Cup Captain Naresh Kumar into a suspect category. Coal could be sold legally in India only by three public sector coal companies. Just as it drove the strongmen employed by the private coal companies into the arms of the state-run companies as union leaders, truck operators or labour contractors, many of the erstwhile traders and owners of mines had to change the nomenclature of their business to become authorised coal handlers instead with interests in Varanasi. The trade also played the role of nursery in grooming political-mafia leaders. As the centre of gravity of the Indian economy moved southward in the 1990s, the heyday of Varanasi also came to an end to move towards Nagpur. The city had some of the same advantages that Varanasi provided, particularly that of extensive rail and road connections. A new class of politically connected entrepreneurs emerged from this city to create the biggest crisis in the Indian economy since 1991.

The lure of private trade in coal made inroads into the offices of the state-run coal companies too. A few chairmen of the eight subsidiaries of Coal India Limited (CIL) escaped the attraction. Until recently, among India's government-run companies, the highest number of corruption cases every year was registered by these companies. Coal was easy to mine, easy to transport and easier to pilfer from government records.

Just as the colonial government earlier had ignored the risks of flood in the Damodar River to almost ruin its war effort, after a twenty-year hiatus since Mrs Gandhi's nationalisation of coal, signs of fresh tensions began to flare up in the Indian energy sector. Of these, the most lacerating was the long hours of power outage each city was struggling with. Other than Mumbai whose electricity supply was run by the Tata Group and so was lit on most nights, all the metros faced blackouts of ten–fifteen hours as coal supplies ran dry. PV Narasimha Rao and his rookie Finance Minister Manmohan Singh began to hand out licences for setting up power plants to all and sundry. They soon realised, however, that there was no fuel to run those plants. CIL, the holding company for eight subsidiary coal mining firms could not produce more coal as it had piled up a huge debt, was badly hit by corruption and was barely able to pay its salaries.

It was the communist party-led chief minister of West Bengal, Jyoti Basu, who provided a way out to the Congress party-led government at the Centre at this juncture. The most respected political leader of the country at the time, Basu, asked Rao to give coal mines to private companies provided they used it to feed their own furnace—a partial roll back of nationalisation which only his support could ensure since the major coal unions were controlled by the communist parties. The company for whom Basu made the request was that of Ramaprasad Goenka. Four years earlier, Goenka had done Basu a favour buying out the state government's stake in Calcutta Electric Supply Corporation (CESC) that ran the business of power distribution in Calcutta.

Meanwhile, the World Bank stepped in to help CIL through its financial gridlock. The results were not entirely satisfactory. It was the first project of the Bank which was hauled up for shoddy implementation by its own auditors. The Bank had learnt a costly lesson. Still the shortages were somewhat relieved as some of the power plants came into production and coal supply improved.

With no lessons learnt from the episode, it was now time for the next crisis. It arrived when Deve Gowda became the prime minister in 1996, in a quirkiest choice ever for the seat in independent India. His support base within the business community was very narrow — he set about cultivating a new clutch of businessmen. One of them was Om Prakash Jindal, the leader of a new party in Haryana and who went on to become a minister in the state cabinet. His extended family picked up three of the mines. By the time these allotments were stopped in 2008, the Jindals had become the second largest coal miner in India. In the process, the floodgates for coal blocks were opened.

It was again serendipitous developments abroad in energy that provided the next trigger to mess up the Indian energy sector. With the ebb of the East Asian crisis, China began to ratchet up its demand for steel and coal, partly to build infrastructure for the Olympic Games it planned to host in 2008. New entrepreneurs in India saw the connection and began to apply for a coal mine or at the very least a wall of coal — a block.

India's coal policy or lack of it created the setting for the largest of the crisis to hit it, this time with massive political implications. By 2003, seven ministers had marched through the coal ministry with an average tenure of one year each on the seat. To expect continuity in this parade or any sense of direction was an absurd expectation. To expect crises in this setting was instead quite natural. It came!

The entrepreneurs who lined up to apply for coal mines had no experience in the business of mining of coal. This was hardly a dis- qualification as the country had expropriated all coal mines thirty years ago, so all the technical knowledge for running the business was confined to the government-run coal companies.

The eighth minister who came in to the coal ministry with a new government in New Delhi in 2004 made a very interesting choice. Due to compulsions of coalition politics, Prime Minister Manmohan Singh handed out the coal minister's position to Shibu Soren and appointed Dasari Narayan Rao as his deputy. Soren belonged to Jharkhand Mukti Morcha, a party located in the poor state of Jharkhand boasting of India's biggest mineral reserves, including coal.

The patriarch of the movement to create a separate state of Jharkhand had left his mark in New Delhi politics eleven years ago as the low water mark for probity in Indian democracy. In 1993, Prime Minister Narasimha Rao had faced a no-confidence motion in the Parliament. It was going to be a tough one to survive for Rao since his government was hanging together in a coalition tied up with all sorts of parties, including Soren's. The motion, however, fell with the slimmest ever difference. Rao's government survived with a 14-member lead over the opposition. Fortunately for the economy, it was an escape from another general election at that point. But unfortunately for Rao, three years later Soren and three of his party members accepted that they had been bribed to vote for the Congress government. Some of them had regaled and stunned the blasé Delhi circles when they arrived at a bank counter near the Parliament building to deposit the cash. The party was ambitious to capture power in the state; in the quest, money was important.

Eleven years later, as he walked in as the new coal minister, now in Manmohan Singh's government, S Soren began to hand out coal blocks by shovels often overruling his prime minister and a zealous coal secretary PC Parakh. The rush was intense. At one stage, the ministry received 1,422 applications for 38 blocks on offer.

Companies were willing to try any stratagem to get a piece of coal. Movie makers, bidi company owners, truck owners and garment dealers, all lined up outside Soren's office. Money and recommendations flew through the government, including even a forged one from the Prime Minister's Office (PMO). It became impossible to sort between those who applied through the correct procedure and those who were paying sleaze money. Thus, Aditya Birla Group's application for Talabira coal block which was a great example of rectitude faced enquiry from the Central Bureau of Investigation (CBI) as did those for nearly 200 other coal blocks. The enquiry in turn was kicked off by an audit report by the comptroller and auditor general (CAG) of India which laid bare the humungous possible loss to the economy from these methods of allocations. Some of those convictions have begun to roll in though only at the level of sessions' court, but one of those listed involves the possible indictment of Singh. The report has finally brought home for the politicians the risk of playing favourites in the domestic energy games.

The cases grabbed attention. But the bigger impact from the crisis was the creation of another acute energy shortage, enough to paralyze the economy even as the shenanigans continued. Coal nationalisation had only de jure shut out private sector from mining coal; most industrial groups in India had to de facto undertake coal mining since then.

Postlude

In his second cabinet reshuffle after he came to power at the Centre in 2014, Prime Minister Narendra Modi has made a striking change in the portfolios of his energy ministers. He had already clubbed the department of coal with power and renewable energy under his ebullient colleague Piyush Goyal; he has now added the Ministry of Mines to the same domain. It is quite on the cards that in another few months, the coal and mines ministries could be merged into a single entity.

Coal will possibly never figure as a cabinet ministry again, possibly not even as a separate one under a junior minister. Do these changes mean that India has gotten around treating its energy economy as an integrated value chain in the overall economy? It does seem so. For the first time in India since the first cabinet of Nehru, all the energy ministries are held by just two ministers. Even more, since neither Petroleum Minister Dharmendra Pradhan nor Goyal hold a cabinet rank, the overarching direction of India's energy policy finally rests with Modi.

The rearrangement of the ministerial pack does create heft for this government to shoulder the challenge of ensuring energy security, a job left unfinished by the previous United Progressive Alliance (UPA) team.

These challenges are principally three. The first of them is about land and its usage, the next is about environment and the last is the cross-country race primarily between China and India to procure fossil fuel reserves in other countries.

The challenge of land arrived for both private and government-run coal companies together, in the 1990s. New deposits of coal are to be found mostly inside forest areas. Exploiting those reserves means disturbing the lives of the resident tribal population on a vast scale. Else, the deposits are often under semi-urban areas such as Bengal and Jharkhand, which means that the mineral can only be extracted, if at all, through underground mining. This is an extremely costly process and has proven difficult for even the state-run CIL group of companies to undertake.

Things get more complicated from here. The UPA government muddied the scene in 2013 when it got the Right to Fair Compensation and Transparency in Land Acquisition, Rehabilitation and Resettlement Act cleared by the Parliament.

Once this act had come into force, the more-than-a-century-old Land Acquisition Act of 1894 got repealed. The 2013 act provides no wormhole to ease into the law under which coal mines were set up until recently. The new land act has made no provision to decide what would happen to land that is not required for mining any more. There is no retrospective provision in the 2013 act to deal with those.

The environment challenge is even more complex. The environmental lobby with presence from the forests of Madhya Pradesh and Chhattisgarh to as far afield as Australia painted the Indian coal companies into a corner. While their argument for closing the coal mines finds support with the current National Democratic Alliance (NDA) government in Delhi, the demands for growth offers little choice for the economy at this juncture. For instance, a special report on India issued in 2015 by International Energy Agency notes that despite the hoopla about renewable energy, fossil fuel will dominate making up 68 per cent of the supply until 2047, a year appropriately chosen since it is the centenary year for India's Independence. Of this, coal will account for more than a half.

As the demand from green activists to shut the coal mines increases, the sources to finance new coal mines from abroad are tapering off in sympathy. The world's largest pension funds will not fund this business any more, so CIL and private sector mining companies can only finance their businesses from within India.

This is a bad news for related sectors. The Indian Railways, for instance, plan to attract more freight traffic to reduce the carbon footprint of road traffic. Although no major national railway has managed to raise its share of goods traffic in the past fifteen years, it is a laudable aim. If sources of finance dry up from abroad, the railways plan can be upended. Also, renewable energy needs backup when there is no sun or wind—the upshot is that coal-based power plants cannot be mothballed soon.

Given all these constraints, India will have to continue to import large volumes of coal from Australia, Asian and African countries.

Those imports open up fresh challenges. On India's eastern coast, the imports are disorganised; on the western coast, they are large with massive environment costs. Coal transport in open wagons extract massive health costs on those living close to the tracks.

This has created a massive dilemma for the political establishment as it wrestles with the practical need to support coal exploration with the necessity to stake out a pro-carbon footprint.

Imports in turn are the harbinger of the country risk that energy issues so often bring out. India is now looking out abroad to scout for sources of energy. Indian companies had begun to make forays abroad to mine coal in bits and pieces but without any sovereign guarantees to back them up. As their demand for energy has shot up, their scale of investments abroad has also risen. It is now difficult for the Indian government to carry on with business as usual without offering political support. That support in turn is predicated upon shedding its reticence to rejoin the global energy race. This is a learning game which the political class is now beginning to figure out—energy security means abandoning micro managing of domestic sources but establishing strong geopolitical supremacy abroad. India now finds itself in a role that challenges its long held policy of abjuring a race for such supremacy which had seemed anathema to it at one stage. Yet intentions are not enough; if it has to police its supply lines from Africa to Australia, then it has to do plenty of things, including building up a navy and securing alliances with major naval powers, meanwhile. The new theatre where this drama is unfolding is the waters of the Indian Ocean just as it happened in the Atlantic in the twentieth century. The two mega rivals in the Ocean are China and India with immense demand for the dwindling sources of global energy. They are thus competing bitterly with each other.

As Ravi Velloor, associate editor, *The Straits Times*, writes, 'The developing India–US–Japan relationship is a game changer in this scenario because there is no knowing where it may lead; the last thing Beijing wants on its doorstep is an Asian version of NATO'.

If events cascade, a blockade could be disastrous for India. It could happen if China gets aggressive, using one of the puny islands of the Indian Ocean to mount such a blockade. So, it could be one for China if India were to raise its presence in the narrow Malacca Straits.

Along with climatic reasons, temperatures are thus also rising for political reasons in the Indian Ocean. The race to develop renewable energy as a substitute for coal is not exactly a peaceful process. As Adair Turner notes in one of his articles, just wind farms will gobble up 4 per cent of India's total area. Solar panels, even more. India will have to ring-fence sizable portions of the sea to avoid such land grab on shore. Yet stepping on to the sea has political ramifications as China has discovered to its cost. Its forays to Spratlys and Paracel Islands in the South China Sea are driven partly by the lure of their suspected mineral wealth, especially oil. As India pushes for a presence in the Indian Ocean, does it possesses the staying power to handle this new world order?

2

A Nation and Its Contradictions

Refugees and an Industrial Policy

The March weather in Delhi is full of contradictions. This year, the days had become warm too soon, much like the political temperature on the ground, Shyama Prasad Mookerjee reflected.

Far too many gut-wrenching events were doing a cameo on the national stage in March 1948. India was at war within itself and beyond. Another long summer was descending on the Indian subcontinent after the terribly stretched and harsh one of 1947. Millions of refugees were still pouring into the country from the two borders with Pakistan. There was a prolonged war in Kashmir against the Pakistan Army and tribal forces, which had begun in autumn, last year. It had now intensified, as the first spring flowers began to bloom in the valley. Strikes were being called repeatedly by the Communist Party of India (CPI), and the man whom everyone would automatically turn to in a crisis, Gandhi, was not around anymore.

The first industry and supplies minister of Independent India was also a bit lonely in Delhi. He was tasked with the writing of India's first economic policy document, an Industrial Policy Resolution, for the cabinet to approve. It was going to be an awfully significant document, setting the tone for how India would arrange its resources for the first time in its history of a few millenniums. The first priority of the paper would be to turn around the legacy of a 200-year colonial rule over the country that had ended just a few months ago. That colonial rule along with the two World Wars had left the economy in a dreadful condition which was too visible all around. To cap it all, there were no goalposts from before and hardly any from the contemporary world around to guide the exercise to suggest where to begin.

One of the things the minister noticed on arriving in Delhi was the difference in its skyline with Kolkata. In his hometown,

Mookerjee would sometimes espy the occasional chimneys of industrial units and the masts of cargo ships dotting the skyline, isolated signposts of trade and commerce. Delhi by contrast was a desert beyond the Lutyens Zone, hosting a vast sprawl of refugee tents growing bigger every day. Industry was a fantasy. India and China were two countries in Asia, saddled with a huge and wretchedly poor population depending mostly on the crumbs from agriculture, zilch infrastructure and a few economic models to go ahead with. The Marshall Plan for the defeated powers of Europe launched by the USA presupposed a population skilled in technology. It was hardly applicable to Asia, least of all India with an industrial worker base of less than 2 per cent of its workforce. The other model being imposed on Japan, again by the USA, was clearly built on economic and political sovereignty being exercised by Washington, DC. For India, having won a very costly battle for Independence, none of those was going to be acceptable. The Soviet Union had a model based on a five-year template more acceptable to the Indian political leaders, but for its success, it hinged on total state control of all factories. His cabinet colleague Bhim Rao Ambedkar at least had the French, US and Irish Constitutions to get ideas from in drafting the political constitution, Mookerjee reflected. He had to make it up on the way as he wrote the economic constitution for the nation.

Deputy Prime Minister Sardar Patel was seriously ill this March and so was Rajendra Prasad, the chairman of the Constituent Assembly. While Ambedkar was immersed in the writing of the Constitution, others were getting to grips with the running of administration of a huge country with 300 million people on a budget of less than ₹200 crore. The industry minister was not a member of the Congress party and that made a difference in his contacts with the others. The aftermath of the assassination of Gandhi had made the relations within the cabinet strained with the Hindu Mahasabha leader. Even though Mookerjee had vehemently denounced the assassination, the reclusive former vice chancellor of Calcutta University felt the bad vibes keenly.

In the cabinet formation, if Nehru had asked for his choice, then he would have preferred education, his lifelong vocation. It had instead gone to Maulana Abul Kalam Azad and he was asked to lead industry. Since then, his discussions with the prime minister had been few.

The mood at the prime minister's residence Teen Murti Bhawan was in any case downbeat. Nehru was supposedly upset since Edwina Mountbatten was to leave India by June when Lord Mountbatten would step down as the last British Viceroy in India. She was a visible presence on the verandah of the Bhawan during the long, hot summer months of last year as the tedious discussion on the partition of the country dragged on and on.

There was a domestic challenge too in the framing of the industrial policy. A long line of industry leaders had allied themselves with the freedom movement over the years. Ghanshayam Das Birla, Jamnalal Bajaj, Purushottam Thakurdas and Walchand Hirachand were some of the most prominent among them. They were the ones who ran a few industries such as steel, aluminium, power and cement and some banks with which India reached the goalpost of 1947. Post Independence, how would the lie of the land appear for the private sector companies?

The Congress party had thought a lot about it, and so had the industry leaders. In 1929, at the annual session of the Congress at Lahore, Nehru had steered the party to adopt the principle of socialism in its economic policies. The All India Congress Committee had then merely passed the resolution. Frank Moraes' biography of Nehru notes that the Congress members said yes, 'although Nehru confesses ruefully that most members probably did not realise what they were doing'. He and the Congress Socialist Group established in 1934 were moving towards a blueprint that made the businessmen pretty anxious. By the time, goaded by the group, Nehru addressed the Lucknow session of the Congress in 1936, the direction was clear: 'I hope that the logic of events will lead (Congress) to socialism for that seems to me the only remedy for India's ills'.

The next day, twenty-one industrial leaders published what they called a manifesto in *The Times of India*. Sir Cowasji Jehangir, Walchand Hirachand, AD Shroff and Purushottam Thakurdas expressed their concerns about what Congress had affirmed. They now realised that they needed to get deeply involved in the working of the Congress party to steer it towards a middle path. The pressure worked to some extent. When the National Planning Committee was set up in 1938 by the Congress to work out the post-Independence economic model, it had to include members from the Indian business. The most vocal among those who entered the Planning Committee from among the business leaders was Thakurdas. He was more than just a Bombay-based business-man. He had a great ability to build business associations—the Federation of Indian Chamber of Trade and Commerce, FICCI, the Indian chapter of International Chamber of Commerce and so on. He was there as a member in a number of public committees and on negotiating tables.

Thakurdas was clear why business needed to ally with the politicians. 'We (businessmen) can no more separate our politics from our economics than make the Sun and the Moon stand still'.

Despite the presence of business leaders, however, it set the direction the economy would take. 'While free enterprise was not ruled out as such, its scope was severely restricted' (sic), the objective resolution of the Committee noted. The National Planning Committee went defunct as the Second World War intervened; Congress leaders including Nehru were in jail.

Before it could again reconvene to produce a report in 1948, Indian industrialists had taken the initiative in the interim. Eight of them along with Birla, JRD Tata, Thakurdas and Lala Shriram produced a 'Brief Memorandum Outlining a Plan for Economic Development for India' in 1945. Viceroy Wavell called it the Birla Plan but soon it earned the more famous sobriquet, the Bombay Plan.

The Plan was the most curious document produced in Indian economic history. One of the papers on it describes it as living 'a curious, almost spooky, existence. Books on Indian planning men-tion it as a mythical forerunner without revealing any more detail'. It was, however, a practical document. The Bombay Plan clearly asked for economic planning. Every 'aspect of economic life will have to be so rigorously controlled by government'.

The crucial difference was that it wanted private sector to be there in every field even as the state was to get busy with huge invest-ments for the development of the core sector. In the early years, the private sector was to spread itself mostly for the production of consumer goods such as textiles, leather goods, oil, glass, paper and tobacco. 'The suggestion was that while in later years private supply would increase in response to demand, (till then) they there-fore suggested curb on consumption with some form of rationing'.

Coming from business leaders, it was as 'leftist' as possible. It would remove the need for the state for outright appropriation of their mills.

Birla and Tata were clear why they had written the Plan. In the minutes for the Plan, one of the authors John Mathai, soon to be Independent India's finance minister, noted:

> The government might take populist economic measures in a hurry after the war. Such measures were all the more likely if the government faced organised political demands for redistribution of income and wealth. These measures would harm the prospects of long run economic development of India. This possibility however could be avoided by proceeding in an orderly and more caring path of development before such a contingency arises.

It was enough for CPI to see 'red'. They termed the Bombay Plan 'as a blueprint for building capitalism with the aid of the state'. The Congress party was embarrassed and clearly wanted to steer away from a Plan that seemingly brought them close to the business interests, never mind even if the advice was sound. As it is, Birla's closeness to Gandhi was something the party was never clear how to handle.

The Plan was thus a still born. Tarlok Singh, Nehru's first private secretary as the prime minister and one of the first officers to join the Planning Commission at its birth, made the first reference to the role of the Bombay Plan after he retired from the government in 1963.

So, as soon as the Indian Independence Act was read out in the British Parliament, the fault lines in government industry relations were stirred again. The need for a State-led development agenda was clear. What was not clear was the role of the private sector in the schemata. Would there be a large-scale takeover of industry?

The Congress leadership exhausted by the two-pronged fight with the British government and the Muslim League was not keen to take on another fight, though the Muslim League members in the Constituent Assembly, till they were there, kept on nettling the Congress for their supposed proximity to the business leaders.

At the other end, support for the Plan was divided, even within the industry. FICCI refused to finance the cost of producing the document, even though its members feared a rise in support for nationalisation. Sir Padampat Singhania, speaking on their behalf, thought that the Plan had offered a chance to the British to prolong their involvement with the management of the Indian economy. Singhania, part of the JK Group, had a love–hate relationship with the British—he got a knighthood from them but later became a member of the Constituent Assembly.

Some of the authors had meanwhile got drafted into the Congress economic management team. They became cold to the aims of the plan. Other than Mathai, JD Shroff went as a part of the Indian team to the Bretton Woods Conference, and Ardeshir Dalal was appointed for a short term as member of planning and development department in New Delhi.

The other authors, mainly Birla and Tata, got canny in the political climate. It was necessary for them to speak with the same vocabulary the Congress party leaders used in talking to the public. Birla, for instance, supported the partition of Bengal at a meeting held in the Chamber of Commerce in Calcutta in April 1947, virtually second-guessing Mookerjee when the political leader was ploughing a lonely furrow, seeking partition of the province.

Nehru was clearly in favour of nationalisation. The report of the Congress party's Economic Programme Committee released in 1948 was clear on it. Nehru had chaired the committee and even when a private members bill in the Constituent Assembly demanded 'socialisation', he turned it down saying that it was not the right moment.

Yet the business as usual model would also be suicidal for the biggest post-colonial transformation story about to begin in the world. All things considered, the cabinet would have pushed for adopting an industrial policy for more settled times. Nehru, however, would not have it. A nation planning to lead Asia needed to spell out its economic doctrine too, he felt.

He had startled them with that bit some months earlier. The first budget speech for free India read by Finance Minister RK Shanmukham Chetty was modest and dour in every other respect as the members of the Constituent Assembly sat through listening restlessly on a warm September evening. Until he came to the conclusion! It was obvious who had written the stirring section when Chetty began to read it aloud. 'If India, just risen from bondage, is to realise her destiny as the leader of Asia and take her place in the front rank of free nations, she would require all the disciplined effort her sons can put forth in the years immediately ahead'. Nehru's signature was all over it.

In this disordered atmosphere like other right-wingers, Mookerjee had not referred to the Bombay Plan; he was to soon make his preferences clear. The man with whom Mookerjee often conferred was his secretary in the ministry, Yashwant Narayan Sukthankar. At one stage, early in his career, Sukthankar was a close friend of another ICS officer who resigned to join the freedom movement, Subhas Chandra Bose. There was consequently a lot of common history the minister and his secretary would rewind through the afternoons as the fans whirred overhead. There was another man in the ministry whom the former vice chancellor would draw close. It was Sushil Kumar Sinha, a retired ICS officer, drafted in by Mookerjee as the coal commissioner. Sinha was the son of Lord Satyendra Prassano Sinha, the only Indian to be promoted to the House of Lords. Chat with these men and his sharp-at-9 AM coffee were the few delights of this town where none of the sweet shops could replicate the magic of *makha sandesh* of Kolkata. For Mookerjee, uninitiated to the ways of the central government bureaucracy, Sukthankar, who was soon to become cabinet secretary, was a deft support. He helped the minister deal with a confidential letter from Nehru about too many Bengalis roaming in the industry and supplies ministry. Mookerjee in a nicely crafted bureaucratese note moved the complaint to a more theoretical level, arguing that the complaint was about the supposed 'unsatisfactory performance' of his ministry. He only mentioned that it was 'amazingly incorrect' to claim that his eight heads of departments were Bengalis. Neither the secretary nor the two joint secretaries were Bengali. There were only two Bengalis including Sinha in the top ranks.

With the team in the industry and supplies ministry, discussions veered to the absence of any visible signs of industry around Delhi and the larger issue of disquiet among domestic industry leaders about the shift noticeable in the government of India's policy towards them. 'The British have gone and the princes and the zamindars are in the background. The Congress accustomed to a target for its hatred, is now finding only one target, that is the capitalist', Birla acerbically wrote to Govind Ballabh Pant in 1948. The note was forwarded to Mookerjee.

Although Mookerjee had never dabbled in this subject before, the hardening of divisions in the industrial story between the Congress and the businessmen had become clear to the professor.

The one area where there was no debate was that of energy economics. It was puzzling, but a few within the political class thought about it. Yet the Second World War had starkly demonstrated the role of oil and coal in securing a country's economic and political security. Erwin Rommel's Afrika Korps were finally thrashed by Bernard Montgomery's Eighth Army by sealing off their supply of oil. What lessons did these hold for India?

Faced with these contradictions, Mookerjee decided that he would settle for a very practical compromise in the Industrial Policy Resolution the cabinet would adopt on 6 April 1948. The language used for it was also simple. To understand it better, imagine it as a four-drawer cupboard where the minister was classifying the industries. The top drawer was to include industries the government would reserve only for itself. They would be ambitious ones but would not scare the industrialists about the future for their businesses in India, since they were projects for the future. In the list of industries in the top drawer exclusively reserved for the Centre came the manufactures of arms—something India was about to forswear off. The others were the railways. Few outside the government and even within it believed that the mention of the atomic sector in the same drawer meant really anything more than a wish list, even though Hiroshima and Nagasaki had made it amply clear what an atom bomb could do.

Mookerjee now turned his attention to the second drawer. It was in this drawer where the hopes and aspirations of millions of citizens of a newly minted independent country had to be reconciled with the current industrial reality—the reality that the few industrial units that India had were all in the private sector. He came up with a brilliant option. He put six of these industries in the second drawer. From then, it would only be the central and state governments that would build a new capacity in these industries. And then, he came to the most important para that factory owners wanted to hear.

> Government have decided to let *existing* undertakings in these fields develop for a period of ten years, during which they will be allowed all facilities for efficient working and reasonable expansion. At the end of this period, the whole matter will be reviewed ... (And if any company needs a takeover) the fundamental rights guaranteed by the Constitution will be observed and compensation will be awarded on a fair and equitable basis. (sic)

The bottom line was clear—the government would not expropriate industries.

The first among those six industries were iron and steel. The Indian industrialisation aspirations revolved around this sector; it united politicians tilting to the left or to the right. Just as the UK and the USA had bet on energy, especially oil, in the twentieth century to drive their industrial complex, steel was the catchword for the emerging economies. Energy was imperial; steel was communist. Members of the Congress had closely watched Soviet Union's experience with iron and steel where it was positioned as the route out of unemployment and its attendant mass poverty. There was something magical about tens of thousands of workers converged around the Bessemer blast furnaces in huge industrial sheds that made the whole operations seem like a leaf from the heaven of worker utopia. Energy economics which was clearly the driving force of the Second World War was, on the other hand, seen to be filthy. On this, the whole political class was united.

In future, according to the Mookerjee formula, it is only the Government of India which would set up new iron and steel plants. The ones being run by JRD Tata will be retained by him. Mookerjee had managed to carefully skirt around the thorny question of the relationship between industry and the Nehru government. The other industries placed in the second drawer included telecom and telegraph. So was shipbuilding and aircraft manufacture. India did not even have much of an Air Force to speak of and only two baby airlines. The Air Force unit was in fact so puny that the government committees deciding on partition of properties between India and Pakistan had decided to omit it from the list.

This classification ran a risk of being seen as too pro-industry and timid. Mookerjee and Nehru knew that to break that impression, they needed to demonstrate one sector where there will be seismic changes. The changes had to capture the imagination of the people as the economic manifesto for a post-Independence India.

The sector which lent itself to such a radical transformation was the energy sector. Both coal and its mineral brother oil were put in the second drawer by Mookerjee as part of the larger energy strategy of the government. In a smart move, he added a sub-clause with the entry on coal in the Industrial Policy Resolution. It was the only sector for which he added a clause. That clause read, 'the India Coalfields Committee's proposals will be generally followed'.

The report Mookerjee alluded to was a unique report written by a promising Cambridge University alumnus for the Government of India. Kailash Chandra Mahindra had filed the report a year before Independence, in 1946. There was a reason why a non-ICS man was given the job of writing the Indian Coalfields report. Conditions in the coal mining sector had deteriorated sharply, especially during the Second World War. But the sector dominated by the British managing agencies had deep connections within the government, so deep that independent assessments were impossible to carry out. Mahindra had an advantage. He was not involved in a business of coal mining, which made him a rare breed. Since he had already served briefly with the government as the head of the Indian Purchasing Mission in the USA during the war years, he knew how government committees worked. He was picked up for the job by the interim chairman of the Constituent Assembly Sachchidananda Sinha. As the editor of *The Indian Nation* and *The Hindustan Review* in the 1930s, Sinha had once drafted in Mahindra to write for these newspapers. The write-ups had impressed Sinha enough to recommend the young man to Sir Rajendranath Mookerjee, founder of the Indian Iron and Steel Company, for a job and then for a role as the chief of the Coalfields Committee.

After a survey of the existing coal mines, Mahindra recommended that the government should progressively bring them under its control. The only mines which were adequately capitalised and could survive on their own were those run by the Indian Iron and Steel Company and by Tata Steel, he concluded.

Here was an outside expert suggesting to the new industry minister that the government should take over the strategic heights of the sector. There had been a long line of studies by the government on coal, but what drew Mookerjee to the report was its original conclusion—it clearly asked for nationalisation of the coal mines. It was the only template available for dealing with India's energy needs.

Mahindra surprisingly never touched coal again in his professional life. Within a year after writing the report, he made his way to Mumbai to set up the Mahindra Group. He went on to form a joint venture to buy a patent on the popular Willys Jeep for Indian markets. His partner turned out to be an illustrious man, Malik Ghulam Mohammed. Mahindra had met Mohammed in the government corridors in Delhi. Within a year, Mohammed quit the venture to become the first finance minister in the Pakistan government.

Mookerjee could now let the industry leaders breathe freely and yet offer a forward-looking agenda for India's industrialisation. Energy economics did not rank as a key area for possible investment by the Indian industry leaders. Both coal and oil were largely managed by foreign capital. There was consequently no eminent industrial leader in the coal sector to create strong opposition to this plan for outright nationalisation.

Instead, since the treatment of workers in coal mines had been particularly shabby, there was enthusiasm for the change. All the political parties were keen to take up the cause of the workers. CPI had already made deep inroads into those pits of discontent. In the elections for the Constituent Assembly in 1946, the Congress had got a scare. In Raniganj constituency in West Bengal, one of the communist leaders Indrajit Gupta ran a stiff campaign against Congress candidate Deben Sen before he was defeated. More than a century ago, Raniganj was one of the first places in India where the British geologists had struck coal.

The communist inroad in the coal mines was at the expense of the Congress. Even though Congress had the first mover advantage in the coal mines when it worked for political wakening among the workers in the 1920s, it had subsequently forgotten to take their cause forward. The Congress's interest in the coal miners was sparked after Nehru visited the coal mines in Derbyshire, England. The haggard faces of the coal miners and the way they were repeatedly convicted 'on trivial offenses' under the prevailing emergency regulations, as he put it, made him angry. In 1928, when leaders of the Indian coal miners invited him to attend a meeting of their recently launched Trade Union Congress, he promptly agreed. Other Congress leaders also made a beeline for the sector to expand their base. The first of them was Subhas Chandra Bose, Nehru's bête noire, who had already become the president of the Tata Workers' Union at Jamshedpur. The Trade Union Congress made Nehru their president next year. He was pleased, but the Congress forgot the miners thereafter. The All India Trade Union Congress (AITUC) became an arm of CPI.

By walking the path of nationalisation of the mines, the Congress thought it could wrest back the initiative in the coal sector. Within months of framing the Industrial Policy of 1948, Mookerjee came to the Parliament with the Coal Mine Workers Provident Fund and Pension Bill. This bill became a template for workers in other sectors.

The political class watched the energy sector, especially coal, from the prism of the workers. Consequently, Mookerjee was happy to staple coal mining with five other sectors as those where it will be the government which will hold the stirrups. Private sector would be progressively asked to disengage from coal.

Eventually, however, he stopped short of expropriation of existing mines. The global race for securing energy supplies had turned to Asia. Oil rigs were coming up in not only the Middle East but also East Asia. India was an attractive destination for the energy companies as a site for exploration. He knew that despite the lack of towering industrial leaders, the sector was very visible to investors within India and abroad. For the Indian government to start off on a new economic policy capped by seizure of coal mines was not going to sit well with its well-wishers abroad. Instead, it would be seen as a bellwether of how the government would behave with private industry in future.

Days after the cabinet approval, Mookerjee spoke at the annual general meeting of the Eastern India Chamber of Commerce at Calcutta's Grand Hotel. A year before he had used the same platform to argue for partition. This time he told the businessmen of his ideas for the new nation. The era of windfall profit was over, he said. Instead, they would have to keep pace with the times. He assured them that there would be no expropriation, but they would have to find ways to assimilate the needs of the labour.

How prescient this move was became evident in 1956 when the central government decided to break this covenant and press for outright nationalisation of coal. GD Birla, as much a Congressman as an industry leader, was at a lunch hosted by JRD Tata in February 1956 at the height of that debate. 'The feelings of apprehension were quite apparent and (my) attempt to inject some optimism apparently entirely failed', wrote Birla to the then finance minister, TT Krishnamachari.

In those tumultuous years though, these were not the questions agitating the members of the first Indian cabinet. Within less than two years, Mookerjee resigned from the union cabinet in protest against the Nehru–Liaquat Ali pact. The pact was about the treatment of minorities in India and Pakistan. Coal could wait. It had already run up a history of entrepreneurship of 150 years and a few more years would not hurt.

It is worth retracing at this point how coal entered the Indian economic life and became so important in its history. And to do that, there is no better place than a walk along the banks of the Damodar River, the same area which almost wrecked the British war effort at one point.

Opium War and Coal

On the bank of the Damodar River just where it touches Raniganj in West Bengal is a wall, obviously the remnants of a very old building.

The wall is to Indian coal what Drake Well is to oil in the USA. India's first battle on coal policies was fought around here. Geologically, this is a freak zone. Coal mines anywhere in the world offer their best product at the lowest seam. The Raniganj–Jharia belt is the only place in the world where the best-quality coking coal is available virtually at the surface.

The Damodar River makes it easier to locate the mines as it tosses and turns with its load of monsoon waters which cuts open fresh deposits for exploration. The wall at Narayan Kuri is the remains of the first large-scale colliery set up in India in 1837. The entrepreneur was Prince Dwarkanath Tagore, Rabindranath Tagore's grandfather.

Once the East India Company had established itself as the ruling power in Bengal by the late eighteenth century, British steam ships began to call at the Calcutta port in larger numbers. Coal was the base of the industrial revolution. UK had massive high-quality deposits, but it was going to cost too much for the steamships to transport them to India and beyond. Wherever the agents of the East India Company went in Asia, they explored for coal. Almost the first job the Geological Society of London landed with after it was established in 1807 was offered to them by Lord Minto, the governor general of India, to investigate the Raniganj coalfields. India had a rich vein of deposits just under the surface in Bengal and Bihar.

The frequency of steamships calling at the Calcutta port complex had increased for another type of trade the company found very profitable to deal in. It was opium. The British had established a

huge opium industry at Ghazipur in Uttar Pradesh. Large consignments from the factory were being transported by ships on
the Ganga to Calcutta and from there by larger seagoing vessels
to China and other Asian countries. All these ships needed coal.

Coal deposits were found in Sylhet hills in Bangladesh, in
Palamau in undivided Bihar and in Central India. Prospectors
branched out to the dense forests in the Bengal–Bihar border,
moving along Damodar River to stake a claim for a good property.
The Raniganj–Asansol region especially became a favourite for
exploration very soon. Lots of adventurers began to pop up in the
river banks of Bengal, often charming and often creating murder-
ous relations with the local Bengali and the local tribal population,
the Santhals.

The most popular among these adventurers was Guru Jones. It
was a peculiar sobriquet to earn for an Englishman 200 years ago.
But that is what happened in 1812 when Rupert William Jones, a
retired mining engineer, bought the patta for a mine in the area
from the estate of Rani of Burdwan. He found the Indian mines
that were opening up were extremely primitive in their method of
production. None of the technological innovations for safety being
introduced in the English mines was in vogue in the Bengal mines.
Jones became a popular figure among the miners as he went about
introducing some of them in India. He was the first to sink shafts in
the mines. He followed it up by introducing the newly developed
steam engines to pump out water from the pits. The shafts made
it safer to go down longer distance into the mines. The employment of the steam pumping helped Jones to overcome one of the
critical problems of pit coal mining, endearing him to the miners
who bestowed on him the title of Guru.

While these developments were taking place in the coal country,
in the British capital city of Calcutta there was a revival of interest
in business among Indian men of wealth. Some of the landowners
were willing to take risks with their money. Prince Dwarkanath
Tagore personified the new sense of confidence among them.
Already a wealthy man having dabbled in several ventures including setting up Union Bank of India, he had picked up a useful
habit of cultivating the society of Englishmen who came to Calcutta
on assignments. He would invite them to dinners or for soirees
at his home. It helped that he was fluent in English and served
English food at his dos. Dwarkanath kept his distance from the

carnival-like atmosphere maintained by the babus of the city with incessant rounds of drinks, dance girls and durbars. He was seen to be a genteel man whose sense of etiquette impressed the colonial masters. The news of the discoveries of the coal mines soon reached him at one of those soirees. By 1836, the East India Company had appointed a Committee for the 'Investigations of the Coal and Mineral Resources of India'. One of the members of the company Henry Barclay Henderson later took charge of the coal department in Tagore's company. Armed with the information, Dwarkanath bought interests in a set of coal mines in Raniganj the next year.

Tagore's holding company was formed with another Englishman William Carr. To keep the imperial government pleased, he had also taken the precaution of naming the joint stock company with the Englishman's name at the lead, Carr–Tagore and Company. He did this despite being the larger shareholder in the venture. This company in turn floated the Bengal Coal Company to mine coal for the ships at a cost of ₹70,000. The business soon became a profitable venture, demonstrating his keen sense of timing.

The mines that Tagore bought were those where Guru Jones had established those best practices. Jones had also managed to train the local workers, the Santhals, to use crowbars to chip away at the coal faces diligently. By 1836, Carr–Tagore had won the mining rights to begin their operations. By June of the same year, the Marine Board of the East India Company, which regulated the plying of all ships on Ganga including the opium boats, had put up an advertisement for a tender to supply coal for three years to the government.

Tagore applied for and won the award. It was helped as one of the members of the Board, HM Parker, again happened to be a friend of Dwarkanath. The company now needed a tough agent to run those mines. The man Dwarkanath discovered to replace Guru Jones was an English prospector, CB Taylor. Taylor was one of those numerous Englishmen who had set out to strike coal in the hills of Bengal and Bihar. But unlike Jones, the years of tramping about in the dense jungles of Burdwan was unsuccessful for Taylor. He was at least lucky to come out alive. Several perished from malaria, snakebites or simply to the combined ravages of fever, dysentery and heat.

Once Taylor joined the company, he stood like a bulwark guarding the interests of Carr–Tagore at a salary of ₹300 per month. From

Calcutta right up to Allahabad, the company began to establish coal depots on the river systems. This became necessary as the opium boats on the river could not be built large enough to store both freight and coal for the full journey and had to often refuel. The coal depots were the refuelling stops for the boats as they made their journey to and from Calcutta to Ghazipur. To send coal to the depots, the company had to navigate the tributaries of Ganga using its own flotilla of boats. Those in turn needed intermediate stops, and to keep them moving on time, a system of marshals had to be set up to keep the transport logistics working. At its peak, Carr–Tagore and its rivals ran twelve major coal depots across Bengal, Bihar and Uttar Pradesh, employing a fleet of 1,500 boats.

It was a complex coal-based industrial operation that Carr–Tagore managed from Jorasanko in Calcutta. Decades before that house became the hub of Indian literary renaissance under Dwarkanath Tagore's grandchildren, it had made its name as the seat of the nascent capitalist empire.

The Burdwan coal as the Raniganj product was known had to initially compete with the superior English coal. Government records from those times are filled with complaints about the quality of the domestic coal and consequent court cases for damages. The difference in quality had a straightforward reason. Dwarkanath's coal remained exposed at the pitheads and depots for months; the imported coal went from the ships straight into the furnaces. The problem of transporting coal, it seems, has been a recurring problem in Indian history.

There were other challenges too, chief among which was keeping the competition down. As soon as Tagore won the contract for fuelling government steamships, other mine owners rushed in. The company responded through a simultaneous policy of buying out the weaker ones among them and denying access to the jetties on the river to others. One of those rivals it bought out held a mine just a mile down the Damodar River from Raniganj, known as Naraincoory. This is the wall visible today from the river near the present-day town of Raniganj, but now spelt slightly differently as Narainkuri. The owner Jeremiah Homfray remained a bitter rival until Carr–Tagore ran him aground and bought his mine from the bankers to the enterprise in 1843.

In the struggle for supremacy in the coal trade, none of the firms was squeamish about the means they employed. Obviously,

Carr–Tagore, being far bigger than its rivals, had deeper resources to deploy. Snatching labourers, blocking access to the river jetties and court battles were regular phenomena that kept Taylor engaged. For instance, in a stand-off with another firm upstream from Raniganj, Taylor used toughies to sort out the claims. In the courts, the contestants used forged documents, coached witnesses and offered bribes to swing the cases. When quite a few cases went against them, the company began to suspect if a particular judge had been 'counselled'!

Carr–Tagore was clear that they had to retain monopoly rights over coal mining business in eastern India. A letter sent from Calcutta to a local attorney Woomesh Chunder Roy stated it bluntly: 'Our object is to secure all the lines of ghats for ten to twelve miles below Naraincoory to prevent parties in the interior from getting their coals shipped out there'. Until about 1850, the company controlled the production of nearly 70 per cent of coal in the country. This sort of dominance was not rivalled until 1975 when the government of Independent India nationalised production of coal.

Carr–Tagore maintained its primacy through a strict system of monitoring every aspect of production and dispatch of coal from its headquarters. Dwarkanath used his personal rapport with the East India Company to maintain this supremacy. Using the same line of reasoning of free trade that the British government was using in China to claim that the opium route should be kept open, Tagore remonstrated with the government at Calcutta whenever his interests were sought to be curtailed. He also argued about the need for the government to support the development of more mines in India for helping the economy to grow.

As the spectre of the opium war intensified, Governor General Lord Auckland worked hard to open another line of coal supply from Sylhet fields in undivided Assam to keep Tagore at bay. The Indian prince proved himself sharp. When he heard of the rumour, he wrote to Auckland pointing out the employment opportunities his firm had created, the entrepreneurship he and his board had spawned and the fact that coal from his fields were the cheapest among all competing sources. The government had to capitulate assuring him that they indeed wanted the cheapest coal and ended up scotching the rumour.

One of the alternatives Auckland tried next was to import coal in larger quantities from England. Tagore forestalled him here too by buying the coal on the high seas from the importers. The East India Company was consequently forced to compete with Carr–Tagore to buy coal from the shippers driving up prices even further. Since the China-bound ships needed more coal than the Burdwan fields could supply, the shortage was a splendid opportunity for Carr–Tagore to make handsome profit. One of the shareholders in the company Rustomjee Cowasjee reportedly had thirty-nine ships of which at least two were armed enough to fight the Chinese war junks in the wars. These ships transported opium to China via Macao.

The end of the two opium wars and the death of Tagore in the interregnum in 1853 forever changed the dynamics of the sector. The pre-eminence of the river route from Ghazipur to Calcutta was over and with it that of the majestic government-run steam-boats plying on them. While Bengal Coal Company continued to operate, its drive to retain a monopoly position driven by Tagore was also over. The coal sector had lost much of its build-up as the opium-based ship movement began to flag. Several of the coal entrepreneurs began to shift to the next emerging product, that of the cultivation of indigo.

The business of coal mining became scattered as rivals poached the employees of Bengal Coal Company. No large company dominated the sector until the end of the British rule in India. The company in 1846 was producing 0.65 million tonnes of coal. Until 1880, the aggregate Indian production did not cross a million.

Gujarati Miners

Unknown to the Indian businessmen, energy dynamics across the world had begun to shift by the end of the nineteenth century. From the time John Rockefeller had established Standard Oil in the USA in the 1870s, competition for oil had spread to new geographies every year. Multi-billion operations financed by the Rothschilds and the Nobel families had begun a race for oil in Europe too, especially after the internal combustion engine was discovered. Ships manu-factured in Portsmouth, Danzig or Amsterdam began to shift to oil. The days of coal-fired ships were over. British geologists fanned out across India to explore for oil. The only place they found it in India was Assam. Explorations in Burma were more productive. India had coal, but the number of takers for it was declining.

There were however a few like Dwarkanath Tagore, of a generation ago, among the Indian businessmen of the late nineteenth century, to hobnob with the British agents to pick up the news about the new opportunities. They had not kept up with the information about the death of coal as the preferred choice of fuel for the ocean-going ships. The ostrich-like tendency meant that the initiative for the coal business passed on to the British managing agencies until India's Independence, fifty years later. Agencies like the Marine Board in Calcutta had now switched off their demand for coal. To keep the supply lines to the Marine Board smooth, Carr–Tagore had fought to keep away rivals from dislocating the complicated chain from the mines to the coal depots. It was not needed any more.

At the same time in Asia, Russia was trying to edge closer to the Indian subcontinent. The country had always fancied a warm water port which the British was equally determined to deny them. The race for control of Persia and of Afghanistan was now on between the two European powers. Persia was valuable for its ports and the until-then-suspected oil bounty; Afghanistan for its strategic location as the gateway of Central Asia.

The arms race for oil did, however, create a derived demand for coal. It came through the railways. The British viceroy in India, Lord Curzon, had a clear mandate from London to establish a national railway line grid. The lines would transfer troops to north as reinforcements or double up as transport links for the British columns from Peshawar to Tehran to repulse the Russians. Realising the enormous scale of investments required as well as the speed of execution needed, successive British viceroys had opened up investments for laying railway lines to all and sundry. Curzon gave it a sense of urgency. It could not remain a government preserve any more unlike the steamships in the middle of the last century.

It was a call to arms for the managing agencies based out of Calcutta and Bombay. They had been hit hard, as the attraction of the opium trade with China slackened and investment avenues dropped off. The financial capital which used to slosh through Calcutta lubricating the semi-military industrial complex had dried up. The babu culture among the Indians who acted as agents for these business houses in the day and spent it all in the nightlife of the city took a hit. Every year, more absentee landlords and company agents went bankrupt. The decadence of the city which gave it colour and joie de vivre began to give a way to decay. Nationalist feelings against the British found a fertile ground to emerge.

The agencies investing in the railway business including Andrew Yule, Balmer Lawrie and Bird Brothers did not have the time required to invest in coal mines to fuel their steam engines. Instead, they hunted for the best bargains the miners could give. The demand for coal expanded, but the companies did not offer a collective face to the miners to exploit scale. At any time, there was more than one railway company in any region to keep the coal miners interested.

The scale of the coal business for the existing owners slipped back to smaller sizes. It, in turn, lowered the barriers for entry into the sector. In Raniganj belt and later in the adjacent Jharia belt, almost anyone with a pickaxe and crowbar could dig out the mineral. Post 1880s, the demand for the mineral which had cut back after the opium wars began to climb again. By another decade, the Indian mines were producing nearly 1.75 million tonnes of coal. These mines naturally followed the route along which the railway lines expanded into India, creating an informal chain of depots to feed the steam locomotives. The first of those large-scale mines came up in 1862 in the Central Provinces. In Rewa state, commercial production of coal began in 1884.

The setting was right for a more insular and small-scale business model to set root in the coal mines. These were pioneered by the Gujarat-based entrepreneurs who used their own family networks in this second phase of coal exploration. The loose cooperative business model preferred by them allowed for the carving up of the market but blocked any predatory tactics from outside. It precluded the urge to drive out their rivals who were often their cousins from out of the business. They were, however, better off then than the Calcutta-based coal companies whose source of easy finance for expansion had dried up.

There was an interesting reason how these Gujarat entrepreneurs arrived at Raniganj and thence at Jharia. These entrepreneurs who mostly hailed from the Kutch region of Gujarat were initially drafted to work on the railway projects. In eastern India, the Santhals and other tribals who had distinguished themselves in the coal mines were not in demand to construct the railway lines since it required skills like those of measurement and that of reading maps. A generation ago, the British employees of the East India Company had struck up working relationships with the local people to train them. But after the rebellion of 1857, the engineers from England who arrived to work on the railways had no truck with these locals. There was no Guru Jones this time around to wean them into the new line of industrial employment.

From 1856, the Kutch region was hit by four episodes of famine. A big chunk of the population of this region, the Kutch Gurjar Kshatriyas, was a strongly networked community which was more artisanal than agricultural. Their construction skills had been noticed by the Portuguese and even the Mughals in the earlier centuries as they built the beautiful palaces of Rajasthan and Gujarat. As the demand for building more palaces dried up by the nineteenth century, these doughty masons were in search of work elsewhere.

When the expatriate engineers landed in India, they knew that they would need a huge army of men to work on the railway lines. The Kutch community's expertise in stone cutting, lime paste making and brick manufacturing attracted the English engineers as a vast reservoir of skilled people to tap into. The recurrent famines encouraged the community to migrate to the railway sites for work. Long lines of these families on bullock carts wended their way through western India and finally reached eastern India. The hardy men walked hundreds of kilometres beside the carts that carried their entire family, including children and their possessions. Each procession largely comprised one extended family of a village. It was an uncommonly large-scale migration within India in the nineteenth century. Some of them ended up abroad too. Despite being practically illiterate, these masons could digest the drawings for the bridges, the alignment of the lines and were disciplined enough to complete the work on time.

The most intrepid among these contractors from Kutch district was Khora Ramji Chawda. In 1895, he fell out with the engineer in charge of building the massive railway bridge over the Ganga near Allahabad and decided to move into coal mining instead. He had connected the dots between owning the coking coal mines, rise of the fledgling domestic steel and power industry and the demand for steel from the expanding rail network. As he worked on the rail network being spread among the Jharia mines, he decided to move on to a new chapter in his life.

A reminder of those times is the Raja Shiva Prasad College in Jharia town. The college stands at the corner of the road leading from Jharia to Dhanbad. Like everything else in this town, the walls of the college are today blotchy as the coal dust and sulphur from the fires burning in the mines combine to turn everything grey.

The college gets its name from the eponymous raja who sold the first plot of coking coal-bearing land to Chawda. As befitting a raja, none from the family ever showed any interest in mining coal. Instead, Shiva Prasad got into tortuous tax cases in the 1940s over the maintenance expenditure for the dowager ranis (queens) of the estate.

By the year 1900, all the elements of the second phase of the coal story in India were thus in place. India was producing 6.63 million tonnes of coal annually; of this, nearly 5 million tonnes was raised in (Raniganj–Jharia) fields. The total output of coal was brought up to nearly 16.2 million tonnes in 1913. Newly opened steel blast furnaces like Tata Iron and Steel Company (TISCO) and Martin Burn needed a lot of coking coal.

Competition grew intense among the owners of coking coal mines in Jharia, as well as between them and the owners of non-coking coal mines in nearby Raniganj. The trigger for the competition was the First World War. Chawda was incidentally as different a business figure from Tagore as was possible. Tagore personified flamboyance; the Gujarati entrepreneur had never stepped across the Indian shores in his lifetime and no soirees were ever held at his bungalow. There was no hint of an attempt made by him to match the English lifestyle. An austere vegetarian, the daily routine at his home allowed for little ostentations except on religious occasions. District officials referred to him as a multimillionaire, 'one of the first class parties in Jharia'. But that was it. He did not make any attempt to influence the government to expand the sphere of operations by his company.

Chawda purchased two collieries to begin with. Following him, his clansmen from Kutch also bought more mines. By 1914, there were 137 coal mining companies, up from just 34, fifteen years ago. (Their paid-up capital was ₹58.7 million.) An enumeration of the mine ownership made in 1920 shows that Jharia town had a distinct air of Gujarati settlement with ninety-two mines held by entrepreneurs from the state. Of these, fifty were held by the Kutch clansmen of Chawda.

The mine owners faced no questions from any authorities as they went about digging open swathes of land to reach for the best coal available underneath. As soon as that coal seam was exhausted, the owners promptly moved to the next patch. It was the worst form of slaughter mining. Something had to give in this environment. The earlier rules under which Carr–Tagore worked where they had to mine the same fields and apply afresh for new mines had fallen into disuse.

In his seminal history of coal mining in India, Anubhuti Ranjan Prasad writes, 'The owners of the Raniganj coalfield had to face an intense competition from Jharia field.... As such, it led to the coal proprietors to adopt the cheapest mining methods resulting in a great loss of coal owing to fires and premature collapses'.

Abandoned coal mines began to catch fire. One of those was the first mine that Chawda had bought. On a November night in 1930, the bungalow that Chawda had built, strangely above his mine, collapsed into the inferno below. No one was at the bungalow that night. Chawda had died some years earlier. Those fires and the ground collapse were not the last in the belt.

Coal production and consequent problems like fire in the mines began to climb rapidly from the beginning of the First World War. By 1919, India was producing 22.6 million tonnes of coal, doubling the production level in less than a decade. An incipient industrial demand added to the demand for coal from overseas during the war. The mineral was being shipped out as soon as it was mined, so prices soared. To put some sense of order in the coal country, a coal controller's office was set up in 1916 just next door to the governor general's office in Calcutta. Few controllers ever stepped out from the office to the mines.

As the First World War ended, production of domestic coal went literally sky high. But based only on anecdotal evidence, the government concluded that there was a domestic shortage and banned the export of coal in two stages. In July 1920, it stopped exports except for those who had obtained special permits. The next year, even those permits were withdrawn leading to a total ban on coal exports. Indian coal at that time had a flourishing market in Sri Lanka, Aden and all over the Red Sea region since those were huge ports for steamship companies to berth and demand coal to refuel. Production of coal slumped by 21 per cent within a year.

The few mines which survived the vicious swings were those run by the European managing agencies. Indian-owned mining companies like those of Chawda found that they could rarely plan long term. Money was exceedingly costly with interest rates far higher than the average for comparable loans in Europe. Conditions were somewhat easier in port cities as the banks were concentrated there. But they were squeamish about lending for inland business. Coal mining was a business with hardly any entry barriers to block newcomers. The Marwari and Gujarati communities were safe from credit default because of the dense interlocking of holding among the relatives. But that prevented them from setting themselves up as firms with limited shareholding to seek loans from banks. When trade finance became tight, they had to sell out together.

This created another problem. The rapid turnover of firms in coal except for the managing agencies meant that there was no long-term continuity of fortunes associated with it. This was unlike jute where local Indian brokers rapidly bought out the European exporters to establish themselves after the Depression. Taking advantage of information asymmetry that was rife in the jute trade, the Marwari community established its hegemony. Names such as Birla and Goenka became well known in the jute business. In coal, no one survived long enough to establish an information asymmetry which he/she could exploit and build a reputation to leverage for raising debt.

Soda Water and Tea

The man who possibly stood between the shutdowns of a large segment of Indian coal mines in that period was Sir Dorabji Tata. He ensured that Tata Steel, the largest Indian industrial enterprise in the pre-Independence era, would survive. In his efforts, he got a timely bit of help from two Congress stalwarts.

Post war, miners by the dozens abandoned their mines and closed their offices. Demand for coal collapsed for two reasons. The stately steam ships on oceans were changing over to oil. And in steel, the demand had shrunk from abroad as Europe licked its wounds. One of those companies affected by the dipping demand for steel was Tata Steel. At the Mumbai office of Tata Sons in Kala Ghoda, a telegram came from its Jamshedpur office in the summer of 1924. It had terrible news. There was not enough money to pay the wages of workers, the plant in-charge had wired. The company was close to bankruptcy. It confirmed the rumours swirling around the coal belt—Jamsetji Tata's great leap of faith was about to be wiped off from the Indian industrial landscape. Dorabji knew that he had to take a drastic step.

In his personal life, Jamsetji's eldest son had the tastes of a patrician and was not impulsive at all. Polished in his attire as befitting a Parsi gentleman of that era, in his extensive travels through rural areas, his servants would prepare his tea with soda water to avoid infection. He had married late by Parsi standards at the age of 38 to a girl almost two decades younger than him. His marriage with Meherbhai Bhabha had attracted a lot of attention in the social circuit of Mumbai. She died early, of leukaemia, in 1930. His lifestyle was a world apart from that of Chawda, though definitely not a debonair one like that of Dwarkanath Tagore.

But one summer morning, Dorabji did something impulsive. With cousin RD Tata, he walked across to the Imperial Bank on the same street to raise a massive loan. The collateral he offered was his personal fortune worth at that time about ₹1 crore. It included his wife's jewellery. The Tata Archives note that a crore of rupees then would be equivalent to about ₹100 crore in 2015.

He now needed someone to buy the steel the Tatas were producing. In the Central Legislative Assembly, two Congress stalwarts, Motilal Nehru and Mohammad Ali Jinnah, jointly pushed for a large order from the government for the steel rails the company could produce, assuring them of a sustained flow of orders for the next few years. Once Tata Steel's finances were stabilised, happiness was briefly restored in the coking coal mines of Jharia.

Despite Dorabji's heroics, however, the number of joint stock coal companies that had peaked at 276 in 1921 with a total paid-up capital of ₹126 million shrunk in fifteen years to 214 with a paid-up capital of just above ₹100 million. Not all steel or paper mills were as lucky as the Tatas. An incipient revival in the mid-1920s was killed as the world slid into the Great Depression in 1929. The Depression hit overseas demand for steel, cement and paper products, cascading the impact onto coal. Their problems took the bottom out of the coal sector. Even by 1933, the production of coal was 12 per cent less than the peak it had touched in 1919.

The prospects for the sector briefly turned around as the Second World War broke out. But by then, a few Indian mining families were left in the business. India was facing what the government described as 'a coal famine'.

In July 1943, Damodar River breached its banks after torrential rains. Within hours, the water had swept away the railway line to Calcutta, gushed over the Grand Trunk Road and filled the coal mines with water. The British forces in Assam and their reinforcements from up country were stranded with the Japanese army just hours away from the Indian border. There was one division of the Indian National Army marching with the Japanese divisions under the leadership of Subhas Chandra Bose.

Shorn of rail, communications and fuel, the Allied army was just one battle away from losing its Indian foothold built over 200 years. News of the immobilisation of the British Indian Army did not however spread to Calcutta. How any such rumour among the frenzied population which had just learnt of Bose's arrival in Tokyo a month earlier would have played out can only be imagined.

The war government in Calcutta and Delhi launched a massive rescue effort with the help of tribal population commandeered overnight. It was a combination of luck and the fact that the Japanese invasion was delayed by the same rains which helped the British Indian government to hold on until September when the rain waters subsided.

Prices of coal shot up in the circumstances and remained high, forcing the imperial government to pass the first price control order on coal in 1944. Coal mining was clearly not an endeavour for the faint-hearted. It would generate even more heat in post-Independence India in political circles.

3

Nationalisation of Problems

The Private Sector Wants to Do Too Much

On a dense summer afternoon in Delhi, the coal sector was nation-alised by the Parliament. The legislation finally got done a deed that had been in the works for more than two decades. Appropriately enough, on May Day 1973, under Prime Minister Indira Gandhi's watch, the act to bring all coal production under the government, thus bringing to a temporary close a roller coaster journey for the sector, was signed by President Varahagiri Venkata Giri who had soon acquired the moniker Prime Minister's President.

It would again become topsy-turvy soon, but on that summer day, there was a sense of inevitability about the legislation.

Why was it so inevitable? To answer that why, one has to travel to Independent India's first industrial belt at Durgapur in West Bengal. It is the story of this belt and particularly of one company in the belt which describes why within two decades of Independence, India travelled from a troubled existence with coal mining in the private sector to its outright nationalisation.

Durgapur is nicely cradled between the parallel course of na-tional highway (NH) number 2 and the Delhi–Howrah railway line about 150 km west of Kolkata. The town at one stage sported the who is who of India's mega engineering projects. Each of those projects were built to feed off one another as a one-stop shop for all mineral-cum-engineering possibilities; the country's first tryst with Make in India. It was a sort of Silicon Valley for all that could be extracted from coal and iron. They were all built with foreign financial and technological support in the 1950s and 1960s.

The complex included Durgapur Steel Plant and Alloy Steel Plant, Durgapur Chemicals, Damodar Valley Corporation, and Mining and Allied Machinery Corporation (MAMC). There was also a power-generation company built to mimic a self-contained US industrial belt, the Tennessee Valley Authority. The Indian power company was named Damodar Valley Corporation. A ring of some more public sector oil outlets and pharmaceutical companies completed the chain around them.

The model came unstuck, as the coal economy failed to take off in the post-Independence India. Among those which spun out of control first was the public sector MAMC.

Even today, this region is coal country. Underneath the deciduous sal forests, the ground is almost entirely coal, sometimes coming up to just below the top soil. It is just 20 km east of Raniganj, with its rich coal deposits that attracted the Bengali entrepreneur Dwarkanath Tagore and later Gujarati Kutch Mistry clans. But thanks to the missteps in harnessing the coal dividend, most downstream industries in this region have been reduced to the status of small and cottage industries over the decades, or left abandoned.

The approach to the once imposing MAMC factory is today a rubble path. On a winter afternoon driving down from Kolkata, I had to hunt around quite a bit since there was obviously no indicator on the road of where the plant had disappeared. The road to the factory leading off from the highway built at one time to carry heavy machinery for coal mines has degenerated into a vast expanse of dirt and rubbish.

At the entrance to the factory complex stands an obelisk of steel and glass which once had the company name proudly blazoned on it. The mutilated shell stands now in a desolate plaza before the L-shaped plant and administrative office complex. It is a stark reminder of the possibilities which went wrong. A guard stands inside locking himself in from thieves, though after taking a round of the vast premises I found out that there was nothing to steal including even the guard rails. He told me that his job was to switch on a bulb in the evening and help a small water works to run.

Having lived in this town as a kid, it was depressing to see how the bustling town had relapsed into a rural tract of sorts. When the company went belly up in the 1970s, many houses in the township were handed over to the erstwhile employees in whatever condition they stood. Those too are in bad shape, as those people have also migrated out in search of jobs. The once neat roads lined with trees planted in straight lines, a different species for each road, have degenerated into cart tracks. Standing there, it seemed to me that I could see the growth history of the area having unspooled before me.

There was an excellent economic rationale, however, to set up MAMC in 1965 by hiving it off from the older Heavy Engineering

Corporation based in Ranchi. It aimed to produce high-end machinery to be used in the Raniganj–Jharia coal mine belt instead of the country having to import those. It was conceived as a joint venture with the Union of Soviet Socialist Republic (USSR), and in its heydays, Russian engineers and their families were all over the town, sampling fish and mangoes from the local haats, stuff which were quite a rarity back home in USSR.

After a tour through the desolate factory ruins, as I turned back, a cyclist pedalled up to me. He and the guard are the only two employees of the company I had seen that afternoon. The cyclist was crestfallen when I told him the reasons for my visit. 'We stole from the company, our union leaders did and so did the bosses', he said. 'No one told us what the thefts would do to the company.'

Once the coal-fired dream was over, MAMC was in a free fall; the skilled employees left. Many of those who remained literally carted away what they could lay their hands on from the offices. It was asset stripping on a mass scale. Except for the land, the state-owned company now had just nothing else left to offer a buyer.

Socialistic Pattern of History

The divisions between private sector and the Congress government were going to soon come out in the open. Despite assurances from Mookerjee, industry was not reassured. M Visvesvaraya got a Bharat Ratna from the government in 1955, but his concerns against nationalisation were not heeded to. As India's most famous engineer, his was a strong voice and in his pamphlet 'Industrialization Scheme' he made it clear that the government's plan to progressively nationalise some of the sectors has stopped fresh investment in them. It did not help; Nehru had set up an Economic Programme Committee in the Congress party. It asked for progressive nationalisation of industry.

Nehru's cabinet was fighting a larger ideological battle on political economy through most of the 1950s. From the Congress, the socialists were leaving in droves. 'It was becoming very difficult to understand what precisely Nehru was wanting to do (sic)', wrote Ashok Mehta, one of those leaders that stepped out from Congress along with Jayaprakash Narayan in 1948. Narayan was blunter. 'You want to build socialism with the help of capitalism. You are bound to fail in that', he wrote in a letter to the leader of the Congress party. Ranged at an even more extreme position was CPI. Congress, even before the first elections, was getting jittery.

Industrialisation was only a part of this larger battle, but it did MAMC in. The battle took an ugly shape at the silver jubilee function of FICCI in 1952 held just after the first general elections.

It was again in the month of March. In the morning of 29 March, the FICCI president CM Kothari got up to deliver his presidential speech. His audience included Prime Minister Nehru, Finance Minister Chintaman D Deshmukh, who had joined the cabinet after serving as the first Indian governor of the Reserve Bank of India (RBI), Home Minister Govind Ballabh Pant and Lal Bahadur Shastri. The general elections had finished just a month earlier in February. There was of course no surprise in the results. Congress under Nehru had won with a landslide margin of 364 seats. Since some of the results were still coming in, the erstwhile cabinet formed in 1947 was still in place with the few changes made necessary as ministers died (Patel) or walked out (Mookerjee). The new cabinet sitting at the FICCI session was sworn in as India's first republican government cabinet a fortnight later on 15 April.

Kothari was consequently speaking at as momentous an occasion as India ever provided to an industrial leader in its history. He milked it well. There was a lot of feel-good factor — the effusive praise about Nehru's leadership, the expectations about the opportunities that India would take on the path of development. The audience sat through it quietly until he begun to give his opinion on the results of the election.

He was unhappy, he said, at the certain 'stray success of disruptive elements' in the poorest constituencies. These were the constituencies 'where the populace has been suffering the most', he said. Kothari did not mention whom he meant but did not let anyone doubt whom he was referring to. It was the sixteen seats CPI had won in the elections that he was referring to. Including the other socialist parties, their tally in the Lok Sabha was forty-two. One of those seats was Burdwan, where despite Nehru's personal campaign, the raja of the estate had lost badly to Benoy Choudhury of CPI. The Bolshevik revolution in USSR was just two decades old; the communist takeover in China had just happened. The industry leaders were scared about the future developments in India. They wanted an assurance from this cabinet that their companies would not be expropriated. This was the biggest point of discussion in the industry chambers. During the Quit India Movement of 1942, Lala Shri Ram had written to Thakurdas about his fears that the Congress party might lose the plot and there could be general usurpation of private property.

> I am afraid that this sabotage may any day start of private property also. Once the Goondas know this trick, any Government … will find it difficult to control it. Today Mahatma Gandhi may be able to stop it, but later on it may go out of their hands too.

The FICCI president had managed to nettle the prime minister sufficiently that morning. Nehru's response was predictably fierce. Delivering his inaugural speech at the session, he challenged the industry leaders to find support for their position outside the venue. 'Are you not unaware that private enterprise is today the target of attacks from all sides', and added, 'we too (government) are ready to view it (private sector) with suspicion'. Pointing to rising unemployment trends in the economy, he said that an atmosphere was developing where instead of hope and faith 'when people find the future holds no promise for them, they naturally will get desperate'. This was a long way away from the soaring tone of Tryst with Destiny. His conclusion was clear: the companies would remain in private hands but only so long as they behaved themselves. The lines were drawn.

In the Industrial Policy Resolution of 1948, Mookerjee had left nicely ambiguous the question of how further investments by the private sector would be treated in basic industries. He had suggested that private investment should be left alone for ten years for them to be assessed thereafter in line with national priorities. Even this had not assured industry. The rapid rise in the support base for the communists and socialists as unemployment rates galloped upwards along with spiralling prices of daily needs came close to break that covenant by the spring of 1952. Thakurdas in his vote of thanks charitably remarked, 'as far as this Federation is concerned, we cannot expect more from (Nehru) than this'.

The differences carried over to May, when an FICCI delegation led by GD Birla along with Charat Ram and GD Somani among others met the Planning Commission. The government team was led by Finance Minister Deshmukh. It included Gulzarilal Nanda, the first deputy chairman of Planning Commission. Both blamed the industry leaders saying that they were not doing much to tame rising prices by making an attempt to raise production. Birla tried to argue that it was the government that needed to spend more to buy their products to which Deshmukh retorted by telling him this would only add to rising prices when additional production from the private sector was not coming through.

It was a fatal problem. The government was suspicious that the private sector had little finance, was badly organised and was too obsessed with profits to really care about pushing ahead with industrialisation at the scale India needed. The private sector was confident that it wanted to be the principal driver of the investment in the economy but demanded an assurance from the government that it would not change the goalposts.

There was a truce of sorts. The first Five-Year Plan did recognise the private sector as the big daddies and structured the investment schemes accordingly. It did not hold for long! The Congress party leaders were furious at having to play the second fiddle. They got a chance to settle scores within another two years, this time through a Parliament debate!

The debate was a fairly routine one. On 20 December 1954, Deshmukh moved a resolution on the economic policies as a precursor to a new Industrial Policy for the economy, which he explained in his speech meant that the government should rapidly expand its presence in the economy. To the surprise of party managers, the mood in the house turned ugly by the afternoon. Opposition members and even those from Congress tore into the government position. CPI leader Hiren Mukherjee said, 'the Prime Minister is trying to bluff our people into feeling that socialism is being constructed in this country'. These were strong words. As soon as two Congress members including Bhagwat Jha Azad offered an amendment to the resolution saying the industrial policy should state that its objective was to create a socialistic society, Nehru grabbed the offer. Without getting a nod from the cabinet, he and Deshmukh came back the next day with the amended resolution that had three clauses. The second one said, 'the objective of our economic policy should be a socialistic pattern of society'. India's development template was settled. It now remained only to figure out what the word socialistic meant. There would be no more playing around the bush with words like 'cooperative commonwealth' which the Congress deployed as its goal in 1947.

Having brought socialism finally into a government policy paper, ministers now went around smoking the peace pipe. They knew that they had created uproar. Industry leaders within India and investors from abroad, especially US-based energy companies, wanted to know what the hell was happening in India. They particularly wanted to hear Deshmukh. At the Associated Chambers of Commerce and Industry of India (ASSOCHAM) annual general meeting, the minister told his audience that he was convinced that the private sector 'stood with the government'. A relieved newspaper report observed, 'It is not difficult to agree with (Deshmukh) that these proposals cannot spell such grave disaster on the private sector as is now prophesied in some quarters'.

The industry owners, however, needed to be sure that socialism though great in principle would not come visiting their units sooner or later. Each established industry leader ran to extract a promise from the government that doomsday was not around the corner for them. Like Deshmukh, other ministers too were liberal with their assurances. The move to nationalise JRD Tata's Telco was scrapped, and the banks led by AD Shroff, cement by the Kotharis and jute by the Birlas got a reprieve. Coal did not. None of the authors of Bombay Plan and none of the top bosses of FICCI were in the business of coal.

> It has been decided that in future the policy of retaining all new undertakings in coal in the public sector should be more strictly followed and that the additional coal production required to meet the increased demand during the second plan should be raised to the maximum extent possible in the public sector. Accordingly it has been tentatively decided that of the additional production of 22 million tons envisaged by 1960–61, 12 million tons should come from collieries in the public sector, either already existing or to be newly opened and that the balance should be raised by the private sector *only* [italics mine] from their existing workings and immediately contiguous areas. (Second Five-Year Plan document)

With this unambiguous position on coal, there was no chance then that any technological support for the coal sector would come from the Western countries. The government made matters worse by leaking out information that by January 1955, the private coal mines were earmarked for state buyout. Consequently, the second Five-Year Plan had to defer indefinitely the proposed setting up of MAMC to supply state-of-the-art mining equipment for private and public sector coal mines. The offer of technological support for MAMC from European or US firms had evaporated.

Summing up the mood, a report in May 1956 by *Financial Times*, London, headlined 'More state control in India, Government Monopolies Doubled'. To defend the Indian government, VT Krishnamachari as a former member of the Constituent Assembly wrote a letter to the newspaper explaining the rationale of the plan. His voice carried weight, since he also represented one of the leading princely states, Jaipur, until then regarded as restive about their forced amalgamation into the Indian Union. Nehru had to also send out an FICCI delegation to the USA and Europe to assess the mood towards investing in India. It was not positive. The investors there interpreted the government's position as a precursor to communism with a distinct possibility of expropriation of their capital. The World Bank sent a stiff communiqué to the government, questioning the direction of the industrial policy. While the Bank never confirmed it, throughout the 1960s it refused financing for new oil wells, with the first such loan coming up only by 1977, making it congruent with the opening of doors to foreign oil exploration companies.

India had committed a fatal mistake. The energy economy was left to wobble with no promise of adequate government investment and none from the private sector to make up the slack. Every time till 1975 the economy was pushed to grow more, the shortage of coal and oil would jerk it back. The damage was particularly harsh for the coal mining sector. The sector badly needed money to modernise. Coal was being transported in bullock carts from plenty of mines. Production was flat. Few domestic mine owners wanted to put fresh money in their pits. To assuage them that their mines would not be taken over, Nehru's cabinet set up a public sector company National Coal Development Corporation (NCDC) as a compromise. The new state-owned company, it was assured, would only explore fresh mines for coal. But just as technological support for setting up MAMC had dried up, financial support for the new company too did not come from abroad, making its expansion difficult. The government now had to look to the eastern bloc for investments in the energy sector. It took another decade before MAMC was set up with USSR support in 1965.

As the supply of coal stagnated, industries which needed coal as fuel began to convert to oil. The new manufacturing units in southern and western India discovered oil was a cheaper feedstock than coal, even though its price was kept artificially low. The plan documents agreed that it was cost inefficient to transport coal over long distances.

A large number of units in the country shifted to furnace oil, taking advantage of the cheaper imports compared with domestic coal. Oil was to mostly imported, but industry found it a more reliable source of supply than coal mined from domestic mines. A report by the World Bank for the period 1953–1971 shows the percentage use of coal as a commercial fuel dipped from 48 to 26 per cent in India. In the same period, the share of oil rose from 40 to 49 per cent. Along with this shift, the coal miners faced another crisis from their first customer, the railways.

Antim Sitara

Beyond Durgapur where MAMC is located, the flood plains of the Ganga river system and its tributaries, such as the Damodar, give way to the Susunia hills, heralding the onset of Central India's Chota Nagpur Plateau. At their base is a major railway town Chittaranjan located right on the Bengal–Bihar border. It is here that the coal economy lost its biggest battle against oil.

A hundred years ago, the demand for coal to pull the opium ships on the Ganga had spurred the development of Carr–Tagore. The expansion of coal-fired steam locomotive industry for the railways had the potential to do the same for the coal industry again.

It is a peculiar story of how the railways made the switch so early on in Independent India from coal-fired steam locomotives to electric and diesel locomotives. Until the end of the Second World War, the demand for steam locomotives to run the expanding Indian rail network was met by the locomotive factories of UK. Those factories ringing Glasgow counted the different railway companies of India as among their major customers.

Appropriately enough, almost the first industrial unit set up in India after Independence was a locomotive factory. On the same day, 26 January 1950, when India adopted the Constitution of India, in a faraway railway outpost on the Bengal–Bihar border the country's first locomotive manufacturing unit was set up. The works was being built from April 1948, just days after the Industrial Policy Resolution was adopted, but the manufacturing facility became fully operational on Republic Day, 1950. It made swell sense to locate the factory at the tail-end of the Durgapur belt. The steel plates for the engines could be sourced from Durgapur just 60 km away. The factory itself was located in a barren country where agriculture was sparse and other than coal production nothing happened.

But on that Republic Day, a lot was happening in India to keep the union railway minister Sir Narasimha Gopalaswami Ayyangar busy in Delhi. Ayyangar was also a member of the drafting committee of the Constitution and it was impossible for him to leave Delhi on India's first Republic Day. In nearby Calcutta, the West Bengal government under Bidhan Chandra Roy was also being sworn in on 26 January. Travel to the Chittaranjan Locomotive Works was therefore impossible. The works and the project township had been named as a salute to Chittaranjan Das, Roy's political guru who had rivalled Gandhi in popularity in the 1920s. It was a political masterstroke when Roy decided to ask Basanti Devi, the widow of Chittaranjan Das, to inaugurate the works.

Local newspaper reports about the event described it as extraordinary. Workers and railway officers present at the site were vastly outnumbered by the local people from the nearby villages, many of whom even scaled the modest walls to watch the event. It was a striking demonstration of the aspirations of a free nation, even though it took another eleven months before the first steam locomotive built at the Chittaranjan Locomotive Works named what else, Deshbandhu (sobriquet of Chittaranjan Das), chugged out to join service.

The factory was largely built through reassembling a dismantled locomotive works in England, the Vulcan Foundry. The technological platform was offered by the North British Locomotive Company. Soon the Indian Railways with the coal-powered steam engines began to expand its footprint. By 1956, the locomotive works was producing fourteen engines a month. Coal was set for a long safe future as the fuel of choice.

It changed when the French Railways, SNCF, organised a conference in Lille in 1955 on how to run electric-powered trains. The French had pioneered the latest advances in the technology.

Railway engineers from India and Japan attended the conference; both were charmed.

By 1964, Japan had absorbed enough of the French technology to build a 515 km bullet train, the Tokaido Shinkansen electric railway, to connect Tokyo and Osaka by a 3 hour and 10 minute drive. The train ran at a maximum speed of 210 km per hour making the world sit up in recognition of their achievement. Their gurus, the French, paid back the compliment by 1981 installing the TGV which ran even faster. The developments 'electrified' Indian Railways officials.

At the same time when the Japanese were studying the French production process, the Indian Railway Board also decided to go electric. This meant scrapping the coal-fired steam engines being produced at Chittaranjan. There was a key difference though. A French magazine carried a photograph of the Japanese delegates to the 1955 Lille Conference. The caption reads, 'The Japanese delegation was always extremely attentive'. They were—by next year, they had mastered the technology enough to offer to export electric engines to India. The Indian Railway Board had meanwhile decided that trying to master the technology would take time.

The two Asian pupils set two contrasting routes. India lost the momentum to Japan, even though it had a larger manufacturing base. By 1957, the Japanese landed in India in competition to sell their locomotive. They were in competition against a European consortium vying to win the mega Indian order. A French railway team visited India for several weeks and advised India to switch to electric traction. The Indian Railways promptly agreed and put out a tender in May for electrification of about 670 km of track with the technical specifications set to French standards. The Japanese did not back out though. Shiro Seki, their deputy director of engineering, advised the Indian Railway Board Chairman Karnail Singh during negotiations that India should go local. 'Japan intends to assist India so that she can carry out this electrification by herself', but they were outbid by the European joint venture led by SNCF who became the technological adviser for the railways.

The railways began plans to convert Chittaranjan Locomotive Works into a diesel engine workshop. Then they changed minds. After some years, they decided to instead make Chittaranjan the producer of electric locos and shift diesel production to Varanasi.

Steam engines were still being imported in small batches from Austria, Italy and Japan. But the days of the steam traction were over. In 1970, the last coal-fired engine for the Indian Railways Antim Sitara was rolled out from the plant. Because of the indecisiveness, between 1950 and 1967, the Chittaranjan works produced only 259 coal engines to haul passenger trains and 1,908 engines to pull freight trains. The production line for passenger trains ran for only four years from 1963 to 1967. The steam engines remained in service at dwindling numbers as the workhorse for the Railways until the 1990s but had seen the heyday of their expansion get over by the 1960s.

Coal was blighted all around. It was proving difficult to mine, was more difficult to transport and the demand for it began to slack. Through the 1960s, the industrial demand for coal rose by less than 3 per cent, less than even the derisively called Hindu rate of growth of the economy. This did not mean that oil was being produced more. The energy needs of the economy were coming close to asphyxiation again.

The dwindling interest in coal mining killed MAMC. Interest in the state-of-the-art machines MAMC was producing began to dip even as the factory sheds were being painted for inauguration. As production crawled, the hopes of the Durgapur industrial zone died with it. MAMC was the first case of a state-owned company turning sick in India.

Indira Gandhi

Hindi films in the 1960s changed the job description of their villains. Instead of plying their 'baddism' in rustic locales, cornering the village shop and preying on village belles, these men moved on to urban areas. They became 'black marketers'; siphoning off essential commodities became their stock in trade.

The larger context of the 1960s was quite depressing for India from which the popular films picked up their cue. It was a decade when the Indian economy met with something like a hurricane every year. It began with the India–China war and ended with the onset of the Bangladesh Liberation War. In between, two prime ministers Jawaharlal Nehru and Lal Bahadur Shastri died and the USA stopped a food aid programme that had kept India just one step ahead of famines and a long spell of drought overtook the country. 'The humiliation inflicted by the US and the lessons of the war finally brought home to politicians the imperative of food security', notes Shankkar Aiyar in his book *Accidental India*. It forced the Planning Commission to lay off its fight with the agriculture minister C Subramaniam on whether hybrid seeds to raise production of wheat would be desirable, he notes.

Along with these were the political shindigs including the unprecedented defeat of Congress's official candidate in the presidential elections. Neelam Sanjeeva Reddy lost to VV Giri, leading to a split in the party and consequent political instability that led to three general elections in less than nine years.

In this environment, prices soared for almost all products, production rates dipped all around and the government at the Centre decided to give the Five-Year Plans a rest for 3 years. The new leader of the Congress party Indira Gandhi spent a considerable time struggling to put her stamp on the party and as the prime minister on the economy. A contemporary report put the number of man-days lost in strikes in the three calendar years at 57 million, more than the entire preceding decade. 'The years 1973 and 1974 were turbulent. There were food riots in some states'.

The one thing she did not need was an inability to control prices. The government controlled the price of anything it could lay its hand on. Even the price of cars; the ministry of industrial development would set the price of Ambassador, Fiat and Standard cars, the three models Indian factories produced every 6 months. In January 1972, the ex-factory price of an Ambassador car was ₹16,898, about 10 years' salary of a central government officer.

So if prices rose, then the villain was the government. And no successful film would allow the villain to walk away in the last reel as a victor. Incidentally, India in 1971 became the world leader in the number of films produced—433.

The script was clear. The government had to earn a 'victory' in the fight with prices of key commodities like coal. The mineral zoomed in importance for households as India's fledgling urbanisation began to take root. It was now the preferred fuel option for cooking for nearly 20 per cent of the Indian population, the middle class. Another 50 per cent who used firewood or cow dung aspired to graduate to coal as their domestic fuel. Liquefied petroleum gas (LPG) was virtually unknown even among the richest. Its total production in 1971 was 1.7 lakh tonnes. Rise in the price of coal affected household budgets and sentiments harshly. For an astute political leader, facing tough elections at frequent intervals, the implications were obvious.

Coal prices still rose despite a gagging price control on them. Or rather, the prices rose because of the gags. Shortages became all too evident. Price control on coal was begun in the Second World War with the passage of the Colliery Control Order in 1944 that effectively controlled production and, more important, the pricing of coal. It was revised through a more comprehensive order in 1945. The order stayed through India's tryst with socialism to be removed only in 1996. The official price of a tonne of coal in 1973 was ₹42. Fifty years earlier, it was ₹7. The black market rate was closer to ₹100. 'The crisis in the coal industry (was) engendered primarily by the government's price policy of cheap coal', noted a commentator on the sector.

The private miners found that every tonne of coal they extracted added to their losses, as the price of the mineral was state controlled. Since price was controlled and cutting back on the wages of the labour was not possible, they resorted to every possible trick to underreport production. The number of workers registered on the company books were drastically cut back. Workers employed informally could be sacked or paid lower wages. The next step was to cut back on every possible investment including safety measures. At the time of nationalisation, the industry was spending just ₹50 crore annually as investment in the sector. When all of those measures failed to keep them in the black, it became essential for the miners to sell coal in the black market. A coal mafia came into business around the Raniganj–Dhanbad coal belt. We will visit that in the next chapter.

Gandhi gambled with a midterm election in 1971 to return with a clear majority. In one year, eleven states changed their chief ministers; in Bihar, twice. There were enough political troubles afoot. Some were comical like the Nagarwala case where the chief cashier of SBI branch of the Parliament Street withdrew ₹60 lakh (a massive sum then) claiming to be under orders of the prime minister. The case was never solved with the main culprit Nagarwala dying mysteriously in jail. At the other end was the India–Pakistan war over Bangladesh.

The options for the central government had narrowed. Increasing, the price of coal was the last thing Gandhi and her cabinet wanted. Petrol prices had reached ₹1.16 from 67 paisa in 1960, and there were protests in all cities.

Despite her reluctance, a measure of decontrol of coal prices had been introduced in 1967 to encourage licit production. Price of non-coking coal was freed to be decided by mutual negotiations between the coal producers association and the public sector companies. There was however a caveat. Under the terms agreed upon, only those mines which could produce a certificate from the coal controller that they had implemented wage revision as asked for by the government would be allowed the new price.

It came with the worst possible timing. The economy had hit a recession in 1966. Prices in every year rose dizzily. Using 1970 as the base year, the wholesale price index rose by 16.2 per cent. In just one calendar year, 1973, the inflation rate had touched 26 per cent by the end of December.

In a span of 25 years since 1946, the government had appointed 9 committees to study and report on coal prices. None had worked. Coal policies were clearly headed for a denouement but the prime minister needed an intellectual justification to backstop her ideas. She fetched her ideas from the two Industrial Policies written during her father's term. Nationalisation of coal production clearly put on the back burner in 1948 had been put on heat in 1956 for some time. It had been given up but Gandhi was sure that she could pull it through.

Meanwhile, she had a more immediate problem to solve. Nehru's best institutional support system on economic policies, the Planning Commission, was not pulling its weight behind her. The fact that she had signed a three-year plan holiday had not helped improve relations with the commission members.

She approached a close friend KN Raj, vice chancellor of Delhi University and one of India's famous economists, for ideas. Raj had a proposal that suited her immensely. A few years ago, Raj had inspired a young Indian economist to give up a position at the Massachusetts Institute of Technology (MIT) against Paul Samuelson's wishes and come to Delhi as a valued colleague at the Delhi School of Economics. Raj nudged this bright professor to join the Planning Commission as a member. Along with Amartya Sen, Sukhamoy Chakravarty was regarded as possibly the finest economist emerging from Presidency College in their generation.

Gandhi had reasons to trust the judgement of Raj. On several occasions, he backed her calls on public policy. None was as famous as his support for her bank nationalisation. RBI's authoritative history of those tumultuous years claims that Raj had told Gandhi to go ahead with it despite an act passed by the legislature a year ago that had already decided on 'social control' of the banks, stopping short of their nationalisation.

The Commission had meanwhile sort of emptied out in protest against her barrage of nationalisation. The members were certainly not in favour of bank nationalisation just as her finance minister Morarji Desai was not. In 1969, the deputy chairman of the Commission, Dhananjay Ramchandra Gadgil had instead taken up the chairmanship of a study group to suggest ways to direct bank credit into 'socially desirable sectors'. The recommendations if implemented could prevent bank nationalisation, Gadgil felt.

Gandhi did not wait for the report. The Gadgil group report came in October 1969, but before that, in July, she had already got the Parliament to nationalise 14 banks, each having deposits of ₹50 crore or more. Gadgil resigned on 1 May 1971 before his term ended. He died the day after en route to Mumbai in a train. He was quite ill when he boarded the train in Delhi. His wife Sudha Gadgil who was travelling with him arrived at the house of her relative with her dead husband to arrange for his funeral. The Commission did not have a deputy chairman for another 4 years.

Chakravarty joined Yojana Bhawan in June 1971, a month after Gadgil's death. The cabinet minister C Subramaniam held dual charge as deputy chairman and minister for planning. Around the time when Chakravarty joined the Commission, three more members including Pitambar Pant, R Venkataraman and B Venkatappaih also quit. Yojana Bhawan was a desolate place to work in.

Chakravarty was also singularly apolitical according to his contemporaries. Much more at home in the company of books, scholars and abstruse problems, one remembered him in his later years always willing to engage even sophomores in detailed discussions and willing to take lectures on any topic at the Delhi School of Economics. He had returned there after differences with Rajiv Gandhi who led him to quit his position as chairman of the Prime Minister's Economic Advisory Council after 1984.

One of the first assignments put on the epicurean professor's plate by the Indira Gandhi administration was crafting out a national fuel policy for the next 15 years. Although the Fuel Policy Committee had been set up a year earlier in 1970, the work took on urgency after Chakravarty joined as its chairman. This was the first time the government was thinking of fuel as an integrated sector. It still was a far cry from crafting an energy strategy.

Before he joined, the committee's mandate was confined to the technical and organisational aspects of energy planning. Macro ideas for the energy sector were now added, as the debilitating impact of coal shortage played out in the economy. The shortage peaked as the Bangladesh war came to its climax. It came to a head with the onset of the first global oil crisis. As crude oil prices shot up, Gandhi asked Chakravarty to figure out the alternatives. The professor's big recommendation was to substitute oil with coal wherever possible in the Indian economy. In a first of sorts for an Indian policy paper, the committee adopted econometric forecasting techniques and end-use analysis to draw sector-wise energy demand estimates, making liberal use of Chakravarty's domain knowledge. He had completed his doctoral thesis under Jan Tinbergen, one of the greatest econometric theoreticians the discipline has produced.

Putting it simply, Chakravarty estimated that with progressive urbanisation, people would reach out for coal. So, the demand for the mineral would rise even faster. The political implication that Gandhi read was that coal prices should be kept soft. She had found her answer.

She now needed a person who could deliver on the nationalisation. That job went to one of the smartest men in her cabinet, Surendra Mohan Kumaramangalam.

An Air Crash and a Missing One

On Malaysian Airlines Flight 370 which disappeared in 2014 was a Canadian-passport-holder, Muktesh Mukherjee. Muktesh and his wife Xiaomao Bai, also a Canadian of Chinese descent, who were on that flight, revived the horrors of another airline accident 41 years ago which struck their family.

Just like Muktesh, his grandfather was killed in an air crash involving Indian Airlines Flight 440 on 31 May 1973 just off Delhi. In his case, the debris of the plane was recovered. The crash killed forty-eight of the sixty-five people on board including S Mohan Kumaramangalam, the minister for steel and mines. The flight from Chennai to Delhi hit a high-tension wire with a dust storm raging around on its descent to the airport.

A day before, the omnibus Coal Mines (Nationalization) Act, 1973 had come into effect with President VV Giri signing it. As the minister for mines in the Gandhi cabinet, Kumaramangalam had steered the bill through the Parliament.

As a trade union leader and former member of CPI, his interests about coal were, however, different from that of Chakravarty. He approached the sector from the point of view of the workers, lifted from the same blueprint that the Nehru cabinet had flirted with in 1948 and 1956. He described the private sector mines as a relic of the Middle Ages and 'an instrument of inhuman oppression.

> If nationalization (sic) is postponed by 25 years and the industry is given a free hand there will be little left at the end of the period for the country to take over. We will be left with a number of units, which, if not affected by underground fires, and other hazardous conditions would be uneconomic to work.

This was how he summed it up. The figures he had in mind were the coal miners like Chawda and goons like Surya Deo Singh.

It was a colourful exhortation, but it struck a chord. There were reasons to be acutely concerned about the working conditions in the coal mining industry. Accidents were not the only one of those, though they became the signature of how badly the mines were run. In Calcutta, the growing citadel of leftist forces in post-Independence India, thespian Utpal Dutt staged a highly acclaimed theatre *Angar* in 1959, tracking the exploitation of coal miners. Kumaramangalam with his deep connections with the city and his own proclivity did not remain untouched. In his book *Coal Industry in India: Nationalisation and the Tasks Ahead*, he claimed without much evidence that the British government ran concentration-like camps in the mines to increase production of coal during the Second World War. Conditions, he said, continued in the same vein in the next two decades too.

It was a bad line of reasoning. Costly coking coal was diverted because there was little difference in its price with inferior metallurgical coal. Successive governments only appointed more policemen to check pilferage. 'As often happens such economic advantages manage to get around physical controls', Rajiv Kumar made the point in a clearly argued article in *Economic and Political Weekly*. Kumaramangalam or his boss did not want any mention of rising prices.

In a short span of eighteen months from October 1971 to May 1973, the central government took over the industry. Unlike bank nationalisation, this one evoked few protests.

Once Gandhi had made up her mind, the cabinet issued the first order, the Coking Coal Mines (Emergency Provisions) Act 1971 on 16 October 1971. It took over the management of 214 coking coal mines and 12 coke oven plants. Those were nationalised and placed under Bharat Coking Coal Limited (BCCL) on 1 May 1972. The only mines allowed to be retained outside were the captive mines of TISCO in the private sector and those of IISCO Steel Plant and Damodar Valley Corporation (DVC) in the public sector.

On 31 January 1973 followed the Coal Mines (Taking Over of Management) Ordinance for 711 non-coking coal mines, mostly scattered over the Raniganj–Jharia belt and in Maharashtra. Their nationalisation was signed by President Giri on 1 May the same year. By mid-June, the Coal Mines Authority Limited was formed in which all these non-coking coal mines were placed and NCDC merged into it. The president cleared the ordinances without demur. Giri had become the president with Gandhi's support in a fight against the Congress party's official nominee Neelam Sanjiva Reddy in 1969. He was clearly beholden to the prime minister and made no moves to even question her spate of ordinances. In 1972, he had bestowed Bharat Ratna award on her, suo moto. She returned the favour to him in 1975 but only after she had declined him a second term as the president.

Two years later in November 1975, another apex holding company CIL was created in which both the Coal Mines Authority Limited and BCCL were merged.

Just a month later, India's worst-ever mining accident took place in a mine 25 km from Dhanbad. At least 372 miners were killed in Chasnala mine when water from an abandoned mine next door burst on them on 27 December. An estimated 5 crore gallons of water poured down on the miners at the rate of approximately 7 million gallons a minute.

The government, however, could not hold the tragedy as a vindication of its decision to nationalise the mines.

The mine was owned by IISCO, now merged with Steel Authority of India Limited (SAIL). Its other two mines were at Jitpur and Ramnagar. The company had already been taken over by the government in July 1972. Worse, it had also approached the World Bank for support to modernise the mine and one of the suggestion made by the Bank was to dry up the water from the abandoned mine next to Chasnala. It was never done. It was this water that came down on the miners next door when the wall separating the two mines breached.

IISCO claimed that it had followed the prescribed standards which a few believed. After a splendid run since the 1930s, the company had run aground as it failed to modernise its mines or its steel foundries.

While the Hindi film *Kaala Patthar* of 1979 softened the impact of this tragedy showing Amitabh Bachchan and some other miners as survivors, the real life incident did not allow time for any miner to escape. The first conviction for the tragedy happened thirty-seven years later.

India at that time did not have even sufficient pumps to dredge out the water and those had to be imported from countries including Poland, the USA and then USSR. Those took time to come and in any case would have still been paralyzing late. Gandhi said, '[E]verything humanly possible will be done to rescue the workers'. The wives of the miners knew better. After the tragedy of Saturday afternoon, according to a report by news agency Associated Press (AP), none of them turned up on Sunday at the mouth of the mine, 'certain their husbands were dead'. The first bodies started coming out of the mine after twenty-six days of draining the mine, but most were never found.

The tragedy brought home with brutal force the lack of investment in mines by the companies, the lack of records of miners who were employed with these companies and the lack of adequate resources to compensate the families of those killed. Nationalisation had obviously begun on a terrible note.

Despite the colossal tragedy, it was obvious that the government had a few clear blueprints for how to handle the post-nationalisation period. Matters got complicated with the death of Kumaramangalam. The creation of CIL as a holding company, for instance, was mostly an afterthought. Strikes in the company leapt from 278 in 1975 to 626 in 1979. The number of man-days lost jumped from 3.51 lakh to 11.59 lakh.

Twenty-two years after staying quiet about the government's nationalisation of coal, the then chief economic advisor in the finance ministry, Manmohan Singh who wrote those economic surveys, pushed for ways to walk back on nationalisation of coal in his avatar as the reformer finance minister in the PV Narasimha Rao government.

In another interesting twist, the current scion of Aditya Birla Group Kumar Mangalam Birla was named in admiration of the deceased coal minister.

Singh and Kumar Mangalam will come together for another drama surrounding the coal sector, 40 years later. That drama would begin to unfold when nationalisation of coal would literally run out of 'steam'.

Coal nationalisation had meanwhile spawned a huge black market on the banks of the Ganga.

4

Coal on Sale

Varanasi Produces Coal

India's biggest coal-trading centre until the 1990s was Varanasi or Benares. The city has no coal reserves but is located at a fantastic geographical spot. Just south of the city rises the Mirzapur hills which descend into India's coal country further ahead around Singrauli. It is also just an overnight journey from Dhanbad, the capital of coking coal mines in the east.

Varanasi's most famous coal market is the Chandasi coal *mandi* (market), less than 10 km away from Mughalsarai, India's largest railway yard. NH 2 which links Delhi with Kolkata cuts through this hub. Varanasi consequently had a flourishing trade in both licit and illicit coal even before Independence. It looms up almost immediately after one crosses the iconic bridge over Ganga next to Varanasi and the road turns southeast.

Traders with coal trucks find the place easy to reach and the buyers from the Punjab and Rajasthan belt find it equally easy to transport the coal from. Supply comes to this place not only from Singrauli and Dhanbad but also from as far away as Jogighopa coal market in Guwahati, Assam. Nationalisation, thus, raised the importance of Chandasi, Varanasi. Yet the Indian government never figured the importance of this market to the coal economics of India. Even in 2016, only a few things have changed.

Chandasi market is a long row of single-storey shops on both sides of the road with trucks parked in front of them and even lining the road. Traffic moves around the trucks at a crawl for kilometres, digging up the black soil on either side of the narrowed road. Most of the godowns manned with surly guards do not stock any great quantities of coal.

In one of my conversations, a shopkeeper explained why the sheds were empty: *'Police aajkal bahut tang karte hain'* (police harass us too much nowadays). When I assured them that I was a genuine customer, they confirmed that the supply would be sent to me directly once the advance payments were made.

Apprentices from even reputed coal-trading companies, like Rajiv Behal, my interlocutor the day I visited the market, had to compulsorily do a stint at Chandasi to learn the ropes. Thirty years later, he has moved a long way from there. He is now the president director of PT Amiraj Energy Indonesia, a company which gets the handshake done between Indian importers of coal and miners in Indonesia, and elsewhere. 'I do the indenting business between the buyers and sellers', said Behal. Coal trading has now moved offshore.

I find talking to him deeply interesting since he has lived through the Indian coal story. Like almost everybody else in India's coal trade, Behal speaks fluent Bengali and is an excellent raconteur to boot. His father was in the coal business and so are several more of his relatives, he told me. At his office in central Nagpur, Behal dives into the world of coal traders while he plies me with excellent Indonesian coffee.

None of the coal traders was more famous than the one run by the former Indian Davis Cup Captain Naresh Kumar. His company Naresh Kumar & Co. Pvt. Ltd was a coal supplier to the Tatas, the CESC of the Goenkas and others who depended on the coal extracted from the mines in Bengal and Jharkhand. In fact, Naresh Kumar was apparently weaned into the coal trade by Russi Mody of Tata Steel at one of the famous Calcutta clubs in the 1960s. Just as his tennis career moved towards sunset, his coal-trading business took off. But Indira Gandhi's coal nationalisation changed the complexion of this business for Naresh Kumar as it did for countless others.

At a stroke, nationalisation of coal mines in India reduced companies like those of Naresh Kumar into a suspect category. Coal could be sold legally in India only by the three public sector coal companies: CIL, Singareni Collieries Company Limited (SCCL) and Northern Coalfields Limited (NCL). Just as it drove the strongmen employed by the private coal companies into the arms of the state-run companies as union leaders, truck operators or labour contractors, many of the erstwhile traders and owners of mines had to change the nomenclature of their business to become authorised coal handlers instead.

While the main operations of Naresh Kumar & Co. as coal handlers did not primarily span the Varanasi market, it ran a small but profitable business segment at the market. The company sourced rejects from the coal washeries of Tata Steel to sell in Varanasi. These rejects from the washeries sported quality that was high enough for the brick kiln owners from up country to make a beeline for those. Moreover, since it was legal, the buyers were willing to pay a higher premium. As Behal describes it, this was one place where all customers would converge, so it made sense to send the rejects there.

> Every morning we would have to figure out the prices at which the coal arriving at the *mandi* would sell. Disruptions at rival mines (of Coal India) because of strikes, road closures, police actions on illegal consignments—all would go into the setting of the price.

The simultaneous illegal market, which Behal refers to, also has a long history at Chandasi. The market came to life towards the end of the Second World War. The colonial government issued a Colliery Control Order in 1945 to check prices of coal. Coal became an 'essential commodity' like rice and sugar. A black market in coal immediately sprung up that persisted until January 2000, when the price control order was rescinded.

In each decade, the scale of this black market expanded even as successive governments ignored it. The puny coal ministry at the Centre could only look at bridging the demand and supply equations between the large coal miners and utilities like thermal power stations and steel plants. CIL, for instance, encouraged its subsidiaries to sign long-term contracts with these large buyers— these were the fuel supply agreements (FSAs) to get a linkage for borrowers which needed more than 500 tonnes per annum (revised in 2007 to 4,200 tonnes). The smaller players with lesser demand had to fend for themselves. For instance, there was the huge glass manufacturing business in Firozabad and the chemical industry in Agra of whom only the largest had those FSAs.

Before coal production was nationalised, these small players when they could not afford the price of coal on offer at the legal market bought illegal coal from Varanasi traders, who often sold both varieties from the same depots. The cat and mouse game that it set off with the police and the local administration poisoned Uttar Pradesh and Bihar politics, interfered with the development of the region and was the primary source for injecting corruption in the sector, getting worse in each decade.

Nationalisation accelerated the criminalisation process by squeezing the number of suppliers too. For one, it immediately reduced the space for the number of companies which could still operate. While there were many buyers for coal, legitimate supplies could come from only the three public sector companies. The choices for the small and medium factories of Punjab, Rajasthan and Haryana were stark. Their only legal options were to buy from the depots maintained by the state-owned coal companies.

The depots rarely worked. BCCL informed in reply to a Parliament question raised by the former Chhattisgarh chief minister Ajit Jogi that while it had set up five depots with annual capacity of 2,341,000 tonnes of coal, the actual quantity handled by them in 3 years from 1995 onwards had gone down from 24 to 17 and then 15 per cent. Two of them were non-functional.

> The objective of setting up of centralised coal depots in BCCL envisaged that all road dispatches to road sale consumers would be effective from the depots which are situated strategically near to the collieries thus restricting entry of road sale consumers to the colliery premises.

In other words, there would be less theft if the coal from BCCL went to the depots and then to the smaller customers. This hardly ever happened.

Without FSA and with no depot to source from, small-scale units like the glass and chemical units of Agra–Firozabad belt had to tap the Varanasi route or face the prospect of going out of business altogether. The pressure from these industries for coal ebbed only after the Supreme Court (SC) ordered them to shift to gas in 1996 on environmental considerations.

The circumstances encouraged every one which had coal to offer to play in the market. Some of those were companies with FSAs. For instance, if a company got a linkage of 500 tonnes of coal per annum, it would divert some of that to earn excess profit. This happened as CIL was rarely able to accurately assess the coal requirements of individual companies which created opportunities for the latter to gold-plate their demands. It has continued to some extent even now.

'Varanasi had its share of illegal coal traders, possibly more than the legal ones', says Behal. 'There was a tremendous shortage of coal, it was always a crisis every day', he says. Those who needed coal did not have it and those who got the FSA did not need all of it.

A typical situation as described in the government records ran as follows:

> A complaint was registered alleging that for distribution of 7.95 lakh Te. of coal against allocation in favour of UP State Authority from Central Coalfields Limited (CCL). The UP State Authority nominated a state agency who has again nominated a private agency and coal available to the State at notified price is sold in black market at double the notified price. (sic) (Reply by Ministry of Power, Coal & Renewable Energy in Parliament, 2 March 2015 about black marketing of coal)

Diversion of FSA was only a minor source for coal supply to Chandasi. The regular sources of supplies to the market were two others. Of these, the first was the coal tapped from the wealth of illegal mines from as far as Meghalaya. The second option was to employ goons operating as rogue labour leaders or as transporters to capture some of the trucks from consignments that left the CIL mines each day.

Lord of the Markets

'Illegal mines have existed in India from as long as coal was mined', says Subrata Chakravarty, director (technical) at Eastern Coalfields Limited (ECL). The worst affected in this respect is the Raniganj–Jharia belt straddling the borders of West Bengal and Bihar. 'Geologically this is a freak zone', he says. Coal mines at any place offer their best product at the lowest seam. This is the only place in the world where the best-quality coking coal is available virtually at the surface.

The phenomenon was noticed by the British geologists who came out here to explore these coal deposits. The local population soon cottoned on to the implication. Right from the time when the first large-scale commercial mining of coal began in this belt, illegal mining kept up pace.

The mining technology if it can be called that has remained practically the same as was used during Dwarkanath Tagore's time. It helps to keep the prices down from the rates ECL charges in its e-auctions.

The standard procedure for the illegal miners is to rig up a well-like structure through which the labourers descend into the makeshift tunnels to cut the coal deposits. A pulley made of bamboo and rope is used to haul up the coal. Beside the mouth of the well, women break the coal rocks into smaller pieces which are then loaded onto trucks. Those trucks one could see travelling to sponge iron units located in this Durgapur–Asansol region. The Raniganj local directory of business is dominated by these sponge iron units. Few of them source their coal from the CIL depots.

'There was a police action in 2013 so the supply (from these wells) had dried up. The prices of coal at our e-auction shot up', Chakravarty said.

The firms which benefit from this illegal coal mining also provide the finance for the local musclemen to stand guard over these mines and the labourers. The entire Bardhaman district of West Bengal, including Raniganj, is pockmarked with abandoned coal mines, some of them over a century old, uneconomical for ECL to tap into. The Varanasi market also got its supplies from some of these truck consignments.

The illegal mining even now provides sustenance for a large segment of the heavily populated districts. The towns in this region sport a paradox of socio-economic conditions. Real estate rates in towns like Salanpur, Rupnarayanpur, Asansol in West Bengal and Dhanbad in Bihar have escaped the industrial downturn in the region. One of the ubiquitous transports in these areas is the tractor trailers that ferry passengers in the day and coal at the night, often driving dangerously fast, careening across the narrow lanes with their load.

In 2005, when a Bharatiya Janata Party (BJP) member of legislative assembly (MLA) Krishnanand Rai was killed in a gang warfare, the assailants had pumped in four hundred bullets from six AK 47 guns into his car in Ghazipur, next door to the market. 'When the bahubalis move in for the kill, they clearly leave nothing to chance', wrote Alka Pande in a perceptive piece on the region.

State police records show a massive jump in crime with especially that of formation of organised gangs from the early 1970s. Coal was a huge draw and so were tenders for rail and public works. In fact, post nationalisation, as governments began to pump in money, ambitious men from this backward region saw opportunities to milk the contracts.

Travelling from Kolkata to Delhi just after NH 2 enters Jharkhand, you could easily miss a small board announcing the office of the Dhanbad collector. Standing at the mouth of a T-junction, it is the only sign leading from the highway that informs that one is entering coal country. The single-lane road runs for about 10 km when the town of Dhanbad suddenly springs up around you.

Far more prominent is a sign at the approach to the town announcing a school—Sri Sri Surya Deo Singh Smriti Gurukulam. The hermitic-sounding eponymously named school stands beside a massive gate, the home of the biggest coal mafia leader of Dhanbad district.

I tried to find how Surya Deo Singh earned the saintly prefix. The principal of the school, Tahseen Ahmad, offered little to go ahead with.

'He is the inspiration for this school. We hire the best teachers and none comes in through *sifarish* (patronage)'. The school was set up under a foundation set up by his family.

It is appropriate that Surya Deo Singh's house should stand guard at the mouth of the coal country. He was an MLA for four terms and his wife Kunti Singh is a member from Jharia in the present Bihar legislative assembly. The reverence of the headmaster is a part of the folklore of this region where extraction of coal by any means by any one was lauded, while the role of companies like BCCL to protect its property was often seen as a nuisance.

Surya Deo Singh landed in Dhanbad in the 1950s from the relatively barren district of Ballia almost next door in Uttar Pradesh. The district even now has hardly any industry to speak of. Able-bodied men from there either migrated in search of work to Varanasi in the west or to Dhanbad in the east. Singh went east.

He soon made his presence felt as a muscleman for the coal miners. While he was larger than life presence in the subsequent history of the region, the coal companies connived with him to keep prices low. Ahindra Chakraborty, former independent director at Western Coalfields Limited (WCL), says that the mines in the district worked on a practical principle. 'Each mine was run by an agent. Coal company executives went around asking for quotes for the cheapest coal. In turn the agent hired workers from mining contractors in bulk. It was an either or situation', he said.

Singh learned to play the hiring game. From there, it was only a short haul to emerge as a labour leader. Once the workers got long-term employment post nationalisation, he became the numero uno leader of these workers. As soon as plans for nationalisation were announced, there was a predictable rush among the workers to get absorbed in the new company. There were two obstacles.

Mines like Chitra Colliery which used to operate 11 mines employing 3,600 workers had by 1974 slumped to half that level as investment in the sector was squeezed out. So, there were fewer active workers on the rolls. The second problem was in the process. Each worker had to fill in a form known as Form B detailing his/ her current status. These forms disappeared from the market. An *Economic and Political Weekly* article of 1983 describes the process.

> Prices for the B form ranged from ₹500 to ₹1,000 at the time of the take-over. Most of the old workers could not raise the sums required; some others who put in all their savings and handed them over to unscrupulous agents still did not procure the identity cards which went to others who impersonated them.

The others were men like Singh. Little changed post nationalisation:

> Corruption is rampant in the recruitment of new workers and the going rate for employment in the mine is ₹5,000. Once employed the workers have to hand over various kinds of illegal deductions, forcible subscriptions to unions which they do not support, and even coerced contributions to religious functions. One such occasion was a large scale yagna held in 1983 whose expenses were borne by the 2,090-odd workers who had no choice but to hand over sums of money ranging upto ₹50 each from their wages. The yagna was ostensibly organised by the community but according to the workers it was the agents of the dominant trade union who had conceived of the yagna which was being held for the second year in succession. (ibid.)

Names such as Babloo Srivastava, Brijesh Singh and those who organised caste-based gangs such as Hari Shankar Tiwari and Virendra Pratap Shahi straddled the Chandasi market and the mines of BCCL and ECL.

On the day I came to Dhanbad, the road was chock-a-block with supporters of the ultra-leftist party Maoist Coordination Committee parading their candidate for the Jharkhand legislative assembly elections. At frequent intervals, the procession would stop to pay homage to the memorials on the roadside for some of their leaders slain in the gun battles with these musclemen, battles which made the district so notorious. It was these events which heightened the drama of films such as *Gangs of Wasseypur* based loosely on Singh Deo's life.

His men not only controlled the workers but also the output from the collieries including a share of the trucks that were filled with coal each day. While the shotgun methods to keep the cowed workers attracted attention, it was the theft of coal-laden trucks that was far more insidious.

ECL was the most notorious for coal theft and labour problems at the coal mines. BCCL and CCL came up next in the dubious honours list. To break the phenomena, ECL and BCCL came up with a system of tenders for transport companies which gave priority to ex-servicemen to run these truck agencies. Those too got infiltrated.

These transport companies came under the *Benami* ownership of the goon leaders. Even a decade after Surya Deo Singh was dead, in 2001, the allegations were so severe that the Ministry of Defence constituted a task force from the office of the director general, Relief, for random checking and surveys. In its report, the task force noted that the companies were deploying vehicles far in excess of the prescribed norms, a tell-tale sign that coal was going somewhere else than where it was supposed to. New coal mafia lords were obviously coming up from this nursery.

The truckers in turn complained that rates for loading and transportation were not revised for decades. To review those, CIL commissioned PricewaterhouseCoopers. But in spite of the new rates, complaints against the ex-servicemen-run companies surfaced again.

When the coal ministry suggested introduction of tenders for transportation of coal with a specific quota of work reserved for ex-servicemen companies, the defence ministry under Pranab Mukherjee objected. The issue had become so vitriolic that Mukherjee had a face-off in a meeting with minister of state for coal Dasari Narayana Rao in 2005. In this meeting, it was agreed that director general, Relief, would conduct investigations on all the complaints relating to malfunctioning of these companies.

It did not help. 'As on today, Ministry of Coal has not received any report on such investigations from DGR, Ministry of Defence' (Induction material, Ministry of Coal, 2014).

Throughout Chandasi's history, no state or central government could devise a system of checks to monitor the origin of the truckloads of coal that came to the market daily. The entire trade ran on *kutcha* receipts (scribbled acknowledgements) with a pittance of sales tax or excise inspections to police the operations. CIL at one stage tried to measure the amount of coal that was being stolen. The holding company asked both BCCL and ECL to come up with some measures. None of them did it; any evidence of large-scale theft would have started heads rolling among the managers responsible for blocking the thefts.

There is consequently no record in the Indian coal industry of how much mineral was stolen, per annum or per decade. Forget the pre-nationalisation period; even from 1973 until 2014, in an amazing display of faith, no government was willing to put a number to the theft. The soft approach was because men like Surya Deo Singh had wrested huge political support. In 1990, one of the few visits that Chandra Shekhar managed to make during his four-month term as the prime minister was a visit to Dhanbad and a dekko at Singh's house. A fulminating district magistrate, who had issued several warrants for Singh's arrest, refused to accompany the prime minister for that visit to the coal lord's office.

Years later, Tapas Kumar Lahiry, the feisty chairman and managing director of BCCL, told me that his first visitor on the evening he took charge as chairman was another political leader. Lahiry did not name the leader, but his assistants informed me that it was Shibu Soren—just removed as the coal minister. Soren apparently came ringed with muscleman for an assurance from Lahiry that the recruitment of miners to the company would be vetted by him. Lahiry claimed he stood down the political leader. Even as late as 2016, the Russian Consul General in Kolkata complained to Jharkhand Chief Minister Raghubar Das about a ruling party MLA Dhulu Mahato from Baghmara in Dhanbad district 'of obstructing work of a Russian company engaged with (BCCL) in his area while demanding money and jobs for locals'.

Showdowns were rare. The CIL management was more comfortable with a soft approach; the state governments were also willing to sing along. As a result, the black markets flourished. Traders, commission agents, buyers and musclemen thrived in India's coal markets besides the river Ganga. In time, like Singh, they ripened into the first breed of criminal-politicians.

Just as Singh lorded over Dhanbad, there was Mukhtar Ansari in Varanasi, who went on to become an MLA in Uttar Pradesh assembly. He became even more famous after the kidnapping and murder of Nand Kishore (Nandu) Rungta who was one of the richest coal traders of the area. The case was never solved despite Rungta's position as a Vishwa Hindu Parishad leader.

At its height, the market used to receive daily over 1,200 trucks in the dusty parking lots. The coal would be dumped in the open-air godowns of the coal handlers. 'Once the coal entered the market, no police could track the origin of the consignment', says Behal.

The central government's stock answer was that black marketing of coal happened to be a law-and-order problem and so concerned the states.

> Complaints of black marketing of coal have been reported from time to time. It is not possible to specify the exact quantum of coal black marketed and loss of revenue on account of black marketing of coal. However, raids are conducted by authorities of the concerned State Governments. Law and Order is State subject and hence, primarily, it is the responsibility of State/District administration to take necessary deterrent action to stop/curb black marketing of coal. However, when any incident of black marketing of coal comes to notice of the subsidiary companies, First information Reports (FIRs) are lodged and appropriate action taken against the guilty.

Though it did obliquely acknowledge the scale of the problem, a government document stated as follows:

> In respect of black marketing of coal Northern Coalfields Limited (NCL) have reported that CBI Lucknow and NCL vigilance dept. had jointly conducted surprise check at 7 small scale industries at Kanpur, Ramnagar, Chanduli, in Uttar Pradesh on 25.03.2011. CBI has registered cases against 5 of the said units. Pursuant to surprise check by CBI and NCL Vigilance Department, NCL has suspended coal supplies to all 22 small scale units with whom Fuel Supply Agreements (FSA) had been entered into. The FSAs of the said units have since expired. The units have filed a writ petition with the Hon'ble Allahabad High Court for the renewal of the FSAs with NCL.

Old habits die hard.

As the centre of Indian manufacturing industry moved away from North India towards the West and manufacturing centres like Agra shifted to gas as fuel, the Chandasi market declined in importance in the 1980s. Its position was taken over by Nagpur. The final nail for the market was the introduction of e-auctions for coal from 2004 onwards which cleared up a lot of rubble in the coal business and which is why ministers like Soren onwards used every occasion to stifle it.

Coal and Crime Move South

At Nagpur and its hinterland, the manufacturing centres of Maharashtra, Karnataka and Gujarat, the dynamics of the coal trade altered. Instead of the small and medium traders who dominated the buy side of the Varanasi coal *mandis*, the demand from companies south of the Vindhya hills was larger. They could not depend on random consignments arriving at Varanasi like *mandis* to run their operations, and coal linkages from CIL were getting scarce.

Nagpur is the headquarter of WCL standing at the centre of the Deccan Plateau. Two other CIL subsidiaries, South Eastern Coalfields Limited (SECL) and Mahanadi Coalfields Limited (MCL), are located an overnight journey away from this gateway to southern and western India. Like Varanasi, Nagpur also had road and rail networks to make transportation of coal easy.

However, a different problem emerged in the city of Nagpur. Unlike the uniformly rich grade of coal in all ECL and BCCL collieries, or those owned by Tata Steel whose rejects too were prized, the quality of coal in WCL varied substantially across collieries. This variation was sought to be captured through the premium that buyers were willing to pay for the coal.

The colloquial term for this premium in coal pricing in Nagpur is 'on'. To put it simply, every piece of coal has a grade. 'On' refers to the premium which that grade of coal would fetch over the price fixed by CIL. The premium for good coal, 'On', was consequently going to be high.

CIL pricing until recently did not account for these variations like the level of impurities, the size of the coal pieces and so on in every kilo and every tonne of coal. Yet even for the same grade of coal sourced from two collieries, the quality could be different.

Industries needed to stay abreast of these differences when buying coal, as it affected the quality of their production process and the amount of coal they needed to burn.

It is akin to pricing of mangoes in Indian summer. Connoisseurs know that despite the classification of mangoes into different names, the orchard from where it has been plucked, the ripeness at which it has been harvested and so on determine how it will be priced even with the same name.

So companies could not rest assured with the papers that gave them linkages to a particular grade of coal. They needed to get coal of a particular variety or premium within that grade but which those papers promising them coal supply or linkage did not specify. They needed liaison agents who could 'impress' WCL and later SECL and MCL marketing staff to allot the right collieries producing those premium coal. Those agents consequently needed to trade information about the current production status of each colliery. A new avatar of the coal trade was spawned.

This is a far cry from the cottage industry-type operations of Dhanbad-based coal miners who relied on abundant human labour but managed to pilfer less than a million tonnes per annum from the mines. The Vidarbha region's illegal coal business was an industrial operation by comparison.

> A complaint was registered alleging that some industrial units like Rolling Mills and other material manufactures situated in Nagpur District are lifting coal at subsidized rate from WCL and without consuming the said coal in their industrial units, they are selling the said coal in open market illegally and at the same time they are using imported coal/hard coke/electricity in their industries. (Parliament question on black marketing of coal. Question no. 649, answered on 2 March 2015)

There were other methods to obtain coal which traversed a fine line between legality and illegality. They were also planned on a trans-Indian scale. We had referred to coal from Meghalaya earlier. This state in the Northeast has surprisingly large deposits of good-quality coal. But because of their isolated locations and difficult terrain on the India–Bangladesh border, CIL has not moved to mine them. North Eastern Coalfields under CIL, for instance, operates only around picturesque Margherita town in Assam.

Local entrepreneurs moved into the breach. Even now, they use migrant labour from across the border to mine the coal, run cross country hikes with donkeys to transport the coal and then reach the Guwahati market at Jogighopa, from where the mineral is transported to the rest of India. Parakh had remarked that when he introduced e-auction of coal in 2004, he was informed that it had undercut the premiums on each rake of such coal from the Northeast. It was about ₹25 lakh for one railway rake.

The Meghalaya coal had a good calorific value which made it attractive for users from as far as Punjab's Mandi Gobindgarh and Haryana. Despite high sulphur content, the coal is often more sought after than the equivalent grade of CIL coal in the Varanasi market. One of those sought-after varieties is called Nangal coal, since the Punjab traders made it their first preference.

The same type of coal was being demanded by the emerging companies in Gujarat, especially in the chemicals and textile sector. Since Gujarat is also located far off from any deposits, the prices were in any case bound to be high for them. The Nagpur-based traders figured out the potential profits they could earn if the Meghalaya coal could travel to Gujarat.

They were helped by the Indian Railways. Because of the asymmetric trade with northeastern Indian states, the railways often run rakes loaded with rice and wheat going to Guwahati and beyond but return empty. The coal consignments made wonderful news for the divisional railway managers located in the Northeast. Instead of coal coming via roads in earlier decades from Guwahati to North India, it began to come via rails for the longer journey to Gujarat. The railway ministry was happy with the consequent profits.

Nobody in the policy-making corridors thought about the costs of this happiness. The consequent harsh exploitation of the men and mineral that accompanied this trade was a 360-degree disaster. The lop-sided coal economics contributed to escalation of tensions across the national border, allegedly funded secessionist groups and shut the door on the desperately poor states from getting a share of their legitimate revenues. All it needed to correct this state of affairs was a possible relaxation of the exclusive public sector marketing rights for CIL. Would the incendiary problems of coal have got whittled if this were done? It is a tantalising question to ask. As the transport of Nangal coal from Meghalaya showed, coal could be transported profitably across long distance in India. This stood the conventional logic of the Indian planners on its head which said that the economics of the mineral did not permit such travel.

Entrepreneurs from Nagpur started scouting for other opportunities to source coal from within India to feed the mills of Gujarat and Maharashtra.

In 1991, for instance, soon after MCL was incorporated, it found out that there were no takers for the coal it was mining. It announced a policy of free sale of coal from the pitheads. This was in addition to the coal linkages being given through the Ministry of Coal. Behal's was the first company to take up the offer.

'Although it had lower calorific value than Meghalaya, the coal also had lower sulphur content. For industries in populated areas this was an attractive difference', he said. His company bought the coal, transported it to Paradip Port in the state and sailed it along the coastline to Gujarat. At ₹1,700 a tonne, it cost just a fraction more than the coal promised as linkage by CIL which was above ₹1,400 but which rarely materialised. Tata Chemicals bought Behal's first consignment.

Once the traders had run consignments along the shores, the next stage was a short hop to cross the Indian Ocean to procure supplies from afar. In the same year, South Africa sent a cricket team to play its first test series in India after the lifting of apartheid; it also exported its first consignment of thermal coal to India. Coal imports became a viable option.

Nagpur had established itself as the centre of India's coal business in the private sector, much as Varanasi had done in the earlier decades. Its geography helped and so did its location as a junction for rail and road connections to South and Western India. The hardy entrepreneurs of the city did not have the advantage of nurturing sugarcane plantations unlike the millers near to the coast. One of their few options was to dabble in coal trade. The number of coal traders listed in the trade journals for the city is massive. The Central Provinces Club where Behal meets me in the evening to continue the conversation and The Gondwana Club next door to the WCL head office were the places where many of them walked in to settle some of the deals. It was in this milieu that the central government decided to relax the rules for owning of coal blocks.

Coal on the Cricket Field

Manoj Jayaswal loved to play cricket on holidays with his employees. From the owner of Abhijeet Group, messages would go out to his employees to spend their Sunday at one of Nagpur stadiums. The boss apparently enjoyed batting for long stretches while they bowled and fielded.

The second son of a quiet business family did not start out with those streaks of flamboyance when they travelled the underbelly of India's steel sector from the 1950s onwards. It was acquired later on in life. The family business founded by his father Basant Lall Shaw was that of a small-scale foundry unit in Nagpur, Jayaswal Neco. The family traces its root from Bihar, but the elder Jayaswal worked as a scrap dealer in Calcutta moving onto Nagpur as business opportunities moved out of eastern India.

The quiet business environment of the 1970s and the 1980s in Nagpur were about to change as the government of PV Narasimha Rao came to power in 1991.

Fresh legitimate business opportunities were still difficult to find for new entrepreneurs in the India of the 1990s. The business of coal offered little profit if one worked legitimately as a trader under CIL. Shortages made bending rules far more attractive.

This picture began to change from 1993. The Rao government handed out three licences for coal blocks to CESC of the Goenkas, Hindalco of Aditya Birla and the state electricity board of West Bengal. Yet as these were established players, the move did not attract much of an attention.

In 1996, the new United Front government under Deve Gowda, however, did something that made a lot of companies sit and take notice, none more so than the coal traders of Nagpur who could sense the implications. Within a fortnight of being sworn in, the government cleared four coal blocks for private mining. One of these cleared was a coal block in the thick forests of Mand Raigarh, located 50 km from the nearest railway station in Raigarh.

The coal block Gare Palma IV\1 until today remains the largest ever given out in India to a private sector company. It was won by Jindal Steel and Power Limited (JSPL), which was owned by a relatively unknown member of the Haryana legislative assembly at that time, Om Prakash Jindal. He had joined the Haryana Vikas

Party under Bansi Lal, who became the chief minister just weeks before Deve Gowda took over as the prime minister on 1 June. Bansi Lal's party was a member of the United Front coalition. Jindal's son-in-law Sandeep Jajodia-run Monnet Ispat & Energy also got a block in the same hill range, Gare Palma IV\5 a day after him.

The word spread that new entrants had a chance to score in coal mining. After the 1998 general elections, the new member of parliament from Nagpur was Vilas Muttemwar from Congress who went on to become a member of the house committee on energy and also the convenor of one of its sub-committees on coal. These committees egged the government to bundle a coal mine with a power or a steel plant, or for setting up washeries. In the city's business circles at the Central Provinces Club and the Gondwana Club, the new possibilities of tapping coal instead of buying linkages from state-owned CIL began to be taken seriously.

The traders of Varanasi were too set in their ways, and their financial base was eroding fast for them to match the Nagpur entrepreneurs.

The Jayaswals applied for a mine. They were in a venerable company. A year before, the president of the local chamber of commerce, Vidrabha Industries Association, Govind Daga, had earned a block for his Central Collieries Company Limited.

The coal rush was on. Daga as the president of the local industry association knew first-hand the intense demand for coal. A mine seemed a wonderful opportunity to scoop up in the circumstances. The fact that the coal ministry had imposed an end-use restriction seemed only a minor hindrance that had to be dealt with.

The veteran businessman found out a way. His Central Collieries Company was given a mine to bring up coal for his washery which in turn would be used as feedstock in a power plant. Instead, he forged an approval from the coal ministry to inform the Maharashtra state government that until the time the plant was up and running, he had the right to sell coal in the open market.

A *Hitavada* newspaper report said,

> The (company) had submitted copies of the relevant pages from the mining plan retained with them and allegedly submitted to Government of Maharashtra. This was strongly rebutted by the Department of Coal, which submitted that the approved mining plan retained with the Department has no such provision.... [O]f

the mining plan approved by Central Government one copy was retained in the department and one was sent/given to (the company) who were requested to give original to State Government and retain a photocopy with themselves.

The state government's mining department swallowed the story, hook, line and sinker. As the Delhi High Court observed, the captive coal mines were given by the Centre, and the state had no business to decide how the mineral would be used.

Strangely enough, though the coal ministry claimed in its affidavit to the court that 'under mysterious circumstances the petitioners had got the mining plan altered', it did not ask the state government to punish the delinquent officers who had accepted those papers.

According to Central Government, (the) State Government unilaterally on July 31, 2001 permitted (Daga) to split the project into two phases and granted permission to sell the washed coal, which is contrary to law. Inspection conducted on July 3, 2000 by Department of Coal officials revealed the full capacity of the coal mine was about to be reached but there was no physical activity for setting up either the washery or the power plant. (ibid.)

The template was set. Setting aside Daga's mischief took more than a decade. The case for cancellation of his allotment came up in the courts 10 years after he had been allotted a mine in 1998. Meanwhile, there was zero loss for the state government officials who were caught bending. Coal could thus be purloined from the mines and sold to the highest bidder.

The Jayaswal family also borrowed the template as did so many others. What they soon realised was that the game would need a political support to play with to make up for the weakness of their balance sheet and their relative lack of experience. The Jindals had shown the way earlier. The Jayaswals also scouted for some support.

The first block which was allocated to them was located in the same forests where Jindal and Monnet had got theirs. The mineral from Gare Palma IV\4 instead of landing up at the washery and thence to the sponge iron plant as they had promised to the government to do went elsewhere.

As the profits rose, the cricket matches became more frequent. Manoj turned the taciturn family business into an in-your-face entity. At the height of his expansion, he and his brothers held ten coal blocks even as his operating style began imitating the film bill boards that dominated this city.

As a *Mint* newspaper report put it pithily,

> Manoj and his wife Manisha currently occupy a penthouse in JP Heights, a building in Behramji Town, a tony neighbourhood in Nagpur (this was 2012). Although he has largely managed to stay out of the media eye in the past 10 years, Jayaswal displays all the signs of a man who has made a lot of money very fast, according to the first associate. He owns at least one private jet, is a regular at high-society parties, and has held plenty of his own. When his daughter Swatee got married in Thailand in 2009, Indian wedding blogs gushed that the event was the most expensive ever to have been held in Phuket.

From the many photographs of Jayaswal that crop up in society pages, his sartorial choices seem to lean towards loud shirts, velvet jackets, and glitter and applique jeans. In most of these images, he sports a thin moustache framing a broad white smile. In one of his heady years, the coal man hired Indian rapper and hip-hop singer Hard Kaur to perform in his birthday party in Nagpur. He followed up this act next year, according to guests who attended his birthday celebrations with a Mumbai film style do. The guests were treated to a film set lookalike that was a throwback to an Amitabh Bachchan starrer where Manoj himself appeared on stage sporting a jacket studded with disco lights and holding a guitar. A group of fair-skinned dancers posing with him completed the show. The halcyon days of the nineteenth-century entrepreneurs, it would seem was black.

In the middle of the fun and dance jigs though, Manoj Jayaswal made sure that

> [the coal blocks] were allotted to Abhijeet Infrastructure Capital (which was renamed Abhijeet Power Ltd in November 2010, and is now his empire's flagship). During the split with his family, he ensured that Abhijeet Infrastructure remained under his control. His modus operandi was simple: showing coal blocks and power purchase agreements with distribution companies, he managed to get loans out of banks. He followed up the coal block allotments with agreements with states such as Jharkhand to build power plants. Financial closure followed.

Abhijeet was the name of his son; the company finally went in for a share flotation in 2011. It did not happen.

When Chinese Premier Wen Jiabao visited India in 2010, the group was among those who signed big ticket deals with Chinese companies. These included an MoU to buy power plant equipment worth $2.5 billion. It has run up an unpaid bad loan account of ₹4,500 crore owed to a clutch of dozen lenders. Adani Group and India Power had bid to take over the business but that too has not gone through.

The company at one time ran its operations from the sixth floor of one of the busiest malls in the city, Landmark on Wardha Road in Nagpur. It has now moved to another location leaving several of those rooms unoccupied. Photographs of Jayaswal with almost all top Indian politicians including one with president of India Pratibha Singh Patil were sent out by the company's publicity wing at one time much like that of another infamous business buccaneer Sahara Chief Subrata Roy.

In that snap with President Patil in the centre, Manoj is accompanied by Vijay Darda. This is the political connection he was looking for. Pretty close to Jayaswal's office in Landmark on Wardha Road is the office of *Lokmat*, the Marathi daily newspaper owned by Vijay Darda and his brother Rajendra Darda. While Muttemwar was a member of Lok Sabha, Darda is a Congress member of the upper house. Rajendra was a minister in the Maharashtra government.

Darda and Jayaswal formed a well-known pair in the Nagpur business circles—referred to as Jay–Viru, the celebrated pair of friends from Hindi film *Sholay*. Darda picked shares in one of the companies floated by Manoj Jayaswal and his brother, AMR Iron and Steel Private Limited. The story as it broke in *Mail Today* newspaper claimed that the shares were allegedly given free to Darda because of his help in securing the Bander coal block in Maharashtra for the company. The MP who has an eponymous art gallery on the main road had written to the prime minister making a strong pitch for Jayaswal to get the coal block. This was one of the last sets allotted by New Delhi made in May 2009 before the window of discretionary allotment was closed after handing out 218 coal blocks.

Darda did not stop there. Along with his brother Rajendra, he promoted JLD Yavatmal Energy which got a coal block, even as he was penning letters for Abhijeet. Some of those investments have paid off. Rajendra Darda's assets had risen from ₹6 crore in 2004 to ₹75 crore by 2014. Vijay Darda also had seen his assets rise to nearly ₹50 crore, though he moved around in only a Nano.

As the coal blocks were seized from Abhijeet and related group companies through a SC order, by February 2015, the Calcutta High Court ordered the winding up of Jayaswal's Corporate Power Limited, his flagship company.

Nagpur-based merchants cornered close to 40 per cent of all the blocks the government handed out. All of them wrote in their applications to the screening committees that they would use the coal to run either a sponge iron plant or a washery. Indian coal has high ash content. A washery is a coal handling and preparation plant. These plants remove soil and rock from coal, crush it into graded sized chunks and make it ready for easy use wherever it is needed as fuel. The process cuts down on the ash content of the coal, makes it commercially more valuable, reduces transport cost and is environmentally better. Like everything else, CIL was short of washeries too with only one facility set-up until 1990.

The coal merchants knew that in the demand-asphyxiated market, it was not really necessary to wash the coal to remove impurities. Rather the margins from washing coal were less than the value they would get for selling the unwashed coal. Even CIL was not willing to wash coal. Its chairman Narsing Rao said, 'We will go for washeries but let the demand come from the consumers'.

So with no particular demand from consumers for washed coal, those who had bid for setting up washeries began to undercut the process. 'It was literally a case of unloading trucks at the front gate and using another truck to pick up the same consignments from the other end of the plants', said one of the investigators into the scam. Entrepreneurs of various hues were attracted to the opportunity.

A report by a think tank said,

Installed capacity of washeries for non-coking coal remained almost constant from 2002 to 2008, in spite of the declared desire to take up washing earnestly in 2002. In 2008–09 there was a huge spike in the installed capacity, with practically all the additional capacity coming from private washeries. (*Prayas Coal Report*, January 2013)

Suddenly, there was a huge jump in the ratio of washed coal. The yield, that is, ratio of washed coal to raw coal feed, of private washeries went up from a poor 34 per cent in 2005–2006 to 74 per cent in 2009–2010.

The washeries were consequently prime targets for investigation. The income tax department raided one of those, Aryan Coal Beneficiation (India) Limited. It was alleged that the Delhi-based company had set up a washery in Chhattisgarh from where it sold the coal it got from WCL and SECL into the black market. Its chairman Captain RS Sindhu was the son-in-law of late Sahib Singh Verma of BJP, one-time chief minister of Delhi. Sindhu had also served as the co-chairman of Industry Chamber ASSOCHAM's national committee on coal in 2009. One of the places the tax people checked up on during their raids was Nagpur.

Despite my attempts, Manoj Jayaswal proved elusive to meet. But I had better luck elsewhere. One evening in the city, I met Padmesh Gupta, chief of Gupta Corporation, one of the largest coal handlers of Nagpur. At one stage, he had several washeries. Gupta also has had a run in with the CBI recently and is consequently not too keen to meet an inquisitive journalist. But he relented after I chase him throughout the day, across his offices.

His office Gupta Towers is easy to locate in the centre of the city. It is on the top floor of a mall just as Jayaswal's office was. In fact, his people describe it to me as the Pantaloons mall building. Auto rickshaw drivers immediately cottoned on to the location and took me there. Coal business has given a major push to real estate in the city. Gupta, however, was very willing to talk about the coal business once I got past his understandable reticence. In his office room which is quite small and bare, there is the ubiquitous platform for Ganesha above. He was wearing a ghee-coloured shirt—but except for the rings on most fingers, there is no sense of soaring presence.

Shishir Arya of *The Times of India* has extensively tracked the antics of several of these merchants. Because of this intimate knowledge, his reports on several of the coal cases over the past few years have been filled with absorbing details. Shishir informs me that lenders have now pulled the plug on Gupta's coal washery firm, Gupta Global Resources Private Limited. 'All the washeries in the region belonging to this company have stopped operations since three years. Though the closure was not purely due to business reasons', he adds.

Gupta's firm was closed after state-run power utility Mahagenco filed a police complaint alleging breach of trust by this company and terminated the contract to buy coal from it. The complaint is the same; coal sourced on behalf of Mahagenco did not often reach the state government-owned generating company in the quantity or quality they had signed on for. It instead was allegedly siphoned off from the market as 'rejects'.

But Gupta blames the quality of coal supplied by WCL or SECL as the reason why he could not stick to the washing standards. 'If there is 25 per cent stone in a consignment, how I could deliver 95 per cent of the coal I received as washed coal', he argues. He has a beautiful parable to explain his choices. 'When you have to travel in a train with your family for an emergency wouldn't you bribe the ticket examiner', he argues.

It made sense to build washeries to pilfer coal 'to bribe the ticket examiner'. The coal companies did so liberally. The easiest way to do so was to promise to set up a sponge iron plant.

There was also another good reason to build sponge iron plants. As the world economy recovered from the trough of the East Asian crisis, demand for all commodities had shot up. Steel became especially prized in the market. Sponge iron manufacturing, an intermediate in the steel production process, consequently became lucrative too.

Sponge iron gives almost the same quality for downstream products that need steel but not for the quality that conventional steel products demand. Set up as units with production levels of less than a million tonnes annually, plants were 'user-friendly'. The plants bypass the expensive blast furnace process for making steel as well as substituting coking coal with coal of lesser quality, using a low capital-intensive process known as direct reduced iron (DRI). It was essentially easy to diversify into production of sponge iron to get a coal mine in the bargain.

'The China bubble had made life difficult for DRIs as coal prices rose', says Ujjawal Chatterjee, chief operating officer of Tata Sponge.

Until 2002, only five companies producing sponge iron had applied for coal mines. In 2003, seven companies did so. In 2006, a whopping 47 sponge iron producer picked up shares in mines. By 2009, there were 80 of these companies holding mining blocks, mostly through joint production contracts.

In a written reply in the Parliament, the former coal minister Sriprakash Jayawsal noted that

[O]f the 195 blocks allotted to companies (other than CIL), 96 blocks were given to government owned companies or to the ultra mega power projects (UMPPs; those came through bidding). Another 27 blocks were allotted to private companies in the power sector, and two were for coal to liquid projects aimed at bringing in new technology into the country.

Of the rest, fifty-five blocks were allotted to sponge iron manufacturers, some of them with funny money. In the CBI roll call of thirty-nine cases in the coal scam, most came from this group.

'Some of them figured their best bet would be to sell off the mines if commercial coal mining was allowed through a change in government policy', says U Kumar, former SECL chairman. He was not making any inspired guesses. In the year 2000, the NDA government had introduced a bill in Rajya Sabha to allow commercial mining of coal. The sponge iron companies had, therefore, good enough reason to feel that a change was just around the corner. It is a different matter that the bill has not moved from there since. Even otherwise, the high price of coal gave a spur to the application for mines. Under the ruse of mining for consumption as end use in sponge iron plant, coal could be sold in the markets. It was literally free for all.

As coal blocks kept coming on the table every year from 1998, business found new ways to tap profits but again by tweaking the terms of the contract like Daga. None was more enterprising in this respect than EMTA, formerly Eastern Mineral and Trading Agency. EMTA pioneered an 'asset-lite' model for the capital-intensive power sector.

While the rules for captive mines made it clear that companies had to have some end use plant or washery as a pre-condition to obtain a coal block, Ujjal Upadhyay, the reclusive chairman of Asansol, West Bengal-based EMTA found a way to duck under the rules. Ujjal, or rather his father Sideshwar Upadhyay, came into prominence allegedly with the support of West Bengal Chief Minister Jyoti Basu in 1996. Around the same time when Basu wrote his letter of support to Ramaprasad Goenka for Sarisatolli, he handed out two coal blocks won by the state electricity boards, Tara East and West, to EMTA to provide coal supply for Bakreshwar Thermal Power Project.

EMTA per se did not play around with rules like Jayaswal, Gupta or Daga. But without issuing any tender, West Bengal State Electricity Board handed over the management of two coal blocks to the company. This company, in turn, formed a joint venture with state-owned West Bengal Power Development Corporation offering it a 20 per cent stake and Durgapur Projects Ltd another 6 per cent stake as Bengal EMTA Coal Mines Ltd with a paid-up capital of just ₹5 crore. In the venture, the two government companies just had the negative rights to block change in the nature of the company but no management control.

EMTA promised the state government that it would supply coal at a lower price than what CIL charged. For instance, in 2015, while the CIL price for the coal was ₹1,100 per tonne, EMTA claimed a price of ₹880 a tonne. What the state was losing out on was the extraction cost for EMTA which worked out to ₹350 a tonne. The extraction was in turn run by one of the group companies of EMTA. The terms of the agreement between the state government and EMTA committed the former to buy coal at a price which is 19.5 per cent less than what CIL charged. The sub-contract for digging coal went to EMTA Coal, which is wholly owned by the Upadhyays. Bengal EMTA, the joint venture, paid this firm 98.5 per cent of what it received from the government-run company. Since the price of coal mined was linked to CIL price, it had seemed fair initially since the company was not asking for a cost plus model. But post 2006, as coal prices were being raised by CIL, its owner Ujjal Upadhyay was sitting pretty. As a *Financial Express* article pointed out while the state companies whined that they were overcharged for coal from their own blocks, they could do little to get out. So Bengal EMTA remained a sort of shell company, while the difference earned from EMTA Coal was what Upadhyay family pocketed.

No one in the state government when the deal was signed bothered to do a fact-check on the markdown of the cost of coal that should be insisted upon. If the discount had been deeper, then the state would have got coal cheaper and produced electricity at a lower rate. It is interesting how a former sand supplier to CIL, EMTA, learnt the ropes, while the public policy-makers did not.

The chairman of West Bengal Power Development Corporation S Mahapatra told us that coal accounted for 70 per cent of the cost of power generation. His thermal power project at Bakreshwar required 20 million tonne coal annually of which 4 million tonne comes from EMTA.

Soon the father–son duo took the model to other state governments. In Jharkhand, it made a presentation before the minister of state for mines, minerals and geology department, Ravindra Kumar Rai. The company wanted to conduct a geophysical study of the newly formed state. As a then newspaper report noted, 'The company, which has coal washeries and is working for the *restoration and rehabilitation of the ecosystem in different parts of the country* [italics mine] and abroad, has expressed its interest in granite, iron and coal block mining in the state'.

It also tapped other states which had won coal blocks but lacked the ability to mine them. In fact, it is difficult to figure out why states like Punjab or Karnataka would want a coal mine. Having done so, both of them and even Maharashtra swallowed the offer from EMTA. Of the nine such bids from state government-led joint ventures to bid for what was known as case 1 projects, seven involved EMTA. Six of those were for mine development operations with the profits to be shared in the ratio of 74:26 in favour of the Kolkata-based company. Case 1 projects are those where the power-generating company has no assured coal supply and so can build the consequent higher costs into its tariff. It is a high-risk venture that typically government-run entities would enter into.

One of the officers in a state government said that the Upadhyays were a methodical group. 'They would work on the details for hours and days to satisfy us', he said. There was none of the sewn-on-lights on jackets razzmatazz of Manoj Jayaswal about them. The only claim to the stars was the Lamborghini parked at their central Kolkata office. It would be a sight when the low-slung vehicle would come out very early in the morning rolling past the rickshaws and *jhalmuri wallahs,* roaring under the bonnet.

By the time the coal block allocations were halted, the EMTA group had become India's third-largest coal supplier after CIL and JSPL with fourteen blocks under Upadhyay's belt. His venture like the one with Punjab State Electricity Board promised to build a host of social infrastructure projects at mines like at Pachmara in Jharkhand. None of those promises materialised, but those defaults were obviously not enough reasons to haul him in. He was questioned instead for having taken up commercial mining of coal in two of those joint ventures. Of these, one was sewn up with

Himachal Electricity Board which is the only one where EMTA put itself in the records as a mine owner.

EMTA's story did not end there. It jumped back in the fray when the NDA government reallocated some of the mines back to the states in 2015. In both Punjab and Karnataka, the state governments rehired EMTA to become the mine development operator without going through a tender agreeing with the company that it had the right of first refusal. Piyush Goyal's ministry came down like a ton of sack on the two states serving them with a show cause notice which promptly acknowledged their error and cancelled the orders. EMTA has now taken the two states to courts.

As the CBI launched an SC-monitored investigation into the two decade-long allotment letters, pictures of all sorts of people tumbled out of the coal galleries. The portraits were mostly murky as many of them won through political connections. This was not new, however. Right from the time when Ramaprasad Goenka got political support for the application for a coal block in 1993, political leadership at the states had considered it their duty to offer patronage. In the high noon of allotments, this became the norm than the exception.

In SKS Ispat, which got three coal blocks, the brother of the former central minister Subodh Kant Sahay allegedly sat on the board. On his part, Sahay denied that he had lobbied for the company to get one of those blocks, Vijay Central. He quit the cabinet ahead of a reshuffle by Singh in 2012. Congress MP Naveen Jindal's final score of JSPL was five blocks.

The list went on and on. IST Steel & Power, a company promoted by the son of Rashtriya Janata Dal (RJD) Rajya Sabha MP Prem Chand Gupta, was allotted a coal block. Gupta, a former importer of watches, was a central minister in the UPA-I government holding the portfolio of company affairs, a role that included monitoring corporate accountability.

Minister of state for information & broadcasting, S Jagathrakshakan of DMK, at one stage during his tenure notched up a record number of applications for visits abroad. But despite the visits, he found time to become director of JR Power Generation Pvt. Ltd which within a week of its incorporation entered into a MoU with Puducherry Industrial Promotion Development Corporation. That MoU was the basis on which it was allotted a coal block in 2007. The minister, however, said that he had resigned as the director of the company before he filed his nomination to run for the Lok Sabha in 2009 elections.

There were film barons too. SPS Sponge Iron sharing space with Tata Sponge at Radhikapur was headed by Bipin Kumar Vohra who was a well-known producer of films. Incidentally, one of his films *15 Park Avenue* contained a graphic portrayal of coal mafia culture in Dhanbad.

Among all of these shenanigans, Padmesh Gupta refuses to ascribe too much blame on Manoj Jayaswal for why he applied for the coal blocks. 'There were several queues available to get coal from the government. The queue for the small and medium industries without any linkages was the longest. The queue for those applying for a block was the shortest. Wouldn't a person jump?' He compares the behaviour to that for people waiting in a line for cinema tickets.

In an obtuse way, he is correct. From the 1970s in Varanasi, through the transformation of Nagpur into a coal city, entrepreneurs had seen the travails of trying to obtain coal supplies for those trying the legitimate route. Shortages had instead got hardwired into the sector. One of those shortages played out as a 'theft' of a coal mine.

How Much Coal Does a Power Plant Need

Some of the murkiest battles over securing coal supply were fought in Singrauli in Madhya Pradesh. Just across the hills from Varanasi, it was bound to be a war zone on coal. Abundant coal, water and a thin population density made Singrauli a fabulous location for mega power projects right from the beginning of the post-Independence phase. One of India's first hydel power plants was built over Rihand River in 1961. The very first projects of state-owned National Thermal Power Corporation (NTPC) were the three thermal power plants it set up here using the coal reserves of the district.

The private sector companies began to make inroads into the valley post 1991. The approach to the town from the Vindhyachal shows how little these companies have ploughed back money into the local infrastructure. From Mirzapur town in Uttar Pradesh as soon as one leaves the Kolkata–Delhi highway to climb the hill, the road loses its black top. The three-hour ride into Singrauli over the hills is dusty with no hint of even a decent halt on the way.

Singrauli town however makes up a lot for it. It is clean and the roads are fairly spacious. The district headquarters is a rather neat affair too. The crowd at any point through the day is never heavy, and our work with the staff to examine the land records was done very fast. Outside the office, the Jayant Morwa Road leading to the Sasan Ultra Mega Power Project (UMPP) has the usual mixture of à la carte traffic on Indian roads—bullock carts, trucks and SUVs.

Those too soon empty out as the hills take over a little beyond the town. Singaruli sits at the base of the Chitrakoot hills nestled amid thick sal forests and the myriad jutting arms of Rihand Dam. Driving down the uneven road out of the town, a new skyline soon takes over. On each corner of the horizon, one can see the chimneys of power plants—of NTPC, Reliance Power's Sasan project, Essar, Hindalco and Jaypee—and there are still others coming up. This is India's thermal power valley. It is quite appropriate that some of the pitched battles over industrialisation are being fought here. While some of them concern environment issues and some concern land, others concern the seamy aspects of politico-industry nexus.

Just about an hours' journey from Singrauli town centre, close to one arm of the Rihand Dam is situated the Sasan UMPP. It is one of the two that have come on steam out of the eight the government began to bid out from 2006. The other one is the Tata Power's Mundra power project in India's west coast.

On the same day in August 2012 when the explosive coal audit report by the CAG was tabled in the Parliament, another report was also tabled. This was a performance audit of 'Ultra Mega Power Projects under special purpose vehicles (Ministry of Power)'.

Although the report was a critique of the functioning of the power ministry's handling of each of the 4,000 MW projects, it caused a larger collateral damage in the coal ministry. But the din from the coal report drowned this one out for some time.

The background of the CAG's UMPPs report was straightforward. The 3,960 MW Anil Ambani-owned Reliance Power Limited (RPL) project at Sasan was awarded two coal blocks, Moher and Moher Amlohri extension in the Singaruli area. These blocks had an estimated total reserve of about 600 million tonnes of coal. Since the plant at full capacity would need about 18–20 million tonnes per year while these blocks could produce only about 12 MT, the government decided to provide it another mine nearby named Chhatrasal with an annual capacity of 5 MT.

Things got complicated from here. The company had initially agreed that it needed the additional mine but three months later told the government that it had improved on its technology to produce the necessary coal from the first two mines. It asked for permission to use the coal from Chhatrasal to fuel another 4,000 MW power plant the company was building in the same neighbourhood at Chitrangi. This position was curiously supported by the Madhya Pradesh government.

An extraordinary group of ministers, Manmohan Singh's pet ploy to deflect decision, debated it at two meetings. It sanctioned the use of 'the surplus coal from blocks allotted to Sasan UMPP by other projects of RPL subject to (some) undertakings'. The CAG objected noting that change vitiated the level playing field for future developers and asked for reviewing the decision. It also estimated that the 'post-bid concessions extended to RPL in Sasan UMPP resulted in financial benefit to RPL to the tune of ₹29,033 crore with a net present value of ₹11,852 crore'.

The subject of surplus coal did not leave the coal ministry until the government changed in 2014. In between, several ministries and departments tried several options to wriggle out of the charges of 'crony capitalism' which this decision by the group of ministers generated.

At one stage, the issue was flagged by yet another group of ministers now buttressed by an opinion from the then attorney general Ghulam Vahanavati who said that the change was broadly okay. The group of ministers led by the finance minister Pranab Mukherjee gave their approval for which a gazette notification had been issued earlier in 2010. At the same meeting, they also mulled over a Planning Commission paper which claimed that there should be a policy to allow more such captive mines if they came on line before the connected project was ready, to sell their coal as surplus. Other ministries pointed out that selling of coal as surplus from mines which the companies had got free from the government would tantamount to backdoor revision of coal nationalisation. It would give the companies an incentive to 'never show interest in bringing up the end use plant'. The larger debate got referred to a committee of secretaries for further examination. It has not emerged from there since.

In response to a questionnaire from a Parliament committee, the coal ministry also admitted that it did not have the ability to police projects like Sasan UMPP to ensure that the coal they mined was first used in the existing project before the surplus was sent to other plants like Chitrangi. It pushed the onus for that to the power ministry. Like many other coal cases, the CBI picked up the papers concerning this one too from the ministry.

The curtain came down on the unsavoury episode when the government affidavit submitted to the SC in the coal case showed only two blocks—Moher and Moher Amlohri stood allocated to the project. Chhatrasal will now get other bidders. The right to trade in coal as the dispute over Sasan project was all about did not end here. The dispute simmered, like several others, on the tray of coal policy dishes that were yet to be finalised. As the returns from the coal mines slid, in another four years, Reliance Power would approach New Delhi for permission to mortgage the two coal blocks to foreign lenders. The spunk had gone out of coal business. While it lasted the injury from the dirty tricks, business in coal would go on to create a deep political crisis.

5

Notes from an Auditor

A Long Walk

On a balmy afternoon in March 2015, Congress leaders walked in a show of solidarity to former Prime Minister Manmohan Singh's residence just half a kilometre from their office at 24 Akbar Road.

A few days earlier, a CBI special court in Delhi had sent out a summons to Singh. He was summoned as an accused, no less; an ignominy no Indian prime minister had suffered except for Indira Gandhi. Her summons was at least for a political case. The Allahabad High Court had issued the summons to her for alleged electoral malpractices in 1974. This was the case which triggered her declaration of the Emergency in the country. Singh was being summoned for a criminal case, for the alleged wrong allocation of a coal mine to a private sector company Hindalco made in 2005. Singh held the additional charge of the coal ministry at that point.

Singh would have found several known faces in the CBI special courtrooms in central Delhi's Patiala House, if he had appeared. The dust-caked rooms cooled by noisy air coolers with smoky tube lights were situated less than 2 km from Singh's office of the prime minister on Raisina Hill. The courts had become the unlikely converging point for corporate czars, their wives, ministers and senior government officers in a most horrible indictment of the Indian economic story from the summers of 2013. These people instead of appearing with Singh in his office began to make trips to those courtrooms often to walk into jail by evening as undertrials.

On most days, at lunch time, there would be an unusual spectacle in the CBI special courts. Once the judge left the courtroom, the accused, their relatives and sometimes even the police would share the food sitting on the floor, scrambling back to order once the orderly came in to announce the afternoon session. Next doors, the regular armies of undertrials from various jails in the city for offences ranging from pickpockets to grisly murders were being produced before trial judges from morning until late afternoon.

The coal cases, just like the telecom ones before, showed how the ship of entrepreneurship in India had run aground on the fatal hazard of shifting government policies, run up by pliable bureaucrats and conniving ministers, to help companies run by fortune hunters. More headlines were emerging from the courts than from press conferences on future business plans of corporate India. Because of these shenanigans, the list of accused was getting longer and reaching into the boardrooms of companies that had built up stellar reputation otherwise. One of those was Hindalco.

Bharat Parashar, the additional session's judge picked by the SC as the special judge for the coal cases, enjoyed the reputation of a tough taskmaster. He had already warned the CBI director Ranjit Sinha, telling him that he would be 'directly responsible' if the probe team's work in the investigation of the cases fell short of acceptable standards. 'One of those shortcomings', Parashar said, 'was CBI's reluctance to question Singh for his role in the allotment of coal blocks'.

So when on 12 March in the afternoon Parashar came back to his podium to announce the list of accused the CBI had to produce in court for the Hindalco coal allotment case, an air of uneasy expectation spread in the room. The judge read out the six names from his list slowly. It included Kumar Mangalam Birla, chairman of the Aditya Birla Group and owner of Hindalco; the former coal secretary PC Parakh; Hindalco Group Executive President B Shubhendu Amitabh; and Managing Director D Bhattacharya. 'There were gasps in the packed court room when Parashar first named the five accused, paused, and then called out accused number 6 as the "then coal minister"'. He meant Manmohan Singh. They were to appear before the court on 8 April.

The Indian Express report headlined next morning, 'Accused No. 6 Manmohan Singh: Court summons former PM over Hindalco coal block'. It was a huge embarrassment for the Congress party.

The party scrambled for the right response. The decision to stage a walk to the residence of Singh was meant to assure him that they would fight the summons together. The larger message was a public acknowledgement that the Congress party stood by his decisions in the coal allotments. The show of solidarity was, however, eleven years late in the making. The party should have stood by him in 2004 when Singh pushed for changing the rules for coal block allocation into an auction route. Instead, as the Congress party then depended on a clutch of regional parties to retain a majority in the Parliament and some of those parties opposed the auction method, Singh had to oblige.

If that sounds complicated, then it got worse thereafter. Since he gave out one of those coal blocks through the pre-existent route of allotments, the CBI special court was now eleven years later looking suspiciously at the decision.

Ambush in a Court

On the last Friday before his retirement from the SC, Chief Justice Rajendra Mal Lodha faced an ambush proceeding in the coal case being argued before him.

The counsel for the CBI director Ranjit Sinha, Vikas Singh, had entered the court of Justice Lodha before the proceedings began that afternoon. His client Sinha was not a party to the case but he had a hunch that Sinha could become one soon.

The case was a follow through from the same court order in August which had held illegal all allocation of coal blocks made by the Centre since 1993. It was now hearing arguments about what to do from here.

Just a week earlier, Sinha had been arraigned before another bench on accusations that he had met some of the accused in the coal case at his residence. The evidence was a visitor's diary that came from a whistle-blower to the lawyer Prashant Bhushan, arguing the case against him. On that Friday, Bhushan was also arguing the coal case on behalf of a non-governmental body, Common Cause.

Sinha's lawyer suspected that the issue of his clients' alleged culpability could again be raked up. True enough, Bhushan referred to the diary, saying it revealed that Sinha had entertained some CIL officials allegedly close to some of the accused and so wanted him removed from the probe about the allocation of some of the coal mines. According to Bhushan, the entry register of Sinha's residence allegedly showed that a 'Coal India official met Sinha three or four times a day for the past 50 days. Congress MP Vijay Darda and his son Devendra Darda, both accused in the scam, also apparently met Sinha as per the diary records'.

The tension between the lawyers was so high, newspaper reports noted, that the bench had to tick off Singh. 'It is very unfortunate that it is happening in the highest court and that too in the first court', Lodha told Singh, 'You cannot hijack the proceedings. You don't teach us'. These were strong words made more so as the battery of lawyers arguing the case before Lodha included the attorney general of India Mukul Rohatgi, a former additional solicitor general Vikas Singh and pretty much the who's who of India's top legal fraternity.

There are slightly different versions of how the day's proceedings panned out but those were minor. A CBI spokesperson later assured me that the broad details were accurate, as reported in the newspapers.

This was the most compelling commercial case that had come to the SC ever. Compared to the Minerva Mills case of the 1980s which was a rare textbook case for law students wanting to pick up corporate law as a career, the second half of the UPA government had yielded a rich harvest for them. Every past few years, the bar had moved up. The Vodafone case on retrospective taxation and the 2G spectrum allocation had been exciting standard setters. Still, the coal case was colossal even by those standards. The scale of possible losses for each party was a reason enough for them to have marshalled the best lawyers in the business.

There was hardly any sizable Indian manufacturing company which was not linked to the case. Tata Group, Aditya Birla Group, Vedanta, Essar, JSW, JSPL, ArcelorMittal as well as public sector SAIL, NTPC, National Mineral Development Corporation (NMDC) and National Aluminium Corporation (NALCO), each had a stake in the judgement. The list of those allotted numbered more than 100 such companies.

Almost each Indian state, including Arunachal Pradesh, was an interested party. The stakes were consequently high for them, for the central government as well as the civil society unused to making its voice heard in these battles until then.

The scrap in Lodha's court showed up how the wires had got tangled. In the Google chart for most-searched words, crony capitalism had peaked at 10 per cent of all net searches among Indians by April 2014, fitting almost equally with 'coal scam'.

In his practically last order as the SC chief justice next Wednesday, Lodha cancelled the allotment of all coal blocks made since 1993.

Our judgment (of August 25) highlighted the illegality and arbitrariness in the allotment of coal blocks and these 'consequence proceedings' are intended to correct the wrong done by the Union of India; these proceedings look to the future in that by highlighting the wrong, it is expected that the Government will not deal with the natural resources that belong to the country as if they belong to a few individuals who can fritter them away at their sweet will; these proceedings may also compensate the exchequer for the loss caused to it....

A large part of the Indian economic history has to be written anew. A line in the judgement noted that the individual cases where the CBI thought it had reasons to push for charges will continue. Singh's case was one of those. But to get a sense of the events, we shall have to back-pedal a bit.

Early Morning Call

The term of the government headed by PV Narasimha Rao was punctuated by frequent dramatic episodes. The summer of 1992 arrived with the breakout of the Harshad Mehta scam in the stock markets. The winter began with the demolition of the Babri Masjid in Ayodhya which rewrote Indian political history.

They dwarfed the two events of 1991 which had surrounded the coming to power of the Rao government.

During the election campaign after former Prime Minister Rajiv Gandhi was assassinated, a surprised Narasimha Rao became the overwhelming choice within the Congress party to become the prime minister. On the evening of 20 June 1991, the day he was elected the leader of the Congress Parliamentary party, the cabinet secretary Naresh Chandra met his new boss to hand him a briefing note. It was an eight-page note that summarised the list of 'urgent tasks' for the new team. The note is the usual one a cabinet secretary prepares whenever a new team takes over at Raisina Hill, compiled from the inputs given by different ministries. Veteran in the government for several decades, Narasimha Rao had seen quite a few of those. This time, however, the tone of despair in the note drew his attention. He remarked after he read the note, 'Is it that bad?' Naresh Chandra replied, 'No Sir, It is worse.' Among those urgent priorities, however, coal denationalisation did not find a mention.

Coal and energy economics was not even in contention for an 'honourable mention in the dispatches'. As Vinayak Chatterjee, chairman of Feedback Infra, put it, 'CIL was away from everyone's radar pretty much making a mess of digging up and bringing out coal from the mines'.

Rao had to, meanwhile, find out a finance minister who could carry through the tasks that Naresh Chandra had shown him. There are several accounts of who actually made the connection between Rao and Manmohan Singh. The most credible version was penned by Rao's friend PC Alexander, Indira Gandhi's principal secretary until her death. As the external affairs minister in Gandhi's cabinet, Rao had developed a close working relationship with Alexander and at this juncture, it is to him that the prime minister designate turned to.

Within the party, Rao had two claimants, Pranab Mukherjee who had made a re-entry after a long spell out in the cold under Rajiv Gandhi and ND Tiwari who too had been a finance minister for a brief spell. While Tiwari was a lightweight, Mukherjee had formidable credentials having been finance minister under Indira Gandhi. He had the experience of handling the political fallout of taking out a loan from the International Monetary Fund (IMF). Since India was already committed to the next loan before Rao took office, it would have made sense to appoint him at North Block. Rao was picking up a lot of those men who had hit the dust under Rajiv Gandhi, which included Mukherjee, but then decided to appoint him to the relatively less important post of deputy chairman of the Planning Commission.

None of those who claimed to be close to Rao during those critical months has explained why Mukherjee did not make the cut. Jairam Ramesh who was officer on special duty (OSD) in PMO notes, 'it was a surprise to almost everybody'.

In his memoirs, Alexander wrote that Rao told him the same evening after meeting Naresh Chandra that he wanted to ap-pointed an economist as the finance minister. Alexander pitched for Manmohan Singh from the thin list of probables. 'I could see that Rao was very happy at my wholehearted endorsement of (Singh)'.

The former Indian Administrative Service (IAS) officer turned policy adviser recounts in his book *Through the Corridors of Power* how the next morning of 21 June at 5 AM he rang up a jet-lagged

Manmohan Singh to come to Rashtrapati Bhawan in a few hours to be sworn in as cabinet minister.

It is a hilarious description of how Alexander woke up Singh despite his servants' protests. 'Upon insisting that I had to talk to Dr Manmohan Singh very urgently, (Singh) came on the line', writes Alexander. But he did not tell the finance minister designate what he wanted to speak about so urgently. When Alexander arrived a few minutes later at his residence, Singh had gone back to sleep. Considering that before and after Singh, prospective ministers in every government have spent sleepless nights awaiting the call, Manmohan Singh, it would seem, had created history even before he became a minister.

The possible names for the post of the finance minister were already doing the rounds of Delhi before the election results were out. The man had to be someone who would be comfortable with the IMF–World Bank negotiating team for a long time to come. That obviously narrowed the field to economists instead of politicians, almost all of whom nursed a deep distrust of these institutions, except a few like Mukherjee. According to RD Pradhan, home secretary during the Rajiv Gandhi years, the three names in that order in the list in the air were the three RBI governors from the 1980s. Top of the list was IG Patel, who had just stepped down as director of London School of Economics after his stint with the RBI. But Patel declined and suggested Manmohan Singh instead. If Singh too had declined, the next choice would have been the then current RBI governor S Venkitaraman.

Former chief economic adviser in finance ministry Kaushik Basu writes in his memoirs that Singh just before his 'wake-up call' had estimated that his public service days were over and had come over to Basu looking to rent a flat at Mayur Vihar-I in East Delhi. When Alexander came to whisk away Singh to the Durbar Hall at the Rashtrapati Bhawan, the latter had just finished his term as the chairman of the University Grants Commission.

Ramesh claims that India's executive director in IMF, Gopi Arora, had asked from the new government for a laundry list of reform measures to be launched within the year. Predictably, the government could not give him any such official list, but Ramesh says that he wrote out one which he showed to Narasimha Rao. 'Clearly Rao wanted to maintain an element of deniability in case anything went wrong, or the note leaked'.

Ramesh's laundry list to Arora mentioned a package for the involvement of foreign companies in oil exploration plus a package for private sector participation in power sector. It was more or less what the IMF had itself suggested to the Indian government at the time of negotiating the loans.

There was no mention of coal though. The absence continued in other government documents written around the same time. The eighth Five-Year Plan document which Mukherjee wrote soon after for the period 1992–1997 also did not speak of any reforms in the coal sector. It mentioned coal mainly as an administrative problem which refused to offer any solutions. There was no mention of the need to bring in the private sector or indeed of any other entity to mine coal.

Yet within a year and a half, the government would open coal mining to private companies. But the process of opening up was not going to be easy. Rao's team was steering a rocky boat of governance and did not want to get into difficult waters like rolling back Gandhi's nationalisation scheme for the sector done just 20 years ago. Relations between the prime minister and Gandhi's daughter-in-law Sonia Gandhi remained frosty. It did not help that Rao resuscitated the careers of several diplomats and politicians sent to the dog house by Rajiv Gandhi. Mukherjee was the most notable but so was Alexander who had been packed off as high commissioner to London. Years later, this would be one of the principal reasons why Alexander would miss out on a chance to become the president of India. In 2002, when the government led by Atal Behari Vajpayee put up his name for the post, the Congress party with Sonia Gandhi as the chief refused to back him. APJ Abdul Kalam got the nod instead.

Rao was consequently aware of the limitations he had to maintain. He focused as the IMF advised on what he and his team felt was the more pressing needs in the short term, managing inflation and accepting devaluation of the rupee and fighting through a new industrial policy.

For the next phase, the IMF advised the Indian government to focus on reforms in two sectors—agriculture and power. (They gave five macro themes for the government to work on—reduction in public expenditure, reform of the tax system, liberalisation of trade, de-licensing of industry and restructuring of public enterprises.)

Agriculture was a state subject which meant that creating any traction on it was difficult. Rao's economic management team zeroed in upon power sector reforms instead. The team's priority for the power sector was to secure additional investment into generation, as the note by Ramesh showed. India was facing one of the worst power crises in the world, and it made sense to make room for more private investments. There was enough anecdotal evidence on top of the dismal data from state electricity boards to make reforms in power an attractive option.

In October, Singh and Commerce Minister Palaniappan Chidambaram travelled to Singapore to tell business people there that India wanted to bring in foreign investment in power and other sectors. It was a pioneering visit from Indian politicians in decades. Unlike some of the sporadic visits of the 1980s, this one was well organised, showed evidence of background research and also involved some inter-ministry coordination, quite unusual for India. As a report by *India Today* on the visit put it, a foreign banker present at the event noted, 'For the first time Indians are willing to say yes. That's big news'. The team distributed videos and diskettes at the event laying out what India had to offer and even handed out application forms printed with names of contact officers to show how keen the government was to procure investment from abroad. Mandarins from the Ministry of External Affairs assured Indian media back home that there would be plenty more of these visits to other potential investment centres. 'Trade and industry waited with bated breath each year for the annual import policy popularly known as the Red Book', a play on Communist China's original, writes NK Singh. Chidambaram cut the source of the *Red Book*—the office of the controller of imports and exports.

The investment climate did not improve much. It was much like the state broadcaster which purveyed such a lot of insipid and repetitive stuff that when BBC news came to Indian television in 1992 a news report noted, 'it was the biggest turn on'. The Indian bureaucracy was too set in its ways to really convince anyone that it had turned over a new leaf. As another report by *India Today* later that year noted, when the managing director of German Asia-Pacific Business Association Dieter Haury arrived in New Delhi in December 1991 to figure out the changes in the business climate happening in India, he was greeted with a lost suitcase at the airport. Haury who represented several hundred German companies for their forays abroad had to travel back twice to the airport during the course of his visit and sign volumes of papers before he could get his suitcase back. 'Never before have I put my signature in so many places to get something done. The big problem here is that you continue to have too many procedural delays', he told the news magazine.

The bad habits within the bureaucracy were getting reflected in plenty of things. The government had set up the Foreign Investment Promotion Board (FIPB) within the PMO as a clearing shop for investors from abroad, but still the concerned officers were reluctant to approve projects quickly. When officials of Coca Cola, General Electric and General Motors travelled to Delhi to meet the board members headed by Rao's principal secretary Amar Nath Verma, they were asked to submit concept notes instead of investment plans. Those notes would be the basis for further detailed negotiations among the FIPB officials. Only after those negotiations were concluded would the companies be told to come back with actual investment plans which would be scrutinised still further by the FIPB. None of the Asian Tiger economies when they were opening up had made investors run around in circles like these.

Three years later, Rao's political team thus found out that there had only been plenty of such sideways movement within the government. Nothing much had moved forward. Verma's team discovered that while China had received $58 billion in foreign investment in 1992, India had scraped together just $600 million in foreign investment in three years. Most of those were in consumer appliances.

Long-term and large-scale investments like those for power sector projects were impossible to attract in such an atmosphere. That atmosphere got more polluted when the Harshad Mehta-induced stock market scam and the demolition of Babri Masjid happened in the same year, 1992. The government added to it when Rao had to let go off his Commerce Minister Chidambaram. The minister had admitted to holding shares in Fairgrowth Financial Services Ltd, a mutual fund company which came under investigation in the course of the stock market meltdown. On the same day, 9 July, the government had to agree to set up a joint parliamentary committee to probe the scam.

Rao's minority government seemed just one disaster away from toppling over. He lost his temper at the World Economic Forum meeting later that year when investors repeatedly asked him questions about the stability of his government.

Consequently, power reforms despite the series of notifications issued by the government to encourage entry of privately owned generating companies into the electricity sector were not going to happen. The amended Electricity Laws (Amendment) Act of 1991 passed by the Parliament to allow power developers to also enter into long-term power purchase agreements with the state electricity boards which would guarantee them long-term returns did not find any takers.

As the difficulties of getting power sector investments off the ground proved more and more intractable, the government espied another problem cropping up in a related sector—coal. Unsung within the government, CIL had begun to sink. It had run up a massive pile of debt—₹2,600 crore. The company needed a bailout just as the Indian government had needed one and approached the World Bank for it. The Bank made the bailout conditional on the company cutting back on its scale of investments, especially those where there was no evaluation of the possible rate of returns.

Many of those investments were planned in areas where rail network had not yet reached. CIL was essentially digging up coal from the mines leaving it to pile in massive stocks beside those mines. From 1980 to 1991, the Indian railways had increased their network by just 1.8 per cent. If one accounted for the fact that in the same period the meter gauge lines had been reduced by about the same length, it meant that there was effectively no expansion. So even if thermal power plants were going to be set up, the coal supply to those from CIL would be irregular at best. To make reforms in the power sector happen despite these constraints, the government had to think out of the box.

It was paradoxically from the stiffest anti-reform segment of the Indian political spectrum at this juncture that liberalisation of the power sector and with it that of the coal sector came to Rao.

It came from Jyoti Basu. By 1993, Basu as the long-serving chief minister of the Communist Party of India, Marxist (CPIM)-led government in West Bengal had come to don an awesome aura. The Soviet Union had collapsed, but the communist movement in India had not dimmed at all. Unlike the 1950s, when the post-Stalinist tumult in USSR had weakened the Indian communists politically, in the 1980s and 1990s, the CPIM was winning consecutive elections in West Bengal and alternately in Kerala. Basu's rule brooked no opponents as even Pranab Mukherjee had discovered to his cost.

Days after the Rao government took office, Basu's West Bengal government in a striking departure from established norms of state–Centre behaviour had released a document, 'Alternative Policy Approach to Resolve the BoP Crisis'. States in India often disagreed with the Centre, but none of them until then had ever publicly ticked off the Centre's right to take an international position. But instead of chiding Basu, Finance Minister Singh and then Rao sent detailed letters to him explaining their policies and soliciting his support. A frown from him was enough to unnerve and could even force a change in the central government's policies.

By 1993, Basu had consolidated his position even more within his party and within the Indian political firmament, while Rao's had weakened with the stock market scams and the post-Babri Masjid riots. As the Centre struggled to get power reforms off the ground, Basu offered a surprising alternative.

There was a background to the developments. Early in 1993, Rao had entrusted the job for making changes in the coal economy to another promising member of his cabinet, Purno Ajitok Sangma, who held independent charge of the portfolios of coal and labour.

The minister soon discovered what he was up against. The Coal Mines (Nationalisation) Act of 1973 and its amendment of 1976 had extended a blanket ban on coal mining in the future by any entity except those specified by the government. Any change in that list could only be brought through an amendment of these acts through the Parliament. The only exceptions allowed were for captive mining by private companies engaged in production of iron and steel and sub-lease of coal mining to private parties in isolated small pockets 'not amendable to economic development and not requiring rail transport'.

Alok Perti is one of India's most knowledgeable men about coal. Unlike many IAS officers who traipse through departments, Perti has stayed with the sector for a long time and even after his retirement as an adviser. He told me that Sangma shocked the cabinet by bringing in a proposal to reverse the nationalisation. His cabinet note asked for letting private companies again begin to mine coal for sale in the open market. Typical of government bureaucratese, it was to go through as an amendment to the Coal Mines (Nationalisation) Act instead of asking for a repeal of the act. There was a precedent to his note. Just a month after assuming office in 1991, the government had done something similar rolling back industrial licensing. It allowed for foreign investments and even permitted sale of public sector companies terming the new Industrial Policy an extension of the earlier Industrial Policy statements from 1956 onwards that had progressively blocked these avenues.

Sangma argued with his colleagues that it would be healthy to let CIL compete with the private sector. About the obvious challenge from the labour unions of CIL, one of the toughest among the public sector, the minister felt that he would be able to bring them around. He had served as the minister for labour in the Rajiv Gandhi cabinet and had established his credentials with vast sections of the organised sector. They had come to respect him as a consequence of which he was able to steer a couple of labour reforms proposal through the cabinet and the Parliament. He was sure that he could carry on from that innings to make the unions accept his logic.

Rao's acumen told him that there was no hope this could sail through. He was proved right. A similar amendment moved by the NDA government eight years later, in 2000, is still pending in the Parliament thirteen years later.

It was mothballed for the future. It was at this juncture that a curious proposal arrived from veteran industry leader Ramaprasad Goenka and countersigned by Basu. Goenka had just taken over CESC which had the monopoly rights to supply electricity to Calcutta and was investing in a power plant in the outskirts of the city. He wanted to own a coal mine for assured supply of coal for the plant. Jyoti Basu wrote a letter supporting the proposal. The union cabinet was now galvanised. There was another curious appendix to the proposal. Bihar Chief Minister Lalu Prasad Yadav had also sent a letter of support with the proposal, even though the state had no economic interests in the investment. As a faithful idealogical follower of Basu, there was no surprise that the Bihar chief minister would support the former. What was surprising was the obvious need Basu had felt to buttress his position with that of Yadav.

No one has ever made the connection why the communist patriarch made the inconceivable pitch. Coal nationalisation was carried through by Indira Gandhi but the communists became the flag bearer of the decision in later years. It is, therefore, stunning how Basu supported the unprecedented proposal.

Chaos Theory

Calcutta was the first Indian city to get electric supply. It was the seat of the British colonial empire in the east in the nineteenth century and so got lit up within a decade of London in 1897. The same company CESC which brought electricity to Calcutta scored another first after 100 years.

It was brought on by a crippling coal shortage in the economy. By the late 1980s, power shortage was the big talking point in urban India. Power companies such as CESC found that there was hardly any coal available to keep their generating units running to feed the city. CIL was not able to meet the expanding requirements of the power plants, even though it was set up twenty years ago as a culmination of the nationalisation of the coal mining sector for this purpose. Faced with a crisis, CESC applied to the central government for permission to run its own coal mine in 1993. The central government in a pioneering move gave the permission which made CESC the first private sector company to own a coal block reversing the two-decade-old public policy of keeping all coal blocks nationalised. Being a part of two such momentous events should have assured CESC's place in history.

It was not enough. Within another twenty years, CESC would go on to score its third date with history and again in conjunction with coal. In February 2015, it became the first power-generating company to win back its coal mine via an auction. The auction was made necessary after a SC order five months earlier in September 2014 took away the block along with 213 others.

If this sounds chaotic, then it is not surprising. The energy economics of India has been chaotic over the past hundred years lurching from one extreme to another. Coal has been its most visible example.

The chaos is pretty much like the traffic converging from all directions at the foot of the headquarters of CESC in Kolkata's prime office district. A guard held the traffic at bay as I got down from a car and dashed across to the massive gates of the century-old building.

The chairman of CESC Sanjiv Goenka met me at his boardroom in Chowringhee Square. My meeting with him happened just days after the SC had cancelled all coal block allocations. We were standing at the fourth floor of the building having left the unruly traffic below. Looking out from the windows, even the high decibel messy traffic below at times seemed pretty. It was quiet there, much like the tone in which Sanjiv spoke. As an entrepreneur in the Indian power sector, there are a few who have stayed the course longer than he has.

I wanted to understand from Sanjiv the reasons which made CESC venture as pioneer into coal mining in a tumultuous period of Indian history when most companies were just holding on to their existing investments.

We talked about those events as Sanjiv walked me through his office corridors decorated with the works of some of the best artists of India—Reza, Hussain, Bikash Bhattacharjee and Ganesh Pyne. At every turn, there was a surprise discovery of another great work of art. Sanjiv, I noticed, also has a passion for sculpture. The collection at the RPG office has often been noted upon by the art cognoscenti. Few industries survived the thirty-four years of left party-led rule in West Bengal, even fewer were left with money to buy pieces of art, not even the government-owned Victoria Memorial. The CESC collection possibly saved many of the best works from leaving West Bengal, just as Dwarkanath Tagore did 150 years ago.

The building itself is one of the landmarks of the city. Victoria House as it was known earlier looks out serenely towards the Hooghly River which flows just beyond the Maidan, home to Kolkata's soccer clubs.

In an interview to a newspaper, Sanjiv had once said that he prefers tees and tracks on weekends, but at his office sitting across from me, he still managed to look comfortable even in his buttoned-up shirt sleeves. But that morning, he was uncomfortable talking about the details of the pioneering allocation process of 1993 which was largely steered by his father Ramaprasad Goenka. 'We didn't want the mine. It was forced upon us since CIL said we cannot give you the coal we promised', Sanjiv remarked on those events.

Ramaprasad would have had reasons to be surprised with the turn of events. The Goenkas are an old business group tracing their ventures back as far as 1820 when the first of them arrived in Calcutta. Business houses in the imperial city were at that time dominated by English and Parsi names and sometimes Bengali ones like Tagore. Since then, the different members of the Goenka family have moved into banking, textiles and jute, but they had never ventured into coal business. Ramaprasad also would not have done so until his hand was forced.

It was a combination of circumstances which did it. By 1977, a coalition of communist and socialist parties had banded themselves as the Left Front to win power in West Bengal state assembly. By 1989, the Left Front government had come back to power for a third successive term and seemed settled for a long haul in future too. Chief Minister Jyoti Basu had little patience for capitalists and even less for criticism.

Basu had a problem with CESC. Electricity distribution in West Bengal is a political hot potato and so remains a state-owned venture even now, thanks to the strong leftist political ideology. In the last century, under the Left Front led by Basu, it was even more acute. But for a long time through the vicissitudes of West Bengal politics, CESC had managed to retain its position as a private sector distributor of electricity for Kolkata, an oddball. It was even odder because though a private sector firm, it was the state government which exercised rights over its returns and dividends despite its position as a minority shareholder.

Jyoti Basu needed the cash that CESC could generate from its business besides, of course, the electricity but did not want the mounting hassle of running the company. The CESC plants were old—the one at Mulajore established in 1944 produced 20 MW and cost 18 MW to run it. There would be no advantage for his government if those were to be made state owned. The state finances were in shambles. No company in India was willing to step in to supply electricity to the 'city of processions'. Ramaprasad Goenka in these circumstances offered to buy out CESC. There was a huge upside to the deal for the state government. Basu would not have to accept in public that he was selling out to a private sector firm since CESC was not strictly a government-owned company. And power supply to Kolkata might actually improve.

Kolkata had run into massive spells of load shedding as power outages in the city came to be referred to. Trams were left stranded midway through their journey, cinema halls cut down on their shows—the city had become the sordid advertisement of what socialist government rule would lead up to for the rest of India. Basu, as they say, needed a break.

Jyoti Basu had enjoyed a great relation with the elder Goenka. In 1979, just 2 years after the Left Front government in the state began its first innings; Goenka cut loose from his network of family firms to set up RPG Enterprises headquartered in Calcutta and began a decade-long spree of acquisitions. RPG was the 'takeover king' of the 1980s as *The Telegraph* newspaper put it in its obituary. He was one example for Basu that private industry could flourish in West Bengal.

Among his acquisitions were CEAT Tyres, Dunlop, Gramophone Company of India Ltd, now Saregama India, International Computers Indian Manufacturers (ICIM) and finally CESC. He made four of these takeovers in 1989, including CESC. This was one of his bets that seemed a spectacularly correct one, or that is how it would have seemed then.

Soon after taking over CESC, RPG realised they needed to expand the generation capacity of the company by setting up another thermal power plant. But CIL, the monopoly supplier of coal, had run out of its capacity to provide an assured line of fuel supply to the project. The only alternative for CESC was to run a coal mine or commandeer coal from the black market.

RPG reached out to the central government in Delhi to gauge the possibilities. It was helped by an offer from CIL. The company's then Chairman SK Chaudhury handed over a list of 143 coal blocks to the Ministry of Coal which neither he nor Singareni Collieries Company Limited, a joint venture between the Andhra Pradesh state and the Centre, would be able to bring into production for decades.

A few months later, Goenka submitted an application to Sangma for award of a captive mine.

Within days, a similar request came from Tamil Nadu Chief Minister J Jayalalitha for a lignite-based project. Years later, when there was an aborted proposal to make Basu the prime minister, Jayalalitha and Lalu Prasad would vigorously lobby in his support.

Recommending coal mines for allotment to private parties had not become a dangerous pastime for chief ministers at that point unlike in 2015. Odisha Chief Minister Naveen Patnaik is now perilously close to finding a CBI summons at his door for making the case for Talabira II for Hindalco.

This was a great opportunity. There was obviously going to be across the board political support for fresh investments in the power sector, provided the government could also give them a coal mine bundled with the project.

The union cabinet was now willing to move fast. Captive mining by power-generating companies, cement and sponge iron plants was going to be allowed just as iron and steel companies were allowed this leeway from 1976 onwards.

But despite the lifeline, it took Sangma one whole year to steer those amendments through the Parliament. At one stage, Sangma even considered an ordinance to make the bill sail through. But the law ministry nixed it. Finally, in June 1993, the president put his signature on the bill to make it an act.

The opening up of the sector was finally a recognition that twenty years after coal mining was nationalised and a state-owned company CIL was set up, conditions in the sector were more or less back to the same position again.

The amendments of 1993 must rank among the briefest ones ever made into an economic sector law in India. The entire bill was a two-page gazette notification without any explanatory clause or scope to write detailed rules under it. Once the amendments were in place, Sangma's team at the coal ministry was sure that the central government could notify coal blocks to companies that could show they needed one. The logic was used in other cases too as, for instance, in the devaluation of the rupee.

'The two-step devaluation of the rupee, for instance, was not only hastened but also pushed through by executive fiat. It was agreed that Rao would manage the uproar after the deed was done', as Shankar Aiyyar stated in his book *Accidental India*.

No newspaper picked up the news about passage of the coal amendment through the Parliament. There were too many political developments playing out for anyone to take notice of the momentous changes. Harshad Mehta's stock market caper was still unspooling when he stunned the country in July with an announcement that he had carried a bribe of ₹1 crore for Prime Minister Rao. By August, Congress leader Arjun Singh had resigned from the cabinet setting himself up as an alternative power centre to Narasimha Rao. The government seemed to be immobilised by the allegations of corruption.

The corporate sector didn't take note either. In an interview to a newspaper shortly after the Parliament had cleared the coal amendment, VK Hajela, executive director of the supervisory board of RPG Enterprises, ticked among his concerns plenty of stuff. He was concerned that their pioneering power project had taken 18 months to get an environment clearance, but he seemed blissfully unaware of the import of the news from the Parliament.

Yet from the pieces of legislation from that first burst of reforms, it is this one which has created the largest impact twenty years later. The entire coal scam was played out because the SC held that the notifications were not permissible under this amendment to the Coal Nationalisation Act. But in June 1993, the coal minister had reasons to feel confident that he had scored a major victory.

Sangma Gets a Committee

One month later, the minister called several officers from CIL to join coal ministry officials at his office in Shastri Bhawan in New Delhi for the meeting of a committee. It was to be known as screening committee. Shastri Bhawan stands as the most visible landmark on the Rajendra Prasad Road in Lutyens Zone in Delhi. Built in the early 1970s, in honour of Lal Bahadur Shastri, it was the first and until now the only government building to be named after a person in that zone. Today, it houses more ministries than any other government building in Delhi. Even two decades ago, it consequently attracted a swirling crowd of cars, buses and pedestrians, each keen to bend rules to get in the front, throughout the day. But, of course, there were no TV cameras to record the moments leading up to that first meeting.

On Wednesday 14 July 1993, these officers created history when they converged for the first meeting of this committee. Sangma had passed the order to set up the committee a year earlier, but it had to wait until the amendments were cleared by the Parliament. Companies wanting a coal block would get them through this committee, the minister figured. The economics of allocation of natural resource was moving to a starring role in the new India.

In Mumbai film industry too, a new kid on the block was also trying to figure out the role he would take on. Shah Rukh Khan starred in *Darr* and *Baazigar*, playing negative characters with panache, which marked him out as the star to watch out for. He later did a forgettable film, à la Amitabh Bachchan, based loosely around the coal mines—*Koyla*. While SRK acquired the hero's mantle very soon, the screening committee came to be known by another decade as the villain of the coal sector of India.

The Indian committee systems owe their origin to the Indian Parliament which got its first committees from 1919. There is a lot of safety in the committee-led procedures. Officers find scope to rope in their colleagues to decide on stuff whenever they discover the rules for deciding that some things are not laid down in manuals. Each year, dozens of them are set up and die. Few achieve immortality the way the screening committees did.

There were three proposals on the plate for the first meeting of the screening committee. In depositions before a parliamentary standing committee in later years, the ministry noted that of those three, one was from Coleman Associates, an Australian mining firm which sought permission to mine lignite from Rajasthan's Barsingar mines, the next was from a joint sector company Jayamkondam Lignite Power Corporation from Tamil Nadu 'to implement integrated lignite-based power project' and the third was a proposal from CESC under the RPG Enterprises for setting up of two units of 2 × 250 MW plant near Kolkata.

All the three applicants were called for making a presentation before the committee. 'Comprehensive details about the applicant, the group, performance of the group, financial strength, readiness of the end-use plant, etc. were placed before the committee so as to enable it to make appropriate recommendation', a coal ministry record from the meetings noted.

Goenka's CESC got the nod to set up a captive coal mine at Sarshatali. It would be ten years before it would begin producing coal from the mine. Within a few months, another company this time from the aluminium sector, Indal, had applied for a coal mine at Talabira in Orissa to power its captive power plant.

The companies were happy to get a chance to approach the central government for their projects. In the 1990s, the process of obtaining a mine from state government bureaucracy was insane.

Jharkhand does not Know Its Mines

The secretariat of the Jharkhand state administration in Ranchi still functions from the abandoned head office of Heavy Engineering

Corporation. But from this office, the state cabinet secretary Ram Sewak Sharma carried out a revolution of sorts. In 2012–2013, he transported all the clearances the state was authorised to issue to an online platform. One of those put online was data on how many mines the state had and of them how many had been allotted to whom. For six years during the global commodity boom from 2002, the state was unable to put that data up on its website.

Unless one walks the corridors of the state government in that complex, it is impossible to figure out how transformative was the step. I had occasions to visit it several times when Shibu Soren ruled the state in three terms from 2005 onwards. In between his terms were two terms of President's Rule. Each administration left its share of detritus, especially in the mining sector. State officers played around with clearances to run up massive fortunes that made the state capital seem like a rich city. Hotels and housing colonies expanded the city in every direction way beyond the original hills where it was originally located as a sleepy resort town.

The clean-up is fairly recent, but it has swept Jharkhand all the way up to third position in the league of Indian states in terms of ease of doing business rankings carried out by the World Bank and the central government's department of industrial policy and promotion. The scope for playing around with clearances has disappeared. Sharma had to use the iron broom to clear the state administration.

During one of the cool Ranchi evenings, two of the top officers from the CAG of India regaled me at their leafy homes standing in the middle of spacious gardens with many tales about postings in the economic departments in Ranchi, each more bizarre than the other. I could have brushed them aside as hyperbole, except that all of them had figured with painstaking evidence in the audit reports.

For instance, it was a fact that during the peak of the allocation of coal and iron ore mining leases, the state department of mine was seriously understaffed in terms of technical people. There were only six geologists in Jharkhand mining department against thirty-three vacancies when Soren was in charge and leases were in high demand.

The audit reports made scathing observations but a few legislators from Soren's party were inclined to read them, certainly not any of the other chief ministers, all of whose terms came and went in a blur after him. One of those reports points out that in the twelve years since the time the state came into being in 2000, various government departments took out cumulative advances of ₹13,543 crore from the state treasury of which 51 per cent has gone missing. 'We in the audit are unable to provide an assurance as to whether the advances drawn have been utilised for the purposes for which those were sanctioned', the report of the CAG noted in 2012. In plain speak, the auditor said that the sum was looted. No other comparable state had this problem, as the same report points out.

Equally serious were stuff which could not be put in the reports. These are the allegations about the state government officials who are sorted into slabs for money to be paid to them as bribes. Incidentally, one of the authors confided in me that he was in the habit of recording conversations with all government officials, so deep was the level of mistrust in the state. The peculiar combination of IAS-dominated senior bureaucracy and a poorly trained staff meant that mining project appraisals was often a formality and the only conduit was the flow of cash to settle all arguments.

Going by the evidence the auditors uncovered, Jharkhand's problems seemed strikingly similar to those faced by some of the mineral-rich countries in Africa. The state was engulfed by a fatal combination of extremely attractive booty in its mines, an administration that ceased to exist in the war for state power and a public too poor to be able to demand accountability—the states' actual per capita income at ₹19,000 after netting out the earnings of mining companies (state government estimate) in 2013 was 44 per cent lower than the national average. The middle class was entirely dependent on government jobs.

This created a buccaneering spirit of an earlier century, right in the middle of India of today. As a result, the listed companies at many points ceded ground to the rogues. Even public sector SAIL had to wait more for almost a decade until February 2011 to get a fresh lease on Chiria hills, one of India's richest deposits of iron ore.

At one stage, Soren was succeeded by Madhu Koda who created a record of sorts clearing forty-one files for iron ore mining leases in a single day during his stint. Koda himself remained the state mining minister from March 2005 until August 2008. It was during this time that the state government found that it had no records on its mines since the year 2002 to be put up on the state government site. Without the records arrears in collection of revenue from minerals, corresponding income tax revenue and others were impossible to build up. An estimate prepared by an audit report put it at ₹763 crore in just 2013.

One of the agencies claimed that since 2005, none of the iron ore mines opened up for private mining by the state was given without a bribe. The report also added that the state government bureaucracy repeatedly delayed sending up to the Centre the list of bidders until the 'favourites' were included in the list.

One of those allegedly was the Vini Iron and Steel Udyog Ltd which got a coal block in Jharkhand's North Rajhara. The company, supposedly a front for Koda, played an important role in the iron ore mining scam too and then went on to get a coal mine. The owner of the company Vijay Joshi was also allegedly the middleman for Koda who acted as the conduit for the investment of money that Koda collected through bribes.

The money used to be laundered through Dubai and come back as white money for investment in the front companies through 'accommodation entries'. 'Shri Joshi had also confirmed the accommodation entries provided through M/s Lackyproject Pvt Ltd', notes a CBI statement to the special courts.

By 2015, Madhu Koda also had been summoned by the courts. Parashar, the same judge who had asked Manmohan Singh to appear, told Koda along with the former union coal secretary HC Gupta and former state chief secretary Ashok Kumar Basu to appear in the case about allocation of coal blocks to Vini Iron and Steel Udyog Ltd.

In this environment, honest government officials felt more secure transferring the rights to allotment of mines to the central government. Sangma's officers and those who came later were sure that this was the best course of action. One of them was Parakh, who finally put Singh in trouble.

Who Rings the Bell

I met Parakh at his home in Secunderabad. He was the coal secretary from March 2004 to December 2005, possibly the most famous IAS officer who turned whistle-blower in a public policy issue.

In an unhurried tone, Parakh explained to me the origin of the problem with the coal amendment that Sangma steered through in 1993. Sporting a thick pair of spectacles, he has a habit of fixing you with a long stare.

Parakh was speaking about an era, eleven years since June 1993 when the screening committee came into life. Manmohan Singh had become the prime minister in the first UPA government in May 2004 and a new chapter in India's energy economics was about to roll out. As Parakh held forth, I realised why his ministers such as Shibu Soren and Dasari Narayan Rao, members of the Manmohan Singh team, were keen to let him go once he reached his retirement age. His mastery over the facts of the case would have been disconcerting for them had he continued.

He said,

> See the problem is that, when Sangma amended the law, it was not clearly indicated as to who is authorized to allocate coal blocks. There was a vacuum. So (the) Screening Committee was also not set up through any amendment to the act. It was through an executive order of the government.

It has been a decade since he had quit government, but Parakh can still recall the details from memory. In between talking to me, he got up to open the door for frequent visitors to his modest flat in a quiet lane of the city. They had various requests. One of them wanted him to be the chief guest at a railway officers' function. Even in a city teeming with retired IAS officers, Parakh had a powerful recall value, I realised. In 2013, when the CBI raised questions about his role in the allocation of a coal block to Hindalco, the Andhra Pradesh cadre officers rose publicly in protest.

> By not specifying in whom the authority vests to allocate the coal block, the government made a mistake. In respect of all other minerals, the applications for mining leases were to be made to the state governments. Coal is the only exception, where those applications were not to be made to state government. The '93 amendment which allowed entry of new categories of miners—the private ones, did not specify whether the applications will be made to the central government or to the state government.

He said that that was the loophole Lodha's court had pinned in the judgement to say that nobody is authorised to make allocations. 'That is why they have held that it is illegal. Not that the policy was wrong', he added.

As I listened to him, I figured out that each government officer who tried to make transparent rules for handing out natural resources faced the same dual opposition. Those were from the political masters and businessmen. Since the benefits would not become apparent until later, the support from the public through the legislature would be indifferent at best. It was a lonely battle to wage.

Parakh said that he was aware of the flaw between the policy of 1993 and the process adopted since then. 'So in 2004, I proposed that we must issue an ordinance to bring about a change in the Coal Mines (Nationalisation) Amendment Act to permit auction through an open bidding'. By the time Parekh made his proposal, the screening committees had allocated 39 coal blocks in its 11 years of existence.

Beginning with a trickle, the pace had picked up in Prime Minister Deve Gowda's period when OP Jindal and his son-in-law picked three; those were rapidly followed by the Jayaswal family beginning the rise of coal rush from Nagpur.

As Vinayak Chatterjee, chairman of Feedback Infra, put it to me 'the allocation process reflected crony capitalism, but the objective was fine. You needed more coal to feed sectors like power'.

By the time Parakh arrived at the coal ministry in Shastri Bhawan as secretary, eight ministers had travelled through the ministry after Sangma moved out in 1993. Prime ministers rarely gave the honour to a newbie. Dilip Ray, NT Shanmugam, Shahnawaz Hussain, Ram Vilas Paswan, Uma Bharti, Karia Munda and Mamata Banerjee were all veteran politicians when they arrived at Shastri Bhawan, the competing lobbies in the sector demanded it. The goings-on became even more interesting when in 2004 the UPA government led by Manmohan Singh found Shibu Soren as the fittest candidate for heading the ministry.

Parakh's term overlapped for just a month with Mamata Banerjee. He said that she was not particularly interested in the sector except to ensure that some of her party men were recruited by CIL. Meanwhile, the world economy had begun to recover from the downturn created by the East Asian crisis. A key aspect of the global recovery by 2003 was that of commodity boom, including of coal.

As entrepreneurs watched the contours of the boom spread, they realised that opportunities were opening up for export of steel and also of coal, principally to China. One of those entrepreneurs who came knocking at Parakh's office to ask for a mine was Visa Steel.

The chairman of Visa Steel, Vishambhar Saran, met me at a short notice at his plush home on Alipur Road in Kolkata. His office is in the same building, a rarity in the city where work and leisure are kept apart, zealously.

Saran said that he found the demand for steel rising globally after the East Asian crisis. It was in particularly big demand from China which was building for the Beijing Olympics. Locally too, the demand for steel expanded from the road sector. An assured supply of coal was just the missing link the companies needed to give them the pricing edge in sectors like steel. 'We would not have thought of any fresh investment in the steel sector unless we had captive raw material security' he said in a brisk voice.

To add to the demand from steel mills, in October 2003, the power ministry pronounced a mission 'power to all by 2012' and wrote the omnibus Electricity Act, 2003, building in attractive incentives for generation. The mission envisaged a capacity addition of 100,000 MW of power by 2012 which meant a corresponding increase in coal production. There was now a veritable rush to get a coal block.

How big was the rush?

In a deposition to a Parliament committee, the coal ministry said that it had once issued advertisements for companies to apply for coal blocks.

> The advertisements calling for application for allotment of coal blocks were issued in 2005 and 2006. Before this, no advertisements were issued calling for applications ... 20 blocks were advertised in 2005 in response to which 728 applications were received. In 2006, 38 blocks were advertised in response to which 1422 applications were received....

Visa Steel was one of those applicants. So were most of India's steel, aluminium, sponge iron and cement manufacturers along with power producers.

The genteel atmosphere of the committee system was bound to collapse under this rush.

Businessmen who visit the corridors of power in Delhi know that they are in good company if they can also brandish a political recommendation. The Goenkas and Upadhyays had those from Jyoti Basu. The quality of recommendations dipped thereafter. Manoj Jayaswal had Vijay Darda to plead his case.

As the number of applicants shot up from 2003 onwards, Parakh found it difficult to allot a mine to each one. He asked for a recommendation from the research wing of CIL. They recommended breaking up of the mines, on paper; several companies were allotted sections of the mines known as blocks to extract coal. The ministry often asked the applicants to form joint ventures. Some of those were created by the coal ministry; others saw the necessity and formed those themselves.

Visa for instance came in a joint venture of five companies when it was assigned a share of Fatehpur East coal block.

As the rush deepened, it did not take much prescience to figure out that the sector was offering 'windfall gains' for those who got the blocks. The word became one of the most quoted one in the sector much like the word Rosewood had become following the success of the epic film of Orson Welles *Citizen Kane* in 1939.

In the morning of 28 June 2004, just a month into the new UPA government in Delhi, Parakh called for a meeting with industry chambers and other stakeholders to float his auction theory based on his hypothesis that they were making windfall gain and should consequently share some of that with the government. He had firmed up the theory in a discussion paper, 'Competitive bidding for allocation of coal blocks'.

'I had invited every industry organization. I had FICCI, I had CII, every organization that was concerned with coal mining. And also all the applicants whose applications for coal blocks that were pending with the ministry. I put that discussion paper to them'.

There was a stunned silence in the room as he elaborated on the proposal. 'I could understand it, because if you've been able to get something free of cost then why would you want to pay for it'. Predictably, there were no releases from the industry bodies after that meeting. Neither was one issued by the government too, a costly mistake as it turned out, since it could not take ownership for the arguments. As late as in 2013, CII made a presentation to the Ministry of Coal where it argued that auctions were 'not' the most popular way to hand out natural resources globally.

'Recently a committee of CII analysed resource allocation practices across nine relevant jurisdictions (globally). It was found that only a minority of mining (countries) have adopted the auction process for allocating bulk mineral resources' (Response by Ministry of Coal to Public Accounts Committee of the Parliament, September 2013).

As economist Bibek Debroy said at the time in a great Tweet, 'If there is prospect of losing your coal, you are bound to lose your cool'.

The merits of auction versus the supposed thuggery of the screening committee also emasculated the larger debate within the coal sector—the question of how to get CIL to produce more coal.

The rush of applicants and the supposed weakness in recording the decisions taken were the manifestations of this larger crisis.

The crisis spread since CIL was unable to mine coal at a brisk pace. Its production grew at a compound annual growth rate (CAGR) of just 5 per cent through the 1990s. In the financial year 2003, it was 5.6 per cent. There is a one-to-one relationship between energy and GDP which means that an economy cannot grow at say 7 per cent if the energy sector grows at 5 per cent. The choice for the economy became stark.

India had to import more coal and at the same time increase production from domestic blocks not held by CIL. Imports of coal in the financial year 2003 had reached 21.5 MT. It was a costly choice involving large drawls of foreign exchange, much like the scene for import of crude oil.

The coal secretary briefed the cabinet minister for coal Shibhu Soren and the minister of state Dasari Narayana Rao about his auction theory. He could not have made himself more unpopular.

> By that time I had been in the ministry for about 2–3 months so I had some hang of what it is required. In my briefing I said the major issue for us is to immediately raise coal production. But the higher coal production will not come from CIL.

He was right. CIL production was flat at about 320 MT; there was massive black market in coal. Of the 2,722 units which got an assured coal linkage, more than a quarter were found to be dud, which meant that they were selling coal at high prices in the Varanasi and Nagpur markets.

Yet the ministers kept pressurising the department to promise more coal supplies from CIL to buyers. Soren and Rao were playing a game of crisis. They wanted the companies that were promised coal to complain about the shortage and its impact on their production plans. There would be pressure on the government to resolve the crisis. Because of the crisis, the screening committees would get the requisite backing to continue to hand out fresh coal blocks as an alternative to supplies from CIL.

The strategy worked later too. Years later, for instance, after Parekh had retired several industrialists including Ratan Tata, Anil Ambani and KM Birla forced the government to issue presidential directives to CIL to raise its supply.

But in 2004, even as the ministers and the secretary wrangled, price of coal began to shoot up in domestic and international markets.

Parekh put up a note recommending auctions using a model he had gleaned from his previous ministry that of oil located in the same Shastri Bhawan, one floor above his office.

> I was in petroleum ministry in the eighties. There we had started this auction of oil blocks under the oil exploration policy. That was already in my mind. It was possible despite complete uncertainty about sinking money into exploration, whereas here (coal ministry) we had full exploration data. So if we put it through bidding, people will know the price they will need to pay.

He also argued that it would be cheaper for the economy. 'The people who are going to get coal blocks would get it cheaper because all said and done CIL is an inefficient organization. So those who were going to earn windfall profit should be asked to pay more, by the government'.

This was a lucid argument.

Events on the ground, however, moved in a strange trajectory. Shibu Soren as the minister never argued with his secretary who was a geologist by training. Happily for Parakh, within days after Parakh made the proposal, Soren had to resign. There was an arrest warrant for his role in the alleged murder of his personal secretary. Prime Minister Singh insisted on his resignation and took over the charge of the ministry.

The coal secretary presented Singh with three options. The first was to free coal mining for commercial coal miners selected through auctions. The bill for the same was pending in the Rajya Sabha from 2000. It sought to denationalise coal completely. The second was to allow companies which needed coal as fuel to mine the coal themselves but again through auctions. The third was to sale coal stocks of CIL through an e-auction route.

Parakh said that Singh was unsure about carrying through any of them given the arithmetic of the Lok Sabha. He was certainly sure that the first option would not sail through the government too. The leftist parties were repeatedly taking out what amounted to insurance through the Parliament that the government would not privatise the mines. In each session, at least one member from among those parties (who were supporting Singh's alliance from outside) would ask the government if it intended to privatise the coal mines under CIL. Rao or Soren would in turn faithfully reply that there is a bill for the same pending in the Rajya Sabha since 2000. They would add that bill has been referred to a standing committee and is not expected to move further because of opposition from the trade unions. The insurance cover would remain valid.

Singh consequently thought that the second option was more practical though still difficult. For the third, he asked the secretary to explore available options even as he worried that prices of coal would rise in consequence.

Singh's hesitancy to reform the coal sector was a throwback to the recurrent crisis in the Indian coal sector and the broader energy sector. Right from the set of options worked out at Independence, the subsequent nationalisation in 1973 and even the partial roll back of 1993, each period witnessed suboptimal strategies. Each set the stage for the next crisis with almost clock-like regularity at intervals of every twenty years.

By refusing to bite the bullet to denationalise coal, Singh in particular and the UPA government had again slipped up on a key public policy reform.

Meanwhile, Soren resurfaced as a minister in November 2004 after spending some months in jail plus a short stint underground. He surprised his secretary when the auction issue came up again saying that the prime minister never wanted a cabinet note to be acted upon. How he got his ideas, even Parakh was not sure since he had never met Singh during his flight from the police much less to worry about coal. But he was sure. '*Woh sirf dekhna chahte the*' (The PM just wanted to examine it), he said and buried the note. When Parakh brought up the observations by Soren to the prime minister, he (Singh) called in his principal secretary TKA Nair to talk to Soren and get the file cleared. It never happened.

This was a classic procrastination. The months rolled on. By March next year, demand from industry for more coal had become sharp. Parakh suggested that if the government did not take a quick decision to go ahead with the auctions, then the pressure would intensify to continue with the old system.

'I said we must issue an ordinance to permit auction. By that time, pressures must have got generated on PM also. The response of (Singh) was that we must consult the state governments too'. The delay worked as by July, Rao happily informed the Parliament that the allocation of fresh coal blocks stopped from June 2004 had been revived under the screening committee route.

Meanwhile, the states and the other ministries were consulted through that summer and brought on board. And in September of that year, Parakh put up a revised cabinet note for auctions. The file was submitted to Dasari Narayan Rao since Soren was again AWOL.

> He waited till December end for me to retire and then on 6th of January, he returned the file back to the department, saying that PM has already approved that we can carry on with the current system till the new system comes into force.

The ministry was happy to erase the dangerous diagnosis.

Rao had argued that since the new system would take a long time to become operational, 'let us carry on with the current system as there is no urgency about taking up this auctioning system'. Parakh smiled wanly as he sipped his tea in his living room.

The file for auction was born anew in April 2006 when it was decided to push for an amendment of the Mines and Minerals (Development and Regualtion) (MMDR) Act to bring in auctions. Perti said that in 2004 and even the next year, there was little training within the government to handle auctions. So even if Parakh's recommendations were accepted, there would have been a long lead time before it could have been put on the road. Meanwhile, there was no option but to continue with the committees.

The episode has been visited several times including by the former CAG Vinod Rai in his book *Not Just an Accountant*. Recounting the episode, Rai said, it is 'rather strange that the Prime Minister (Singh) is made to make a statement in Parliament which is contrary to that in government files'. What Rai referred to is the curious phenomena that while the notes progressively made out a case for auctions, the prime minister stood in the Parliament to debunk the auditors claim, justifying the auction of the mines.

'It may not be advisable to indicate windfall gain. It may also not be advisable to quote any figure of gain since the estimates may vary considerably' was what the prime minister told the Parliament. Essentially, Singh was saying that the auction of coal blocks would not be the best option. The Hindalco case, as we shall see later, was an illustration of this line of argument.

By then, the storm from the audit report was at its peak.

An Auditor Comes Home

During Vinod Rai's term, the UPA-II government had got so rattled by the series of audit reports that a day before one of those was tabled in the Parliament, a department which thought it was going to cop it sent out a fact sheet to the media houses. Relations were so bad between the government and the CAG that when Vinod Rai went on his pre-retirement customary call to Finance Minister P Chidambaram, it became prime time news.

In a trenchant article just before Rai became the auditor, Vinayak Chatterjee had said,

> Critics of CAG's functioning point out that it is a 150 year old institution with roughly 50,000 officers and staff that carries out about 60,000 audits every year and that it is already creaking, overburdened and unable to make much of a difference in public life'.

Rai accepted the criticism and simply turned the conventional manner of presenting audit reports on its heels. He asked his officers to add up the costs of misdemeanours of offices audited by them and put the figure upfront.

Few reports showed this aphorism better than the audit report on the coal sector. The report 'Allocation of coal blocks and augmentation of coal production' was tabled in the Parliament in August 2012. It ran on two principal themes. The first theme was the crucial necessity of invoking auctions to hand out a natural resource like coal. It was not the first government document to make the suggestion though. The Ashok Chawla Committee on natural resources had already established the framework of thought, a year before in 2011.

The second theme in the report was the demonstration that the screening committee procedure which was being used instead of the auction route was non-transparent and consequently opened to misuse. This was the most popular take on the miasma from policy-making in the sector.

The report, however, even without the second theme made a robust conclusion. By not opting for the auctions, it established that the government had laid itself open to charges of making a loss to the exchequer. It estimated the loss at a towering ₹1.86 lakh crore—Parakh's windfall gain.

It was a fine piece of analysis that could become a template for plenty of future audit reports including those for companies in the private sector too.

Remember the coal mines were given out without asking for any payment except for royalty payable to the state governments. So, the only costs for the miners were the cost of extraction. To arrive at their gain, the auditors used CIL's average selling price of coal, deducted from it the cost of extracting the coal and added to it a finance charge. The net difference was the profit margin per tonne for the private miners. Multiplying this figure by the total extractable coal reserves of all the mines handed out by the government, Rai got his sledgehammer of a number that delivered a KO blow on the Singh cabinet. There were counter arguments.

The most trenchant of those was from economist Surjit Bhalla. He said that the CAG estimate of coal prices were based on those prevailing in 2010–2011, while 'the so-called sweetheart deals were made well before the explosion in commodity prices post 2006. If tomorrow the international price of coal falls, then will the CAG come out with a reduced corruption estimate?'

He was not quite accurate since of the 214 blocks, 144 were given in the years 2006–2011. The CAG's baseline price for CIL was realistic since those prices had been hardly revised since 1993. At the end of 2011, when CIL attempted to revise them, it was sternly issued a presidential directive to roll them back.

Bhalla was on more sure grounds where he argued that Rai's team had made no allowance for discounting the profit since the realisation from the mines would stretch 25 years into the future. Here too, to be fair, the auditor would have had to raise the price of coal into the future to estimate the gains. However, neither Bhalla nor others ever claimed that competitive bidding was a bad idea.

But Indira Rajaraman, RBI chair professor at the National Institute of Public Finance and Policy disputed Bhalla's observation. 'No one is prevented from constructing a time stream and discounting at any rate of their choice or trying other price and cost configurations. *The issue survives any correction of the sum* [italics mine]', she wrote in *Business Standard*.

The episode was ironic. Singh himself could have come to a similar figure to demonstrate an opportunity cost for the economy and he could have used the offices of the CAG for this purpose. The calculations would have provided ammunition to a determined secretary like Parakh to neutralise the opposition from Soren and Dasari Narayan Rao to bring in reforms in a critical infrastructure sector.

The government instead was left trying to prove that the loss was notional and even if it were not so, it was not anywhere near the scale it was made out. For instance, the ministry pointed out that excluding coking coal and top-grade non-coking coal from the total sales of CIL would have reduced the average price closer to the cost of extraction. The loss would have seemed far punier. But the audit report had gained huge traction made more colourful by the type of entrepreneurs listed as mine owners.

The scope of the debate was not academic. The working of the Parliament came to a stop the day after the CAG report was tabled in the two houses. A furious finance minister sailed into the debate to make it more vitriolic. Chidambaram talked in detail with the press to take the sting out of the report. 'If coal is not mined, if coal remains buried in mother earth, where is the loss. The loss can arise only if one tonne of coal is taken out of mother earth, and sold at some unacceptable price or value'. It was a good argument—the reporters, however, read it as a zero loss theory. The word had acquired opprobrium earlier when the telecom minister Kapil Sibal had used it to nail another audit report from Vinod Rai on allocation of telecom spectrum. It also had claimed a massive notional loss of ₹176,000 crore from the allocations. The coal report topped it by another ₹10,000 crore.

Within 48 hours, Chidambaram was back at another press conference to deny the charge. 'If the coal is not being mined, there is no question of a gain or a loss. That is what I said. So please quote me accurately', he claimed angrily.

Subsequent events moved away from the debate on merits. One after another, Manmohan Singh's ministers slammed Rai for all sort of reasons. Rai was invited to give a lecture at the Kennedy Business School at Harvard University, where he said that as CAG, it was his endeavour 'to uncover instances of crony capitalism and counselled the government to support enterprises per se and not entrepreneurs'. The information and broadcasting minister, Manish Tiwari, said that Rai as the holder of a constitutional post should not have criticised the government abroad. 'I think constitutional authorities, you know, should circumscribe by the *Lakshman Rekha* propriety'.

'CAG has no authority or right to comment on the policy of the government but unfortunately it has questioned its authority, which is totally unwarranted and against the mandate given to them', V Narayanasamy said. He was closer to Manmohan Singh as his minister of state in the PMO. It did not stop there.

Newspaper reporters were filled in with stories of why Rai had produced the audit reports. I had the experience of sitting at one of the periodic briefings held by a group of them at Shastri Bhawan, next to one of the ministers. Inadvertently, I had opened a file placed before me—it was an agenda sheet that clearly said, 'take the fight to the auditor's motive'. One of the ministers I mentioned above smiled blandly as he retrieved the file from me.

A rattled government sunk to the depths to discredit Rai particularly and his team in general. Years later, at an event organised by a policy consultancy group that I and Professor Amitendu Palit run—PolicyAudit—he said, 'I have been told by the best authorities in this country that policy cannot be audited'. It was the worst example of government-regulator face off that would hopefully never get repeated in future. Incidentally, it is peculiar that despite the strong advocacy of auctions, neither the prime minister nor the finance minister thought of putting up the Ashok Chawla Committee report on any of the government websites. That committee provided the theoretical justification for auctions and particularly of transparency in allocation of not just coal but also airwaves, water, forests and mines. Putting up the report which came just ahead of Rai's audit report could have repaired some of the perceived damage but the reluctance to do so remained baffling. Possibly all sections of the government were not sold on the principles put there.

Rai was, however, on a bit weaker wicket when he ascribed the blame for the mess on to the screening committees, particularly their lack of processes. Successive coal ministry mandarins have claimed that this was an unkind cut, as it seemed to paint all of them as players in a long-drawn conspiracy. In fact, it was the perceived conspiracy that had got Parakh's successor HC Gupta into trouble. Yet even Parakh vehemently claimed that the auditors got it wrong in blaming the committee system for the ills of the coal sector and adducing non-transparency. Their anguish is understandable. But there was no way for them to absolve themselves from the shenanigans for a simple reason. The coal ministry had lost all the papers it could have used as a counter argument to defend itself from the charges. Absurd as it may seem, all secretaries of the department since Parakh agreed that this was true.

As the demand for coal blocks shot up (in 2003 itself, the government allocated 20 blocks; between 1993 and 2002, it had allocated 19), one of the first things Parakh as the coal secretary did was to streamline the application procedure by the companies.

Before him, companies applying for a mine did not need to show that they were in the business of mining coal. It was considered enough that the company should have a demonstrated track record of running a profitable business and be able to show an end use for coal in their business plans. But with those yardsticks for every block, there were now applicants in close to triple figures.

The rush was intense.

Ajay Dua, the former industry secretary, described his experience of seeing the working of the screening committee in the post-2003 era as melas (local fairs).

> The additional secretary, coal would be sitting on a dais at the venue. His department officers would crowd around him like in a *durbar*. In the hall there would be a continuous chatter as representatives from the applicant companies would sit clutching their files. As soon as their name would be announced they would rush to the dais and shove their papers to the officers trying to rush through their presentation in the shortest possible time.

To avoid creating a spectacle, no senior officers from other ministries or even state governments would visit this durbar. Was there any space for evaluation of the respective merits of the applicants at these meetings?

U Kumar, the former chairman and managing director of SECL, the largest subsidiary of CIL, had to often attend some of those meetings. He said that the rush in the meetings began post 1998 after the government opened the allocation of coal blocks for other sectors such as cement and sponge iron.

'*Woh tabse mela ban gaya. Thoda gadbadi bhi zarur hui*' (The meetings became like fairs. Some amount of mischief too then happened), he told me. The pressures from sundry politicians and lobbies began with this phase, he claimed. He had a point. Almost all the CBI cases in coal allocation have indicted companies in the sponge iron sector. In the carnival-like atmosphere at the meetings, critical records often went missing.

I asked Vishambhar Saran the same question. He got fidgety as he considered the question. His opinion was then carefully worded and his brisk voice became measured. He argued that there was a reason for the chaotic look of those meetings. 'When you try to include everybody in a meeting it could look a *mela*. But the procedure adopted was elaborate. We never got an impression the process was wrong'. Did his team make a presentation for the meeting? He was sure that they did. Of course, he had no idea whether the ministry preserved those presentations.

Between 2004 and 2011, based on the committee's recommendations, 168 coal blocks were passed on to private and state-run companies. The SC order cancelled all of them including that of Visa Steel named after his and wife Saroj Saran's initials.

'Would you have bid if there was an auction for the mines?' I asked Saran was again measured in his reply, 'But there was no plan for an auction at that time'. 'But would you have', I persisted.

'We plan to bid this time (they did and lost). What is your opinion about the auction?' he asked me as he escorted me out.

As Rai wrote in his book, 'All that the records showed was that the committee met, deliberated and merely recorded the name of the block allotted to a company, and the state where the end-use plant existed. It is left to the reader to decide if transparency was a victim'.

Parakh differed from this assessment. According to him, the SC had only gone by final minutes of the screening committees to castigate them.

Those minutes are a brief record or what happens in the Screening Committee. But apart from what happens in the committee, there are detailed agenda notes which are discussed too. And after Screening Committee's recommendations, every case is examined in fine detail, before the ministry takes a decision. So to make your (auditor) decision merely on the basis of Screening Committee recommendation and say that every decision was arbitrary is a very sweeping kind of an observation, which, in essence condemns every chairman and every member of those committees from 1993 to 2010. So to my mind, it's a very, very unfair observation.

But where were those agenda notes he referred to? They were often not traceable.

Parakh's successor Harish Chandra Gupta paid a heavy price for those missing files. During his term, the screening committees went their merry ways allotting 68 blocks to 151 companies. The allotments had risen after Parakh moved out stonewalling the convening of those meetings.

Many of those allotments are simply not traceable. As the records of the promoters tumbled out, cases after cases mentioned Gupta as the signing authority.

Overwhelmed by the number of cases where he had been arraigned as a suspect, Gupta broke down in the CBI special court. The former secretary said that he had no money to pay for the fees of the lawyers. Justice Parasher, the same judge who had not wilted in serving a summons to Manmohan Singh, was sympathetic but firm. Gupta could take help from a court-appointed lawyer but the cases would roll on.

Amitabh Kant, chief executive officer (CEO) of Niti Aayog, did not shy away from airing his opinion on Gupta's predicament. As the painful drama played out in the court, Kant Tweeted about Gupta, 'He is the most honest officer I have come across in my entire career. Real travesty of justice. Sad and tragic'. It was sad, more so because it stretched out for years. Gupta got dragged in the CBI net in 2013, when he was a member of the Competition Commission of India. As this book went to press, the trials in the CBI court were still on. It is anybody's guess if the cases would reach the SC within this decade.

Parakh and Gupta's troubles with the judiciary threw into stark relief the risks senior Indian bureaucrats now run when they make decisions on economic issues. A decision can potentially benefit a non-State company since most of the sectors have been opened for investment by anyone. Given the 'perverse incentive structures that riddle the top functionaries of the Indian state', as Milan Vaishnav points out, allegations of favouritism in making decisions stick (Vaishnav and Khosla, 2016). For the officers, most of their trouble had to do with an innocuous amendment made in 1989 in the Prevention of Corruption Act. Section 13 (1) (d) (iii) of the Act says, (if a government employee) 'obtains for any person any valuable thing or pecuniary advantage without any public interest', he will be punished. Parakh and Gupta had awarded coal blocks to companies (read pecuniary advantage). It is quite easy from there to infer that the blocks were not given out in public interest.

The onus was on the officer to prove that he met the criteria of public interest. Parakh was hauled over the coals in the case of Talabira II given to Hindalco before he could establish that there was public interest. In Gupta's case, since the files had gone missing, he had no evidence to prove his innocence. The offending section had hit almost all cases of awards of national resource; Shyamal Ghosh, secretary, telecom, was gutted when he told me about the experience of having CBI officers visit his house. 'I had to wage a long and lonely battle in the court', he told me. The case was about allocation of telecom airwaves made in 2002; the charge sheet was framed ten years later in 2012.

Parakh told me that he had just stepped out for his morning walk at his house in Secunderabad when the sleuths dropped in, seven years after he had retired from service.

Kant had once told me his opinion about the games politicians play. 'Politics in India is not in line with the economic realities'. Almost echoing those lines, Gupta told the court that he had written his opinion on the files and sent those up to the minister of state Rao who had presumably forwarded the same to Prime Minister Singh. And just as the Andhra Pradesh IAS officers association stood up for Parakh, Gupta's public breakdown galvanised the officers in New Delhi to stand up for him. It would not help to defuse the court cases though.

What followed next was on the basis of hours of discussions I had with many officers of both the audit department and the coal ministry. Many of these cannot be ascribed by names to the individuals concerned as they are highly sensitive, but they are accurate nevertheless. And the conclusion is sad.

In the process of firming up an audit report, the government departments and the auditors deploy a standard operating procedure. This includes an entry conference between the two to decide on the modalities of the audit, followed by (usually) two exit conferences where the draft audit report is discussed.

In the course of the coal audit, it was clear by late 2011 that the audit team had veered to the conclusion that the auction and non-implementation of it would form a key part of the report. A copy of the draft report which appeared in March 2012 in *The Times of India* captured this line of argument. It was, as we have seen, a cogent line.

What was not so cogent was the ascription of 'non-transparency' to the working of the screening committees. The final coal audit report came out with this startling disclosure at least as far as the coal ministry mandarins were concerned who felt that their point of view was not reflected in the report as tabled in the Parliament.

The report had used two examples to drive home the point. At the 35th meeting of the screening committee for the Fatehpur coal block, of the 69 applications for allotment, only 39 turned up to make their case before the screening committee. The block located in the state of Chhattisgarh was finally allotted to SKS Ispat and Bhushan Steel.

Similarly, it alleged the case of two Rampia coal blocks. Here, the auditor noted that of the 108 applications received, only two were listed for making presentations to the committee. None of the two was selected in the list of six companies whom the committee recommended for allocation of the coal blocks. On the face of it, these would seem to be absurdly capricious.

'Minutes of the screening committee did not indicate how each one of the applicant for a particular coal block was evaluated. Thus, a transparent method for allocation of coal blocks was not followed by the Screening Committee', the final audit report noted.

These were grave charges and rather unprecedented in the history of the Government of India where at the level of the secretary, business procedure of a ministry was never called into question so openly.

According to Perti and Sanjay Srivastava, his successor in the coal ministry, the audit team went wrong in their assessment since they did not 'give a chance to the ministry to rebut the allegations'. Ministry officials at different levels claimed that the auditors looked at only the minutes of the meeting but did not inspect the noting made on the concerned file, namely the agenda notes and others.

The auditors could not have read the notes even if they had tried. In a subsequent deposition before the Parliament Public Accounts Committee, the ministry admitted as much.

The comparative statements (of the companies) could not be found in the records of screening committee files. The screening committee minutes also do not comment on the preparation of comparative statements. However the minutes ... do state that the feedback received from the state governments and ministry of power were taken into consideration ... further the contents of the preparations made do not appear to have been preserved in the file....

For each block, there would be multiple applications. It was the usual method not to ask a company to repeat the same if they had already made a presentation in the same meeting for another block earlier. This happened in the case of Rampia coal block, for instance.

Kumar also supported Perti's contention. 'It didn't make sense to make them (companies) to show their corporate score card repeatedly'.

But he agreed with the auditor's contention that the minutes of the meeting were often 'so shabby'. Some years ago, the record room at Lok Nayak Bhawan where plenty of those papers were kept caught fire. Few files survived that conflagration. In its reply to the SC on case after case of allotment, the ministry repeatedly said, 'it appears that the presentations made by the applicant companies have not been retained on the file'.

The parliamentarians asked the ministry if they had established any system to verify documents; what if there were misrepresentations? The ministry again admitted that there was not any such process.

'As per records available applications do not appear to have been checked for eligibility and completeness before sending to concerned administrative ministries and state governments for examination and comments'. Feedback forms from the companies applying for the coal blocks were at times accepted without signature, it admitted.

It is plainly impossible that a range of officers over a span of twenty years in the ministry were acting in concert. It was the reverse—they were caught napping. The slip-ups in records date from the very first meetings of the committee. When CBI officers called in to investigate specific cases, the ministry had to appoint a committee to fetch many of those papers. A record of Congress MP Vijay Darda's incriminating letter asking for Bandar coal block in which he was a shareholder to the PMO could not be found. It was ultimately retrieved from the PMO.

The committee system as Parakh noted had simply fallen short of the demands made on it. Did the auditor also get carried away ascribing to it a lack of transparency and insinuating mala fide?

Coal was not a 'sexy' topic for a long time in post-liberalisation India. Few ministers took interest to improve its functioning, and fewer officers recognised the importance of the issues it was likely to throw up. Yet there is also no evidence that the quality of civil servants posted to the ministry were in any way inferior to other economic ministries. Parakh was a geologist; Gupta was a member (administration) in the National Highways Authority of India before coal.

Few of them, however, took the effort to secure the interests of the sector from the obvious build-up of attacks from sharp entre-preneurs and wily politicians that began from 1997 onwards. There were enough warning signals for them to be careful, as they were aware of how the system of checks and balances had collapsed in states like Jharkhand. The shattering demonstration of misman-agement of records under their watch instead showed errors of omission—an indication of a larger rot.

What the officials were claiming would seem unthinkable, but they were plausible. Indian government's handling of allotment of natural resources which seemed light years away from the ham-fisted approach of the state governments had collapsed in the post-reforms period. Nobody noticed it though. So, the auditor it would seem was right. Parakh in coal ministry and earlier Ghosh in the telecom ministry had attempted to set those right, but with varying degrees of success.

The chinks they left open expanded over time as Gupta discov-ered to his cost. But then the guideposts were available. The first of those came when the coal scam was in full blast in 2011. The cabinet secretary set up a committee headed by the former finance secretary Ashok Chawla. Under him, the committee worked out a pithy set of rules for how such eight resources including coal, oil, gas, water and telecom spectrum should be handed out by the government. 'In the Committee's opinion, the test of transparency needs to be applied regardless of whether the allocation process is market-related or non-market'. It was a valuable advice but it came too late to undo the damage made in the allotment of coal blocks to private parties. The lack of transparency was visible even in the way the state-owned monopoly CIL was run. Its pricing policies, for instance, created another crisis.

6

Entrepreneurship and Environment

CIL Corner Room

Partha Bhattacharya stepped down after completing an over four-year-long term as the chairman of CIL in February 2011. Bhattacharya had rewritten much of the sordid script for the chairman of CIL during his time to make the company presentable to the world. Under his watch, the company floated its first public share issue in 2009 which was the largest ever in the history of the Indian stock market.

Old habits, however, reared up as soon as he left. For more than a year until April next year, the coal ministry under Sriprakash Jaiswal could not appoint his successor. Although in anticipation, by November 2010, the Public Enterprise Selection Board had short-listed Tapas Kumar Lahiry, the CMD of Dhanbad-based BCCL to succeed Bhattacharya, it got scuppered.

Lahiry's nearest competitor to the post was Dinesh Chandra Garg, the CMD of Nagpur-based WCL. Lahiry is a flamboyant man. At his home in the BCCL town, he would organise *kirtans* (devotional songs, often sung in chorus) every evening where he would invite not only his top officials but also egg on his personal staff including his driver to sing along. He was bitter about the alleged skulduggery that denied him the move to CIL when I met him. 'You obviously know what they did about my case in the selection', he gestured juggling with three mobiles in his office.

Garg had also acquired another variety of reputation in the sector by the time he made his bid for the post of chairman of CIL. There was a clutch of major vigilance cases arraigned against him. One of those was about a bank guarantee of ₹2.24 crore submitted by a construction company to build a project under WCL. Garg as the chairman of the Nagpur-headquartered company had accepted the papers without demur. The RBI found that the bank which had issued the guarantee did not exist and informed the CBI accordingly. It was enough to make the anti-corruption agency to ask for government's permission to chargesheet Garg as he did not make any move against the offending company. But Coal Minister Jaiswal and his team strangely delayed the approval until the interviews for the post of CIL chief were over. In the charming world of Indian public sector, charges of graft are not enough to disqualify a candidate for selection to a higher post unless those are proved. Since proof at the senior level is often elusive (for one, the vigilance officer of the organisation, though independent of the CMD, is still junior to him in protocol and access to resources. In this case, the WCL vigilance head had to ask for protection from the ministry since he was tasked to enquire against his boss) and the charges are not made public, the tarred candidates often manage to march ahead.

There were no charges against Lahiry when the interviews for CIL corner room were held but here also, mysteriously after he was shortlisted, a vigilance complaint surfaced against him. Garg incidentally was director in BCCL before getting the charge of WCL. Some of the allegations against him were about 'social investments' made in the districts of Gondiya and Chhindwara, the constituencies of two ministers in the union cabinet, Praful Patel and Kamal Nath. The coal ministry gave him 'five' extensions until he died as chairman of the company. Lahiry never made it to the CIL corner room. It was not the first time such events gathered around the selection of CIL chiefs. They had taken their toll earlier too.

As the pressure for coal supply from CIL began to intensify from 2003 onwards, the position of its chairman became a hot potato. The coal ministry was forced to remove the then CIL Chief NK Sharma on charges of 'corruption and abusing official position'. He had allegedly signed on coal linkages or in other words made written promises to supply coal to those companies disregarding rules since they offered to 'please him'. There was plenty of excitement when his tenure was cut short but not before CBI had to file a caveat in the Kolkata High Court lest he moved a stay against his suspension. 'Several complaints had poured in against Sharma, but he was always given a clean chit by CIL's vigilance department ... (which) could never establish any charges against him'. The ministry did not feel that it would be able to ask him to go without a court order.

Sharma in turn became chairman after winning a race against another officer of the company, B Akla. This officer could not become chairman as he also faced a CBI investigation culminating in a search warrant. As a result of l'affaire Sharma, issue of coal linkages by chairmen became difficult to execute. In each decade, chairmen of CIL and its subsidiaries did something or other but none were convicted. One of them had run up a personal fortune of over ₹6 crore during his term. The fortune he had made was discovered when he in turn was conned by a fortune hunter to whom he had transferred a good part of that money to invest in the stock market. In the police complaint, the ex-chairman revealed the amount of money he had lost to the conman.

Just as in the case of Lahiry where coal minister Jaiswal made his choices clear, others before him had done so too. Parakh remembered having asked Coal Minister Mamata Banerjee if she had any candidates she would prefer as CIL chairman. Mamata to her credit did not offer any names. But according to Bhattacharya's predecessor Shashi Kumar, she encouraged him to post her party candidates as employees in the company.

The most brazen among the coal ministers was not surprisingly Shibu Soren. Shashi Kumar had described him as 'more or less an extortionist' in an *India Today* news report. Soren's second in command, the minister of state Dasari Narayan Rao of Congress, now arraigned before the CBI special court, 'was also very demanding when it came to money and had (allegedly) asked for ₹1 crore for party funds'. Similarly, BJP's Karia Munda too had allegedly demanded ₹10 lakh from the Coal India ex-CMD, if he wished to retain his post'. Appointment as chairman of CIL did not consequently command respect in the world outside.

Partha still retained his zeal about the coal sector. I asked him once how he dealt with Soren. The Bengali engineer's father Benoy Krishna Bhattacharya was a medical officer with the British Army when he was posted in Singapore during the Second World War. He was taken prisoner when the island fell to the Japanese Army but was released once he opted to join the Indian National Army under Subhas Chandra Bose. Bhattacharya laughed when I asked him to compare whether he had to face more troubles while running CIL than his father did during the war.

It was a rare politician who would instinctively support the key role of energy as the hidden plumbing that needed to be laid well for the Indian development themes to flow. Few things illustrate this better than some of these cavalier selections done for the corner room of CIL. There was rarely a time when some serious thought was given within the government offices of New Delhi about who should get the nod as chairman of CIL or its subsidiaries. It is India's largest state-owned company by market capitalisation, has an almost monopoly position on coal extraction over the third largest reserves in the world and has more cash reserves in its vault than the combined sum of the next five state-owned companies.

Party caravan members, dodgy military hands and bureaucrats with no chances to go higher up the ladder made for a colourful line of chairmen of CIL since it was born with only a few exceptions standing out in this procession. This was in stark contrast to the treatment ONGC managed to secure for itself right from when it was set up under KD Malaviya in 1959. Later too, the long term for Colonel SP Wahi through the 1980s is a good example of corporate stability for India's oil exploration company. With few aberrations, the similar long term for Subir Raha also demonstrated this healthy practice. CIL never got into that groove.

Selection and termination of terms of chairmen of public sector units in India are in any case edgy affairs. The amount of offstage negotiations that precede the handing over of the appointment letter is lengthy, full of negotiations and mostly unfair. Wahi, for instance, was suddenly asked to go by the VP Singh government in 1989 because he was apparently close to the Gandhi family.

CIL had come up as an amalgam of nearly 1,000 mines held by about 300 companies. Considerations of stability should have been even more germane for it, especially because it offers within its empire nine such corner rooms. Eight of those are located in the eight subsidiaries, each run by a chairman cum managing director. And above them there is a chairman of the holding company, CIL. Since the tenure of the respective chiefs does not coincide and every time goes through a long selection process, it is quite probable that at any time of the year, there is at least one vacancy up for grabs.

As the importance of the coal sector shot up in the 1990s, it was inevitable that the degree and intensity of offstage negotiations for these posts would deepen. That it peaked around the same time CIL reached a crisis regarding the pricing of its coal is no coincidence.

Movers and Shakers

As the overhead fans sigh to a stop in East Delhi's overcrowded homes in the lanes of Joshi colony, the income differences between those who can pay for a generator and those who cannot become too evident.

Families which can afford have all invested in diesel generators, often manufactured in the same lanes. Those somewhat less off pool in one with their neighbour; the noisy generator sits in the common passage cased in an iron grill to provide safety from theft. Those who cannot afford even a shared generator have to hit the lanes to get some breeze. Generators are important not because they provide an insurance against loss of a night's sleep but because they power the economy of these market colonies. Beauty parlours, textile shops, DTP job works and everything else run on computers; mobiles need to be kept charged for even providing home delivery of vegetables. Electricity matters, despite the costs.

Between 2011 and 2015, there have been seven revisions in the price of electricity in Delhi. Those revisions are the reasons why a new party under a rookie politician Arvind Kejriwal came to power in the elections for the Delhi state legislature winning an astonishing 67 of the 70 seats. It handed the incumbent Congress government its worst defeat in any state elections. BJP managed to win only three seats.

Electricity prices for Indian consumers in India have ruled the same or higher than in most developed countries, consistently since Independence. This is ridiculous. India imports 78 per cent of its oil and so there is good reason why the prices of petrol and diesel are higher than in the West Asian countries. The country has the third-largest reserves of coal in the world, then why does electricity cost rule so high?

The daily power outage spells are far more extensive daily in the smaller towns beyond Delhi. Uttar Pradesh Power Corporation Limited's chart for daily power supply position for the state as on 18 June 2016 showed that no town in the state had got more than 20 hours of power supply, on an average. Through the peak summer months of May and June 2016, this company had not bought even one unit of power from the electric spot exchange as the prices were still high compared with what the people were willing to pay.

Electricity consumers in India subsidise the coal companies for their inefficiencies. The perverse logic is horrible. Marginal farmers in rural areas and daily-wage workers in towns pay these higher costs because of the political clout of the unionised workers of the three government-run coal companies, CIL, SCCL and Neyveli Lignite Corporation.

Most of Tamil Nadu swelters to keep up for the cost of not only buying expensive lignite from the last of these three but also to pay for the cost of keeping it from getting disinvested. The last time this company came on the block for sale, the Tamil Nadu government moved Securities and Exchange Board of India (SEBI) to drop the plan and instead rustled up the cash to buy the shares.

Just upwards geographically, as Telangana fries in one of the worst heat waves for decades, the state government has debated whether to raise additional cash to buy out the central government shares in SCCL to make it an exclusively state-run enterprise. It is a throwback to the similar reasons for keeping Air India a state-run enterprise. States are willing to spare tax revenue to keep them ticking.

India continues to produce coal at one of the most expensive rates in the world. The output per man shift, that is, the average amount of coal per tonne each employee of CIL digs out from the mines, was less than 6 tonnes in the financial year 2014. This was a third of the global average. At the same time in the last three decades, the minimum wages of the employees of the government-run coal mining companies had risen by a CAGR of 9.67 per cent (1974–2015). Government records show that the lowest minimum wage rose from ₹325 to ₹15,713 per month for all of them. In contrast, average wage in the largely private sector mills of textile sector hovered around ₹10,000.

This is the primary reason why post 2010, the domestic coal sector has had to raise coal prices sharply when the rest of the world has begun to slash cost of production. As successive governments have found it difficult to cut back on this patronage to open up the sector to competition, the lethal combination of low productivity and high wages has pushed up the costs for power generation. The cost of the coal is, therefore, the mover and shaker in the fuel flask of the power sector. It has provided the froth to keep the costs of electricity high for the end consumers and also provided the setting for a revolt of sorts by Indian industrialists.

God's Directives

The man who faced the rough end of the stick because CIL made a hash of the pricing of its coal was the new company chairman

S Narsing Rao, who took over after a 13-months delay from Bhattacharya.

Does it make any difference to the performance of a state-owned company like CIL whether it has a chairman in the saddle? Rao asked a counter-question. 'Does disinvestment in any public sector unit ever change the way it functions?' He held up the example of National Mineral Development Corporation (NMDC). 'For two years that company was without a CMD. Did it do demonstrably badly in that period than when it was run by a CMD?' If the movements in the share prices of India's public sector companies are plotted on a time series, then it is obvious that Rao is right. The markets do not particularly take note of the changes at the top in these firms. But as a one-off exception, the absence of a helmsman in CIL in 2011 did make a lot of difference.

By the time Rao became CIL chairman, the company had thrown Prime Minister Manmohan Singh into hot water. There was a first-class energy crisis in the economy. I met the former chairman after he had resigned from CIL in 2014 to become the principal secretary to the chief minister of the newest state in India, Telangana. On any day, irrespective of the hour, there was a long line of visitors lining up to meet him at his fifth floor office at the secretariat of the Telangana government in Hyderabad. Along with me waiting to meet him were two junior ministers in K Chandrashekhar Rao's cabinet. Ministers rank above all officers, but in their case, obviously those considerations did not matter.

Despite the distractions, Rao was keen to talk about CIL. 'The pressure on us at CIL to import coal started building after the power producers met the Prime Minister. The Presidential Directive followed very soon'. Rao was referring to the famous evening meeting of Singh with the private sector power company chiefs including Anil Ambani and Ratan Tata that was held on 19 January 2012.

A few days before, the coal producer had raised the price of coal in a bid to align them with international standards. CIL claimed that it had been trying to get to this standard for determining the price of coal since 1998 but had been stymied by its major consumers, the power companies.

To help keep the price of coal down since nationalisation, the government had deployed a home-grown formula since 1973. This formula basically allowed CIL to price its coal in terms of its net of moisture and ash content—'useful heat value'. Basically, it meant that while the rest of the world graded each tonne of coal on the basis of how much energy it could produce or 'gross calorific value', India did so in terms of its level of purity of coal like that of gold or diamonds. It was a compromise, meant to allow different types of coal to be mixed liberally in each consignment sent from the mines. There was no way the buyers could argue about the quality and win, but they kept quiet since the price worked out lower than that of coal produced abroad. Yet despite such blatant rigging of the prices, CIL found that its costs were still rising. It was as Parakh noted 'a highly inefficient organization'.

London-based The Children's Investment Fund (TCIF) had bought 2 per cent of the shares in CIL during its public issue to become its largest minority shareholder ranking right after the Government of India. TCIF immediately began to put pressure on the CIL board to raise the price of coal at par with international norms. It argued that the lower price 'only benefitted the politically connected industrialists and not the general public. It also alleged that the government had sold shares to the Indian public and foreign investors based on misrepresentation that there is an independent board and that the price of coal is deregulated'.

After holding out for several months, the CIL board functioning without a full-time chairman caved in. The members, mostly retired bureaucrats and coal sector experts, were no match for the stiff public campaign carried on by TCIF. Jaiswal in turn did not offer any direction to them. The changes as expected raised the price of the mineral all around. On an average, the price rise was 12.5 per cent, but within it, the most important grade of coal meant to fire power plants got hiked much more. In a spectacular display of bad timing, CIL chose the last date of 2011 to carry out the changes. The power companies were furious.

Here was a public sector company supposedly moving against the interests of domestic private sector companies. All through the period of liberalisation, the covenant between the government and private sector was the reverse. Narasimha Rao, Atal Bihari Vajpayee and even Manmohan Singh had agreed that the socialist baggage of earlier era had given the public sector too much space hurting fair competition for the private sector. Coal Minister Santosh Bagrodia had assured the industry four years earlier that despite a global surge in coal prices, CIL would find out ways to keep prices unchanged. It would 'manage' the situation, he told the companies just ahead of the general elections.

As Mihir Sharma puts it pungently in *Restart,*

> More than a century after the Jamshedpur plant opened, Tata Steel trumpets its cost advantage.... But speak to any of its competitors, and they will point out why: Tata Steel has exclusive access to some of the finest iron ore and coking coal mines in the world—practically free.

It was a norm set then; it was a norm industry expected government to fulfil 100 years later too.

The subsequent price rise after the UPA came back to power seemed a walk back from that commitment. As the prices were revised at the instigation of TCIF, a foreign fund manager brought out all the protective instincts of India Inc. against the move. 'The basic issues in the power sector are not being resolved and are impacting generation programmes. The companies will seek quick redressal', Ashok Khurana, director general of the Independent Power Producers Association of India, thundered.

Prime Minister Singh realised that his coal minister had landed him in a major trouble. Jaiswal later claimed that CIL was free to decide prices to protect its commercial interests, and the government played no role in this. 'However, in the same breath, he said that coal prices are kept on the lower side to ensure that consumers do not pay an exorbitant price for electricity'.

The companies thought that they were the consumers the minister meant. The key point they made was that if the coal prices rose, then they would also have to raise the price of electricity they sold. It was likely to raise prices all around, something the government was desperately keen to avoid. The price of Indian crude rose to US$116 a barrel in April 2011. It came down briefly, but by the time Singh met the industry in January, the prices had again risen to US$106. Nobody in power wanted to take a risk.

When Ratan Tata came to meet Singh, he had already announced that he would step down as non-executive chairman of the Tata group by the end of 2012. His successor Cyrus Mistry was there in the group of sixteen company chiefs, yet Tata felt that the situation was serious enough for him to also join up. Others included Ashok Hinduja, Vedanta Chairman Anil Agarwal, Anil Ambani,

Prashant Ruia from Essar Group, GMR's GM Rao, Gautam Adani, Sajjan and Naveen Jindal. Rarely had the top Indian industrialists converged on the political leadership with such a single-minded zeal before or after. Many of them drove together in the same vehicles to the meeting. It was a virtual revolt by the companies against the government policies in the energy sector.

Singh understood the passion running among his visitors. A statement issued by his office after the meeting said that the prime minister had assured them of decisive action to solve the power sector's problems. 'A practical, pragmatic and viable solution will be found to the plethora of problems facing the power generation and distribution sector'. To show them his intentions, Singh drafted in his new principal secretary Pulok Chatterji as the points man for coal.

Since 1985, Chatterji has worked in the PMO, first with Rajiv Gandhi. Chatterji came to the notice of Rajiv Gandhi in the 1970s as an efficient district magistrate of Sultanpur in Uttar Pradesh, nursing the constituencies of the Congress first family. He never severed his links with the party even during the period when the party was out of power from 1998 to 2004, serving as OSD to Rajiv's widow Sonia Gandhi. In 2011, he was appointed principal secretary to Singh, virtually making it clear who would call the shots in economic decision-making from then. By asking Chatterji to set up a committee of secretaries to meet every week until the coal crisis was resolved, Singh was signalling them to call off the revolt.

Strangely, Tata and the other industry leaders found support from a most unexpected quarter. Mamata Banerjee having won a landslide election victory campaigning about political–industrial nexus in West Bengal assembly elections now supported them. Her power minister Manish Gupta wrote a stiff letter to Coal Minister Jaiswal. Gupta went for the ultimate argument against the rise in price of coal. 'This move by Coal India is worst definitely in the public interest and is anti-people' [sic].

CIL rolled back its price rise in the same month, on 31 January. To make it stick, the company was slapped with the first of the two presidential directives—no public sector company in India had ever been served one before. The proposal for the directive came from Chatterji. A phone call might have done the same trick, some thought. By then, Narsing Rao had become the boss at CIL. The directive was meant as much for public consumption outside as it was for the company. It ordered CIL to maintain a supply of at least 80 per cent of the commitment it had signed on with its consumers instead of the usual average of 50 per cent at that period. 'How a company struggling to maintain its level of production could suddenly ratchet it up to 80% was never explained', said Rao.

By next year, the government issued the second directive telling CIL to offer more supply to new power producers. If it could not do so, then it was supposed to import coal to bridge the deficit.

'We were living from one crisis to another', said Sanjay Srivastava, whose term as coal secretary overlapped with Rao. The government possibly did not know what it was getting into. The coal pricing battle stretched out for a long time.

Vinayak Chatterjee, chairman of Feedback Infra, is one of the most astute commentators on the Indian infra sector.

> It was the gathering of demand in the shape of massive addition to power generation capacity that brought up the heart attack in the coal sector. But the socialist mindset of the UPA-I and II government instead of doing a heart transplant ordered a bypass operation.

The bypass he referred to is the policy of offering captive mines that only pushed back the problem of 'transplant' or freeing up coal production to some other day.

The directives were impractical and remained on paper. The former CIL chairman gets annoyed describing the sequence of events.

> It was simply impossible! To provide an 80% level of satisfaction for all the power plants with whom we had signed linkage agreements would have required us to produce 480 MT of coal (from the then 250 MT). Any simple person would say 'No' to this. When you can run for 10 km, you can sign an agreement to stretch it to 12 km. When you know there is no way you can run for 25 km why build in a penalty clause mandating you to run the distance.

State-owned companies are not expected to object to what their masters say. Despite Rao's misgivings, CIL said yes, only for the promise to remain only on paper. The only one from CIL who objected was TCIF. The London-based fund manager argued that selling coal without raising prices would be unfair. It also argued that the central government as majority shareholder was 'improperly exerting pressure on CIL directors'. TCIF filed an unprecedented suit in Calcutta high court against CIL. It was unprecedented because no Indian public sector company had ever been challenged by any shareholding group on allegations of 'breach of their fiduciary duties and for failing to perform their functions with adequate care and skill'. These epithets were supposed to be reserved for mischief sometimes the Indian private sector indulged in.

TCIF claimed that CIL had lost over ₹8,700 crore in pre-tax profits by reversing the price increase. Failing to raise coal prices to market levels at all was bad, it argued, since 90 per cent of such profits could have flowed to the 'Indian people in dividends, and such sums could easily have funded free electricity for all Indian households'. The argument was a fair one. I had wanted to discuss the reasons further with TCIF. But Angus Milne, head of compliance at TCIF, sent me an email thanking me 'for [my] enquiry and [my] interest, but [he had] no comment to make at [that] time'.

According to Rao, TCIF was right as a shareholder to claim that its interest was jeopardised. 'But they are wrong to argue that they didn't know how the company was run. Nothing was concealed. Everything was there in the red herring prospectus, including the limitations on price policy as a government owned company'.

Their demand that CIL should be allowed to sell coal at international prices and there should be removal of all linkages amounted to an interference in the rights of a sovereign government, he argued. But he was even more upset with Singh's emissary Chatterji's orders.

> Do you believe I could produce more coal as the government had ordered? But the government said you should produce it. You can't produce it through just issuing an order whether it calls itself Presidential or God's directives. In all that time no one told us the workers must be *directed* to produce more from their shifts. Nobody even asked this question.

He was referring to the almost flat production trend at CIL for years together from its existing mines. The government went round in circles, but the problems which beset that organisation were left for another day. The festering problem had drastically changed the business models for large segments of the manufacturing sector.

Coal Entrepreneurs

Ratan Tata and the others not only met Singh on that cold January evening, they had also made elaborate preparations on a scale that had not happened for a long time. In February 1956, his predecessor JRD Tata had hosted a similar elaborate lunch for his fellow industrialists to block the government's plan to include the word 'socialist pattern of society' in the cabinet. It did not succeed though. This time, the industry leaders had flown in from Mumbai the evening before to fine-tune their strategy at a dinner. On most days, they would arrive in the city by their respective jets and fly out the same day after finishing their business at Raisina Hill. That Wednesday was different. Throughout the day, the industry captains went round meeting Coal Minister Jaiswal and officials from the PMO and rounded off their visit to the city by calling on Finance Minister Pranab Mukherjee late in the evening. It was quite an entourage through Lutyens Zone.

It was all about coal. Ironically, for none of them, coal was supposed to be the centrepiece of their business plans. The private sector was not supposed to have any truck with coal mines from 1973 onwards except as buyers since coal was supposed to be extracted only by the state. It was a state monopoly.

But the big men of industry sitting in Singh's drawing room that evening were all representing industrial groups that got dragged into coal business over the decades. It was the most emphatic signal about the failure of the policy of nationalisation of coal business. Instead of insulating India Inc. from coal and the larger energy issues, the government had ended up dragging them onto the pitch, somewhat like unprepared batsmen asked to face a furious fast bowler. Particularly so, as the foray into coal has not added to their profits; *Forbes Magazine*'s annual ranking of Indian billionaires for 2012 showed this up clearly. 'Not surprisingly, the wealth of businessmen from the debt-burdened infrastructure sector shrank most. The most notable of them is Gautam Adani, whose coffer is lighter by US$4.3 billion. Among the 10 drop-outs, six, including Tulsi Tanti, have interests in the power sector', it noted. Those miffed by the drop in their fortunes would have found ready support from a wider group of businessmen who may not have been involved directly with the sector but were tied to each by marriage connections.

Prashant Ruia, CEO of Essar, was the son in law of Narendra Kumar Bajoria, owner of his eponymous group. Kishore Biyani had no truck with the coal sector except that his son was married into the family of Anil Agarwal, owner of the Vedanta Group. Kumar Mangalam Birla's sister was married to Kushagra Bajaj who had set up Lalitpur Power Generation Company in Bundelkhand region of Uttar Pradesh. It did not have a coal mine nearby for hundreds of kilometers in any direction and so was dependent on CIL's supply to run its 2,000 MW plant. The Jindals of Haryana were also connected through marriage alliance with Monnet Ispat. Monnet's promoter Sandeep Jajodia became the brother-in-law of Sajjan and Naveen Jindal when he married their sister. Between them, the Monnet and Jindals had the deepest exposure with the coal sector in India.

The union cabinet was consequently aware that the stakes in the meeting in Singh's office would extend far beyond those present there. It was pretty much similar to the developing crisis in the natural gas business. As the possibilities of steady supplies evaporated, fertilizer and power companies spent more time to figure out their options for fuel as feedstock than on plans for their expansion. And few industrial groups' foray into coal described the failure of government policy better than that of the Tatas.

Jamsetji Tata's business empire was built around the steel plant that began production in 1907. It added hotels and a line of chemicals early on, but coal mining was just a part of Tata Steel's insurance against disruptions to its supply of raw materials. By the time India became independent, Tata Steel operated six coal mines located about 180 km from Dhanbad. As the scope of government restrictions on the sale of coal in open market grew, the company extracted only that much coal from its mines as its steel furnaces could consume and left the excess as residue. Those residue were, however, so fine that they created a sought-after supply line in the distant Varanasi coal market. Naresh Kumar and Co. set up by the former Indian Davis Cup captain as coal distributors got a toehold in the business because of his proximity with Russi Modi, the former czar of Tata Steel. By the 1970s, however, the government had pushed for nationalisation of even those mines. JRD Tata's exertions avoided that hubris for his group. The Coal Mines (Nationalisation) Act specifically excluded the Tata mines from its sweep. This was the second time the company secured that reprieve. The first was in the 1946 Indian Coalfields Report.

The turning point for the group, however, arrived in 2001. By then, the company's mines were producing 5 MT of coal of which it used 3.5 MT every year. The government was meanwhile faced with a shortage of coal for the economy that grew worse each year. Hit by the crippling shortage was Tata Steel's neighbour, public sector giant steel producer SAIL. It did not have coal mines. SAIL despite its status as India's largest steel producer was asphyxiating for want of coking coal to run its mills.

Ratan Tata sensed an opportunity to sell the mineral to SAIL. He set up a task force within Tata Steel to decide if the coal business could become a separate profit entity. 'Tata Steel is highly impacted by the cyclical nature of its business, (so) making the coal mining activity a separate and reliable source of revenue would enable the company to become insulated, which in turn will boost its top line'. The proposal stopped just a step short of free market sales. The proposed change Tata Steel was about to make in its business plan was enormous. From a steel maker which had bought coal mines to provide raw material safety a hundred years ago, it was now about to transform itself to a coal-led business model that would also take care of steel.

Sure, Tata Steel was not about to jettison the production of steel, but it was clear that sale of coal from the mines was a 'more reliable source of revenue'. Just two years ago, the company CEO Jamshed Irani had seen a 61 per cent drop in its net income. Workers' flats in Jamshedpur town emptied out as the company began an aggressive retrenchment programme. As governments came and went in rapid succession in the second half of the 1990s ruining the benefit of a five-year stable term provided by Narasimha Rao, the Centre was not able to offer much of a sustained opportunity for business to demand steel. Coal was in a different league altogether along with oil. For instance, just as coal shortage grew, Reliance Industries Limited (RIL) had found attractive and stable markets to sell refined oil products abroad than within India. Coal production within India was not about to keep pace with even the rise in inflation, crimping the existing demand lines.

Tata and his deputy Jamshed Irani had learnt the same lesson that a decade earlier was digested in quick succession by Ramaprasad Goenka and Aditya Birla. The Aditya Birla Group's key line of business in the early 1990s was of aluminium, the same as that of Vedanta but coal business entered its menu because of the need to protect its electric-run smelter. Similarly, the Hindujas were focused on banking and automobiles, GMR was in the business of construction of airports and power, the Adanis in logistics, agribusiness and energy, Sajjan and Naveen Jindal in steel and so on. By the early 2000s, all of them were instead de facto coal entrepreneurs. In the meeting with the prime minister, most of these companies said that they were then interested in owning coal mines.

Of course, the Tatas had to eat humble pie when they tried to get more coal blocks. The company was forced to tie up with a little-known Adhunik Group for a lease for a coal block. Manoj Agarwal, owner of Adhunik, had firm links with Jamshedpur having started out his business career from the city. He was one of the new breed of entrepreneurs who had sort of stepped on the gas in the coal sector. Just as Tata Steel announced its plans to acquire more mining leases to add to its existing six collieries, others big and small did so too. And some by then had begun to move abroad.

Broken Stairs

At the base of the flight of stairs leading up to coal controller's office in Kolkata, there is a warning. 'Old stairs, not to be used by more than three persons at a time. Carrying material by head load prohibited' [sic]. It is the oldest office to monitor the sector in India, set up exactly 100 years ago, in 1916.

I did a double check as I stood there wondering if I should use the lift instead. It looked equally uncertain. The options looked like the Go and No Go challenge Jairam Ramesh as environment minister had thrown before the coal companies.

Amrit Acharya, the coal controller, told me that the warning has decorated the wall for decades. The office occupies the treasury building at Council House Street which stands cheek by jowl with Raj Bhawan. The building would be a film makers' delight if he/she plans to capture the ambience of early twentieth century offices, including even the swivel doors that still operate outside Acharya and his colleagues' room. The West Bengal government has plans to tear it down—less costly than to repair it from within.

Coal controllers were supposed to ensure that the colonial government had enough coal to 'adequately meet the requirements during First World War'. Without any modernisation, Manmohan

Singh-led UPA-II government tried to pitchfork this office into the role of de facto regulator for the sector. When I met Acharya, he informed me that he was the only technically qualified person among the 160 odd staff in the office.

The role of regulator was one of eleven policies or schemes the UPA government conceived of in five years from 2009 to repair coal production business in India. Each of them enjoyed an approximate life span of roughly six months from the time when they were discussed, planned and then jettisoned for the next one to be picked up. The set of eleven did not include any plan to auction coal mines. And for each of them, the midwife was Planning Commission, delivering a still born, each time. As Jerry Rao had once remarked in his feisty columns in *Indian Express* — 'Samson physically destroyed the temple in Gaza. Montek (Ahluwalia) can simply put the Yojana Bhawan on sale'.

Like the rickety stairs at the coal controller's office, none of those policies had a strong base to give confidence to the investors outside the government that they will hold. If the government had instead agreed to commercial mining of coal, then all these permutations could have been jettisoned.

Congress, rather to its own amazement, won big in the 2009 general elections. 'The verdict provided greater stability to the national government and reduced the bargaining and blackmailing capacity of coalition allies vastly. The verdict eliminated the need for a Congress–Left coalition and was widely seen as paving the way for greater economic liberalisation', read a Centre for the Study of Developing Societies, Lokniti post-poll survey. Singh also read it the same way. He was freed of the malevolent influence of Soren in the coal ministry.

He got Mrs Gandhi agree to retain the coal ministry within the Congress party. His freedom stopped there. Soren's replacement for Singh was Sriprakash Jaiswal, a Gandhi family loyalist from Kanpur. He had never dabbled in coal, had a class 12 pass certificate from DAV College, Kanpur in Uttar Pradesh, to show, but most important in a state where Congress foothold had progressively slipped, he had won three terms to the Lok Sabha. He was a muscleman with strong roots among the gold traders from the city. Singh got some freedom of action since Jaiswal was made minister of state with independent charge of the coal ministry. Soren was a cabinet minister. The new minister was willing to listen to the advice of the secretaries in the ministry and from Singh to run the coal business. It would prove invaluable giving him the longest term in the ministry of 5 years.

Singh thought that his problems were over. Except they were not! In the environment ministry, another long-term party loyalist had walked in. Jairam Ramesh had been a part of the PMO and the Planning Commission from the initial days of the Narasimha Rao government. He had no strong political base but with a string of degrees beginning from IIT Mumbai to a stint with the World Bank, he was the party's quintessential backroom boy. Incidentally, before the 2004 elections, Ramesh was also in charge of the Congress economic cell reporting to Singh. Old timers recall the mass of data he would store on his computer that would be the base for any party paper in a matter of hours and his huge collection of music that travelled with him to all his offices.

Like Jaiswal, Ramesh was also appointed minister of state with independent charge. Both saw their route for advancing further to that of cabinet ministers as dependant on who could be the faster draw on the gun. Singh had possibly hardened those positions. He advised Ramesh to introduce transparency and accountability in the environment ministry. To Jaiswal, he said that coal must be harnessed to push economic development. The battle between the coal and environment ministries began in earnest. The party could not blame its alliance partners for it. This was an internecine war.

On 20 April 2011, Ramesh wrote a letter to Jaiswal. While it addressed him politely as Jaiswaljee, the tone was hard. 'It is a general perception of the investors that having got allotment of plots from one ministry of the Government of India, they expect other Ministries to 'coordinate' clearances'.

He advised Jaiswal to exercise more restraint before handing out mines to entrepreneurs. One of those restraints, he advised, would be for Jaiswal to check up with Ramesh's office before handing over the mines that those had got an environmental clearance. The environment minister pointed out as an example that the oil ministry had superimposed the coordinates of their proposed bidding blocks with the protected areas before bidding them out. 'The Ministry of Coal may like to adopt such a scrutiny process in the interest of environmental conservation and the investors confidence through improved coordination between our Ministries' [*sic*].

It was the most unfair bit of posturing. A year before, the coal ministry had conducted precisely the same exercise which Ramesh was asking them to do. The two ministries had carried out a joint exercise to superimpose maps of nine rich coal-bearing areas with India's forest cover. These coalfields were in Talcher, Ib Valley, Mand Raigarh, Sohagpur, Wardha Valley, Singrauli, Hasdeo-Arand, North Karanpura and West Bokaro.

Except, his ministry had turned the mapping exercise around to coin the term Go and No Go.[1] The Go areas are those where mining or other manufacturing industries would be allowed and No Go areas are those where no removal of forest crown cover would be allowed.

Out of possible 602 coal blocks in these fields, 206 were outright rejected by the environment ministry as being inside 'forest crown cover', the epicentre of the forest—in other words, No Go areas. In terms of numbers, it was one-third of the coal blocks, but in terms of area, they formed 4,039 sq km out of the 6,487 sq km which these mines would cover. As the two ministries now squared off, the environment ministry relented on another 51.

Ramesh's action created a first-class crisis for the government. Most of those 155 locked in the No-Go belt had already been awarded to private miners, state governments and public sector companies for exploration. Some were given out in the period between 1993 and 2008. Others were earlier inheritances for CIL. For instance, of the 116 new coal blocks given to CIL, 28 fell in those No Go areas. Another 52 were bracketed in the grey zone as 'Not Defined'.

Jaiswal's men were stunned. They pleaded with the environment team. 'It was thought doing this (mapping) would enable the process of getting FC (forest clearance) much faster. This was the genesis of the attempt at defining "Go" and "No-Go" areas ... in respect of coal blocks', read a coal ministry minute.

They also reminded Ramesh's ministry that 'no forest clearance proposal was turned down (before) till mid 2009'. Until the end of 2009, the rules governing mining projects said that all of them would need clearances under the Environment (Protection) Act, 1986. An environment clearance (EC) remained valid for a mining lease, provided the company had got its environment management plan approved by the government. The clearance held for as long as the mine was operational. The only rider was that the environment management plan had to sit pretty with the environment impact assessment to be done by the government.

In case the projects were located in forest areas, they would need an additional clearance under the Forest (Conservation) Act, 1980, to allow diversion of forest areas. For a mine located in a forest area, renewal of mining lease meant tearing off all the previous clearances and beginning the process from the start.

Everything including EC would be awarded out after fresh inspections. Since a mine licence was often for a shorter duration than the life of a mine and mines tended to be located in or around a forest, this meant as a government document from the mines ministry put it 'the process is similar to obtaining a fresh grant'. (Also remember, most mines in India were already operational to some degree.)

Nobody was more surprised in the government by this turn of events than the two-time Congress party MP Naveen Jindal. His JSPL held the largest quantity of reserves outside the government-run CIL. But thanks to Ramesh, there were now disputes over mining several of those coal blocks like the ones in Gare Palma range as No Go areas. So were several of the blocks of Sandeep Jajodia-led Monnet Ispat & Energy, his brother-in-law.

In his book *Green Signal*, Ramesh notes,

> I had to take a tough stance not because I wanted to be contrarian or play to the enviro-gallery but simply because it seemed to me to be the right thing to do.... On occasion, companies that could not get the green light became implacably hostile to me—somewhat ironical, since many of them were my close personal friends and I had excellent relationships with them.

Ramesh of course did not name any one. In India, it was, however, most unusual for an MP from the ruling party to suffer the spectacle of seeing his businesses suffer so comprehensively from the decision of a cabinet.

As TN Ninan put it, Ramesh took his work 'seriously', unlike some of his predecessors.

> But critics said he had been targeting projects by businessmen who had links to the Opposition: the pro-BJP Ajit Gulabchand, Gautam Adani who is widely seen as someone close to Narendra Modi, and

Vedanta promoted by Anil Agarwal, who had invested in Odisha that was run by Naveen Patnaik's Biju Janata Dal. The problem with this line of argument was that it didn't explain why the projects of Congress MP Naveen Jindal were being rejected too.

One could argue whether the coal ministry had jumped the gun on awarding dense forest areas too for exploration. But until Ramesh arrived in the scene, the ministries had worked on the presumption that there were no areas totally off-limits for exploration. There could be delays of which some would be short, while others would take longer to sort through. The environment ministry under Ramesh changed the government policy on industrialisation but never bothered to get a cabinet nod for the same, as we shall see later. The other problem within the concept was in the definition itself.

Jasiwal said, 'In environment subjects *Hum kuch bhi nahi kar sakte the. File banke aate the ki yeh nahi hoga'* (I could not do anything on concerns raised about environment issues. The files would return to me loaded with all objections).

Did he ever try for a meeting with Ramesh to sort them out? '*Chodo bhai, hamare colleague the, hume kuch nahi kahna chahiye'* (Forget it. He was my colleague and I do not want to talk about it now). Obviously, the objections rankle even now. 'And what about auction of the mines?' I asked Jaiswal. Was that ever considered by the cabinet? He replied, '*Uska environment nahi tha. Hamare sathi dal support nahi karte'* (There was not the political environment to bring it in. Our allies would not support it). He was correct though. The left parties have always opposed dilution of state control over coal or any other sector and despite their weakened political position post-2009, they exercised sway over the UPA government.

The Go and No Go concept drawn up in 2010 was supposedly a model to simply rule and cut corruption as the prime minister advised. To make it work, the environment ministry introduced the concept of 'weighted forest cover' which also other ministries looked upon as highly subjective. Ministries like coal and mines wanted the rules to be laid out with specific conditions showing when either of the two options would kick in.

The mines ministry put up in a note to the PMO,

Instead of mere guidelines ... which will always be indicative and subject to actual applications of the provisions of Forest Conservation Act, the need of the hour is to introduce clear provisions in the forest legislations which enable statutory declaration of 'go' and 'no go' areas.

How did the environment ministry read the rules? It said No Go would be applied for those coal blocks which have more than 10 per cent weighted forest cover or more than 30 per cent gross forest cover. If both these conditions were absent, the blocks would be allowed to be mined.

The mines ministry pointed out that there was no definition of terms such as weighted forest cover or other terms such as moderate cover and so were subject to interpretation by the officers concerned.

Singh asked his old ally Montek Singh Ahluwalia to figure a way out. Under Ahluwalia, the Planning Commission came up with an estimate as part of its long-term coal demand analysis. The paper was a masterpiece recalling some of the seminal work done by the Commission in its heydays.

It showed that as on 2010, of the 619 million tonnes per year of coal producing areas, 59 per cent would be affected in some way by the new definitions adopted. Ahluwalia used the evidence to argue that the policy had done just the opposite of what it was meant to achieve. It was expected that in Go areas, speedy clearances would come quickly and in No Go areas, these would be available in most blocks too but after extensive examination. This has not happened. He was directly criticising the policy formed by his mentor, Singh.

'It has no basis in any statutory provisions. The policy needs to be reviewed in the context of balancing the energy and the environmental requirements'. What he meant was that it needed to be scrapped.

It was. Ramesh was also eased out of the ministry by July 2011 and made a cabinet minister for rural development.

And Changing Colours

Jorbagh is possibly the leafiest neighbourhood in Delhi. At night, Indira Paryavaran Bhawan, the headquarters of the environment ministry, is surrounded by a glow from a row of bulbs whose chromatic keys keep on changing. The building has been designed as 'net zero energy building' as a report in *The Financial Express* put it. It generates its own power from a roof-top solar plant catering to the full load of 900 kW so the building complex with four towers does not draw any power from the grid.

It is the first Government of India building in New Delhi or anywhere in India which has a mechanised underground parking slot for cars. The clutter of cars and hangers on that announce that the presence of a government office in the city was consequently absent here.

Singh would have hoped that with a new minister Jayanthi Natarajan the colours would change at the ministry too, metaphorically. Nothing of the sort happened. The suspicion of the devil in coal mining had spread too thick by then. Under Natarajan, the environment ministry revived another argument—that of a mouthful sounding Comprehensive Environment Pollution Index (CEPI) norms. It impacted the producing mines, this time mostly of CIL.

The CEPI norm as it was called was meant to monitor air, water quality and ecological damage in industrial clusters. It was developed by the Central Pollution Control Board under the ministry in 2010, under Ramesh. A score above 70 out of maximum 100 on the scale would mean that the area has reached a critical level of pollution which meant restrictions would need to be placed on further expansion of industrial activity in the area.

'Coal extraction does not release any chemicals. It only produces dust which soon settles back especially as water sprinkling is a standard operating procedure around open cast mines', said Subrata Chakravarty of ECL. The pollution is triggered where coal is burnt to produce sulphur dioxide and nitrogen oxide like in the power plants, he pointed out. Underground mines do produce methane during production, but 90 per cent of Indian coal mining is open cast where it is not a problem.

But when the CEPI benchmark was applied to eighty-eight industrial clusters in the country, several coal belts fell afoul of it. This happened because power and steel plants had come up in coal belts like Talcher and Singrauli to take advantage of the coal mined nearby. The emissions from these plants, as Chakravarty pointed out, pushed up the pollution score for the belts above seventy. The environment ministry had issued a notification in January 2010 declaring that out of the eighty-eight locations it had examined, forty-three had scores above the critical level of seventy.

This included eight of its largest coalfields including Singrauli straddling Uttar Pradesh and Madhya Pradesh. CIL was asked not to expand capacity in those mines even though Singrauli was partially eased from the list in 2010.

Jayanthi Natarajan re-imposed the CEPI norms on Singrauli in September 2013. The colours at the Paryavaran Bhawan it would seem were unchanged from Ramesh's time.

For CIL in particular and coal ministry generally, Singrauli was a prime battle field. In 2014, the ministry had identified it as one of the four areas from where the bulk of India's additional coal supply would come. The other three were Ib Valley in Odisha, North Karanpura in Jharkhand and Mand Raigarh in Maharashtra.

As the battle over the coal mines spiralled out of control of the PMO, Singh asked Pulok Chatterji who was brought in as his principal secretary to sort through the mess. When that also did not work, he set up the cabinet committee on investments with its secretariat working from the cabinet secretariat.

In December 2013, Jaiswal's ministry sought blanket exclusion for coal mining projects from the CEPI moratorium in this cabinet committee. The government was voted out of power before it could go through. Coal did the Congress party in at the 2014 general elections. There has been no other election to the Lok Sabha in India which played so deeply on a single theme since the 1984 December elections that revolved around the assassination of Indira Gandhi.

It was on demonstration in early May of 2014 as Narendra Modi landed in Valmiki Nagar in Bihar as part of his election campaign. The town is located in a picture-perfect zone, nestling amid the Valmiki Nagar forest reserve. Just out of the town is the Gandak River offering the first sight of the Himalayas across it. There is nothing picturesque about the condition of the town, however, with zilch employment avenues except for theft and kidnapping. Workers from the constituency travel more than 100 km to find work as coal workers in the mines of BCCL and CCL in Jharkhand state, next door.

'Nobody steals coal but these people did. Is such corruption Neech Rajneeti & Neech Karma or not', Modi cleverly juxtaposed the frustration of this largely lower caste-dominated constituency with coal theft. Equating coal theft with metaphorical allusions of *neech* (lower caste) karma went home in the caste-laced language of Bihar politics. Addressing someone as *neech* is asking for a death sentence. People have been killed for using the sobriquet.

The CAG Vinod Rai's report had pinned a number to the size of the coal theft at Rs 186,000 crore. The Congress could not wipe the stigma of those numbers by any means. In the Parliament, Jaiswal's ministry argued that the coal mines were given gratis as state policy to ensure the downstream cost of electricity, steel and cement remained low. Yet there were more than one company like JSPL's Jindal Power plant at Tamnar in Chhattisgarh which sold power at commercial rates despite sourcing coal from Gare Palma 1V/2 and 3 blocks. The charges stuck through the election coverage in the media. Coal got about as dirty as it could be.

In a paradox, none of the other measures Congress took to raise the supply of coal also worked. The failure of those measures painted the Singh government as an expendable one for industry too.

Just as in 1948, the government led by Jawaharlal Nehru had run scared of being painted as close to business houses, 65 years later another Congress government under Singh was running scared under the same aspersion. Unlike the Nehruvian era, the charge of practising crony capitalism had struck this time. As Rai mentioned in his lecture at the Kennedy Business School at Harvard University in February 2013, 'We may not be able to wipe out corruption, but our endeavour is to uncover instances of crony capitalism. Government should be seen to support enterprise per se and not particular entrepreneurs'.

The coal entrepreneurs at their peak had produced less than 5 per cent of the total coal production in the country. In 2012–2013, the total production of mines beyond CIL and SECL was just 10 per cent of total coal production and that included NTPC and those held by the Tata Group. The entire exercise of trying to make CIL loosen its hold on coal production in the country and bring in the private sector prized the Congress party out of power, made for a gripping political drama and created a phalanx of villains with few heroes. No significant change had happened in the coal economy. Nothing more had come from the machinations since Purno Sangma moved the bill to allow private sector into coal mining twenty-one years ago.

Aerotropolis

About 160 m underneath the surface inside the Shyamsundarpur Colliery of ECL, the path is slightly undulating dipping gradually ahead. The walls painted white including the ceiling, the fluorescent lights cased in street lamp bowls, telephone and electric cables overhead and a slight breeze playing along the path, all create the perfect simulation of a deserted town road. The only things missing here are the coal and of course people.

Abhijit Mallick, general manager, ECL, was walking briskly with me in one of India's deepest underground coal mines. The only giveaway from the walk-in-the-town feel was the heavy metal-cased battery strapped with a belt on my hip to power the torch perched on my fiberglass cap.

But most of the time, if one is careful, the light from the street lamps is enough to pick the way ahead. At frequent intervals were road signs indicating the way to the active zone of the mine. Long strips of galvanised iron lied stacked in tunnels that branched out from our path.

On the way, we had crossed small companies of miners returning from their shifts. But there was no sign of the coal being carted out of the earth. I did not see any wagon tracks beside us on the path too.

When I pointed this out to Mallick and Ajoy Sharma, the agent of the mine, they asked me to listen to the hum in the background. 'That is where the conveyor belt with the coal is running up from the mine', Sharma said.

By then, we had walked above 2 km inside the mine and the breeze had dropped off. It was getting hot and humid and slushy underneath our feet. We had left the orb of the friendly street lights sometime ago and it was dark like nothing else on the surface of the earth. We were in the bowels of the earth. After a couple of more turns, Mallick pointed straight ahead.

From out of the darkness, the headlamps of a massive vehicle turned towards us. Hard to see the object, Sharma explained that that was a fully mechanised dumper laden with coal. He pinned me against the wall as the dumper mounted on caterpillar tracks flashing red lights careens past us towards an awesomely massive piece of machinery.

'This is the continuous miner. It cuts the coal from the walls with its grated steel teeth sort of chewing out the mineral', Mallick explained.

He asked an engineer Bipin Pal to offer a demo. A huge shower of water sprayed from the nozzle of the continuous miner keeping the circular steel jaws from overheating as it chewed through the wall of coal in front of us. The wet coal fell in a shower on the dumper which scurried away to the conveyor belt as soon as it was loaded.

In turn, the conveyor belt carried the coal from out of the mine pouring the cargo on to the railway wagons lined up beside the Shyamsundarpur mine.

Welcome to the new world of Indian coal mining. Machines like the continuous miner, as its name indicates, mine coal for twenty-four hours, seven days a week, and have no room for the human miners.

A team of about seven hundred workers is now replaceable with a group of less than a hundred engineers and technical support staff to run a coal mine. 'Mining is now a highly technical job', said Subrata Chakraborty, director (technical), ECL, at his office at Sanctoria, near Asansol, the headquarters of the company.

It is showing up in the statistics too. In less than a decade, CIL the holding company of the eight public sector coal companies including ECL has cut 121,812 jobs. That is more than a quarter of its workforce.

Each year, the companies are shedding staff through retirement and sometimes through voluntary retirement at nearly 3.7 per cent of their previous year's strength. At the same time, the companies have sharply improved their total production. In the same eight-year period, aggregate production of coal by CIL has risen 43 per cent. CIL is mechanising.

Every year, in its annual report, CIL provides a table of how efficiently it uses its heavy-earth-moving machineries—dozers, dumpers, shovels and drills. You cannot do coal extraction sans these machines, all of which are all clubbed as heavy earth moving machinery (HEMM). Since 1969 (three years before nationalisation), the first committee 'to examine the percentage availability of (HEMM) equipment' was set up. Since then, eight committees have investigated the same question. The last one set up in 2013 is a work in progress.

The same audit report which brought grief to the political leaders was scathing on CIL too. It showed that the numbers of these machines have actually declined over the years. There were less machines to go around in 2011 compared with 2009. The number of drills, for instance, which was 696 in 2007 had reduced to 664 by 2012. As machines became scarce, accidents mounted. Average fatality rates also mounted. Since the number of workers has come down and production risen, the uptrend means that more workers are susceptible to accidents. In the absence of adequate investment in heavy machines, pairing workers with them is still subpar as the death of eighteen miners at Lalmatia, ECL's biggest mine, proved. As a result, the output per man shift (OMS) at 5.62 tonnes was about a third of the average of comparable mining companies globally in the financial year 2014. In other words, though it had more men on the ground, it produced less coal than other companies.

Even that was inflated. The company 'overstated its manpower productivity for five years between April 2006 and March 2011'. It was not even sophisticated. To bloat worker productivity, it added the performance of outsourced production to that of departmental workers. Corruption in India is not always business versus the government. As CIL demonstrated, it could become endemic within the government too, mostly because there are no counter-checks. A fascinating paper written by Milan Vaishnav and Sandip Sukhtankar on public sector corruption in India in 2014 got it spot on: '[T]here is little reward to performing well, and worse, rarely any punishment to non-performance. The entrenched power of employee unions and onerous government regulations means that short of murder, it is nearly impossible to fire a public sector employee'.

The supposed increase in productivity came about at the same time when the company went for a public issue, under Bhattacharya. Did it really help though?

This is the picture that the unions of CIL did not want to see for a long time. Nowhere is the change more apparent than in ECL and BCCL, the two erstwhile sick children of the CIL family. As on 31 March 2014, these two companies accounted for 38 per cent of the total staff strength of CIL. But this was a sharp descent from 2005 when these companies held 45 per cent of the total staff strength.

Data sent to the stock exchange by CIL for April–December 2014 shows that production had been 102 and 100 per cent of the annual target in these companies. ECL was then the best among the lot, and BCCL had outstripped both SECL and MCL, the two largest production centres for CIL. These were the hotbeds of industrial unrest until recently in the Indian coal sector. Compare these with any given year in the 1970s; in 1977, there were 344 strikes at the mines. The next year was even worse at 623. In just five years of CIL, the company had seen 2,022 of them at an almost AB de Villiers-like strike rate. On plenty of days in those five years, there were overlapping strikes. The management was left fighting those.

Now, as the demand for a far higher level of production— 1 billion tonnes annually—by 2017 stares CIL, its directors are encouraging the subsidiaries to place mega orders for machines like continuous miners for every underground mines and surface miners for open cast mines. A report by Reuters in 2016 noted that CIL 'also plans to stop filling most vacancies arising from retirements over the next three years, and outsource more mining to private companies'. The same report also quoted those opposing it. '"High-tech mining will mean fewer job opportunities for labourers and no job guarantee for existing employees," said Baijnath Rai, president of Bharatiya Mazdoor Sangh (BMS)'.

Just out of Dhanbad town is Kustaur town with its underground coal belt. Its rich near the surface seam had made it one of the first places in India where coal was excavated from the 1900s onwards. That pace of extraction continues. As our jeep approached the road flanking high above Amalgamated West Mudidih-Keshalpur Colliery, a huge plume of smoke rising from the side forced us to stop. Raju Evr, deputy general manager (environment) at BCCL, accompanying us said that the smoke was from the dynamite blasting of the coal seam. Once the smoke cleared, excavators and machine-mounted shovels moved in to cut the coal.

But these too are becoming history. They are being replaced with 120 surface miners across Indian open cast mines as they are faster and environment friendly to boot. This is chiefly because the machines remove the need for drilling and blasting which threw up enormous amount of coal dust in the environment.

Kustaur town has a permanent haze enveloping it. The coal miners' houses are often on the same side of the hillocks where the coal blocks are located. No wonder advertisements for detergents are so prominent in the town where even houses are rarely painted white.

Surface miners and continuous miners also break the coal rocks into the most right-sized material which increases the efficiency of transport and also saves on the energy requirement for their transportation.

BCCL's Lahiry said that higher production required structural transformation of the mining practices of his company. One of those was adopting the mine development operator route where BCCL had brought in specialised mining companies to produce a guaranteed output. Lahiry said that that was inevitable as productivity had reached a near plateau from the open cast mines.

His ₹16,000 crore underground mining project aims to secure a 6.5 million tonne additional coal production in the next five years. BCCL has roped in global mining giants like Joy Mining, Bucyrus and CME to do the high-capacity underground mining using long wall technology in Muraidih, Moonidih and Kapodia collieries.

At other subsidiaries of CIL, the discussion is on the same lines to increase production while protecting environment. Garg's successor at WCL Rajiv Ratan Mishra had the same ideas. 'Nature has been unkind to us', he said. He had a soft lullaby-like tone as he talked. 'My mines can produce upto 100 MT a year from their average of 40', he said, adding an extra 's' after each tonne. He also is pushing the Kolkata head office to sanction him more machines to reach those targets.

Coal reserves in seams can be found up to a depth of 1,200 m, but open cast mining is generally done up to a maximum depth of 200 m. So mining has to go deep underground if coal production has to grow. And that means more machines and less employment for labour. Coal mine unions mistake the wood for trees by demanding a halt to privatisation as they did in their strike in January this year. The investment plans of CIL show that labour displacement is happening big time in the public sector than in the private sector most of which at single mine per operator would likely to be more labour intensive.

CIL chairman Suthirtha Bhattacharya has said that his strategy would include productivity improvement in mines through technology upgrade in open cast mines with induction of high-capacity equipment.

And one can see the reason why. Operating the coal mines near the towns require a high degree of skill and precision. At some places like Munidih, illegal colonies of migrant labourers sit on top of the mines.

Not just BCCL, at WCL too, Mishra told me that his coal blocks were all situated under thick population cover. At BCCL, the coking coal deposits are pretty much near the surface due to a freak of nature. This means that any caving in can cause huge loss of life. The risks have multiplied as the density of houses above the mines have increased. They have no land rights but the hope that the companies will resettle them is viscerally attractive. In the fire-affected 126 surface locations at Raniganj coalfields, officials discovered that in 46 of those, there were just no legal title-holders to the land. The Lalmatia tragedy happened because there was no room to position the machines on the lip of the mine due to encroachments.

Using machines to cut coal can reduce the risk to miners and to those above. At Shyamsundarpur Colliery, Pal and his colleagues drill 5 ft-long steel screws into the ceiling to hold them up against the vibration of mining down below. The screws come with a colour patch which changes from green to yellow and finally red as the pressure on the ceiling grows.

Just a few kilometres away from this colliery is the aerotropolis the West Bengal government has built. Planes have begun to take off from runways with dense coal deposits underground. The polis will soon sport every other paraphernalia of a modern airport city. The margin for error down below is minimal.

No wonder ECL and BCCL are migrating to machine-led mining, big time. There is another spin-off to their effort. As production shoots up and the furore against mining accidents multiply, the companies find replacing labour with the machines a clear winner.

ECL director (technical) Chakravarty agrees that mining fatalities have sharply come down at the mines that have switched to the new methods. As a result, strikes, once a bane of this sector, have come down rapidly too. From a massive twenty-two such strikes in 2009, there was only one in 2014. The planned five-day strike in 2015 has also not been disruptive. As the unions have realised, they need the officers, that is, the engineers, to also join the strike to have any impact whatsoever.

To keep the workers happy, BCCL is simultaneously removing all coal miner townships from the vicinity of the coal mines to safer places. 'Already 40 such townships have been identified and work on 17 has got completed', he said.

The changing worker profile is also reflected in the environment engineering BCCL has launched at Tetulmari and Damuda, about 15 km from Dhanbad. These are huge tracts of forest that go way beyond the single-layer tree canopy to instead build three layers of shrubs, ringed by small trees to large sal trees at the top. Near

Andal town in West Bengal around Bankola mines in ECL and in Kustaur in BCCL, rows of workers homes are now falling vacant.

Facebook and Industrial Strikes

In January 2015, three days into their five-day nation-wide strike, the CIL union leaders agreed to call it off after a meeting with the power, coal and renewable energy minister Piyush Goyal.

Goyal issued a conciliatory note after the meeting on his Facebook page that night but accepted almost none of the demands of the striking workers except for an assurance that CIL was not going to be privatised. But the strike did notch a success even before it had begun. It again delayed coal denationalisation, which had seemed around the corner after the SC judgement scuttling all coal block allocations to companies other than CIL since 1993. Business chamber ASSOCHAM estimated that 'the country would lose production of over one million tonnes of coal worth about ₹200 crore per day'.

The dowsing of the strike was essential because later in the same month, the government floated a 10 per cent additional share sale in the market. The strike would have killed the market appetite from which the finance ministry eventually earned a massive ₹22,573 crore, more than half of its disinvestment target for the fiscal financial year 2014. In 2009, the UPA government had also earned ₹15,000 crore when CIL listed in the stock markets.

The CIL unions did not forget to strike work, so soon though. In September 2015, they made the company bleed with another strike. But as coal prices have softened across the globe possibly without any comeback, their support for the strike of September 2016 next year did not help. The strike was on the same issue, to register their unhappiness about a further disinvestment in CIL. 'Coal India workers' strike on Sept 2 seen to have limited impact', a wire agency report noted. The company was sitting on a pithead stock of 42 million tonnes and the power stations with a supply for twenty-one days in their backyard, the report noted.

'Every link in India's coal supply chain requires upgrading for coal to fulfill its required role in meeting perhaps one of Modi's most important campaign promises: to provide affordable, reliable electricity to every person in India', the World Coal Association report on Indian coal sector remarked. Redrawing CIL and its legacy of trade union workers is one of those 'links' which has begun to be upgraded. It has begun to work—the complexion of the domestic coal sector has rapidly changed for the better.

Note

1. Jairam Ramesh's Go and No Go definition works out as follows:
   The definitions to arrive at the percentages for weighted forest cover (WFC) and gross forest cover (GFC) are as follows:

$$WFC = (Avdf \times 0.85) + (Amdf \times 0.55) + (Aof \times 0.25),$$

where
   Avdf = area under dense forest cover,
   Amdf = area under moderate forest cover and
   Aof = area under open forest cover.
   The weights 0.85, 0.55 and 0.25 are drawn as the mid values of canopy density class of the three types of forests.

   So, WFC/Total area of the block = %GFC = 100 × GFC/Total area of the block.

7

Winners and Losers

We Are Upfront

On an early New Delhi summer evening in 2015, there was a series of happy moments clicked at an office beside a shopping complex in Connaught Place. Assembled at one wing of the World Trade Center were officers from Vedanta, Hindalco and Jaypee, marquee names in the mining sector who had done their own bit of shopping for coal mine auctions that ran from 14 February to the end of March.

On that evening, they had come to claim their shopping bags, a two-page document tucked into simple rexine folders. Those documents were the coal mine vesting orders that said that the mine was theirs for keeps. There was a photographer in tow to capture the moment as they walked by turns into the room of Vivek Bhardwaj, the nominated authority of the Ministry of Coal, to receive those folders. There were some heartbreaks too among them as one of the companies had failed to get its bank guarantee deposited in time with the government. Its officers got the chance to pose with the folder with Bhardwaj but had to return empty-handed that evening.

It was also the last time the companies had reasons to smile. International coal prices dropped through the bottom within months of those auctions. A Goldman Sachs report says that those prices will never recover. Despite an upturn in late 2016, prices are moving south.

Bhardwaj had laughed when I had asked him for directions to his office earlier. 'It is the first office at the foyer of the World Trade Tower. We are transparent so our office too is located upfront', he had said. Claiming transparency was a big thing for the Indian coal sector, even in the larger energy sward. The pervasive sense of stealth in the sector had hurt business government relations so deeply in 2000s that with good reasons, the slump in the economy for two consecutive years of 2013–2015 was placed at its door.

With a Spartan staff of about ten people, Bhardwaj's office was responsible for giving out those folders partly reversing the process began 32 years ago when another nominated authority had taken away all mines from the private sector in India. Unlike the grandstanding which marked that era when Dhanbad town turned out to witness the nationalisation, this was pedestrian in its simplicity. The winners were naturally proud to have beaten their competitors in a gruelling auction. Even as Bhardwaj signed the files for each company, he discussed with me the coal ministry's plans to put fresh blocks under the hammer.

Within eight months, however, belying his optimism, the demand for additional blocks had withered away. In December the same year, the coal ministry had to cancel the fourth round of auctions, as the bids were low. These were the same blocks for which countless companies had fought pitched battle until a few years earlier to win the rights to mine them. Companies with small purses like Visa Steel owned by Vishambar Saran had taken a 20 per cent right in Fatehpur coal block to run their steel manufacturing business; others made do with even less rights.

Was the coal economics in India built over so many decades just a huge casino? As the auctions made it easy for any company that needed coal to step up, had that casino lost its business? Was the long queue of distraught entrepreneurs in the 1980s literally begging the government committees for coal at any cost over? What about the queues in the 1990s when India began to liberalise the owning of coal mines. One of those entrepreneurs who had stood in the queues, Padmesh Gupta, to feed his string of coal washeries around Nagpur city in Maharashtra had bluntly compared their behaviour with those which used to form before cinema halls until the 1990s. He said, *'Jo line sabse choti hogi uske liye log bhagenge'* (people will watch out for the line which seems the shortest), to explain why entrepreneurs had jumped queues before the coal ministry, willing to ride their luck on any one of them.

The coal deposits still lie within the mines as they had done during the halcyon years of 2003–2008. Yet now even those who had won in the auctions were not happy. Thirty-four mines were auctioned by the coal ministry team among private firms or were allotted to state governments through 2015. Only 10 of those have come into production one year later.

'What had changed was the business dynamics', said Anil Sardana, CEO of Tata Power. His company was one of the few that did not bid for a coal block in the auctions, though the court-mandated cancellations had hit them too. 'The trick to instil confidence in coal mining is to set a time table for auctions for the next three year', he said when he met me at Bombay House. People will not hoard the coal blocks as the confidence sets in about a steady stream of mines that will be made available on tap. Even though the upfront realisation by the governments at the state and the Centre will be less, Sardana argued that the lower price would translate into lower prices for downstream sectors.

It was only a follow-through from an earlier era that made nervous companies such as Sanjiv Goenka-owned RPG, Vedanta and Hindalco to compete ferociously among them to send the prices soaring at the first round of auctions. Once it became clear that more mines would come up for auctions as Sardana had said, the scarcity value of coal disappeared.

Ole King Coal

There are two reasons which felled the demand for domestic coal, India's principal source of energy. With the establishment of a new order of predictability in the domestic business of coal trade, it was then clear that there would not be any other era in future where coal buccaneers would chase the mineral to make a quick buck. Instead, they would have to come along with others to an open market and bid for a piece of the mineral. The rush to grab a piece of the natural resource to sell in a market at a premium because of short supply was over. India had managed to establish the rules of the game for its domestic supplies, though it may have come a bit late.

Companies are now also free to arrange for themselves a regular supply from abroad. It was possible earlier too; in fact, it was a possibility right from 1993 when the imports of the mineral were freed—put under open general licence. The difference now is that India has begun to sense the contours of the global energy business and allowed companies to step up to the plate accordingly. They could now take a geopolitical risk like not only contract supplies from abroad but also own a mine overseas and hope to survive. The fossil fuel order in the economy has changed. Both are compelling reasons for a fundamental transformation of the energy economics in India.

It is hard to juxtapose the change in the demand scenario that happened in less than a year. In Hindi film parlance, the demand for coal mines became a flop instead of the runaway hits as they were during the time when Shibu Soren was the coal minister at the central government.

It was a script impossible to imagine for those tracking the auctions when it was rolled out on Valentine's Day in 2015.

By the evening of 14 February, social media was actively tracking the auctions. What had got them curious was again Sarisatolli. Sanjiv Goenka's heirloom was snatched away from him by the SC verdict a year earlier which cancelled all allotments and instead directed them to be handed out through auctions. The coal block was about to create history for the third time in its existence. It was among the first set of blocks that was put up for auctions. As the bidding for the mines edged into the night, the prices for Sarisatolli swung into the negative zone just like breaking through the sound barrier. The coal secretary Anil Swarup who had kept up an almost running commentary like Twitter feed on the price movements throughout the day tweeted, 'For power sector coal block Sarisatolli reverse bid at 0 (zero). Now bidding commences at (minus) 100'.

Swarup has a fine sartorial sense. His Chinese collar for all his shirts makes him stand out even in staid government snaps. And there were plenty of those when the coal auctions went through amazingly well. 'My friends told me the collars look good on me, so I have stuck to them', he explained. He is quite unfazed even when faced with uncomfortable questions, like the ones I had for him. More than me though, it was the coal ministry that offered a basket of difficult questions when he took over as secretary, three months after Piyush Goyal became minister for power, coal and non-renewable energy. Among Swarup's predecessors, one is battling a court case, another came close to being picked up. Did the minister ask for him? 'I make it a point never to meet my minister till I am appointed. I met him (Goyal) only after the orders came', he said. Although secretaries retire irrespective of government tenure in India, the minister had figured out that the coal ministry needed continuity at a difficult juncture. Swarup has a long enough term ahead. Before moving in, Swarup spent a fortnight as OSD to the retiring secretary Sanjay Srivastava in October 2014. Such understudy positions were unusual for ministries under Indian government and showed what was at stake in the transition.

Goyal and Swarup acknowledged that before the auctions, they had never seriously considered the possibility of how the bids would move on the first day. Sarisatolli had a reserve price of ₹458 per tonne. The rules of the auction said that that was the price at which CIL would mine coal from Sarisatolli, so any bidder who wanted the mine had to be more efficient than that rate. It is known as reverse auction where competitors bid at gradually lower prices armed with the efficiency they can extract from their operations. The power generation companies were to start at this ceiling price and go down from there. For each tonne of coal, that was the maximum cost they could load onto their electricity tariff. If they could extract coal at a lower cost, they would win the block but would then have to commit to build the corresponding lower fuel charge onto their power tariff. It would be great news for the consumers and obviously for the state governments too.

It was sensible so long as the bids for Sarisatolli kept descending. Bidders offered to mine the coal at a lower and lower price until they arrived at zero 'pass through' status. Swarup and his team were stunned. The bids had now become crazy. The companies were promising to 'pay' West Bengal government, where Sarisatolli is located, for the privilege of mining the coal. And still the auction went on. It finally ended at ₹470 per tonne in favour of Sanjiv Goenka.

By the time the auctions would be over on 8 March, each of the nine blocks meant for the power sector broke the zero barriers. The highest or lowest depending on which side of the equation you stood was committed by Essar for Tokisud North at ₹1,110 per tonne.

A CRISIL note commented,

> Reverse auctions for coal blocks in the power sector, which can fuel generation of 9,940 MW (sic) have opened on an aggressive note. Initial bids indicate long-term strategic fuel security is getting precedence over near-to-medium-term profitability—as underscored by multiple bids at zero cost and additional premiums per tonne that will be paid to state governments and cannot be passed on to consumers.

The coal blocks earmarked for non-power generation companies went through the more conventional route of forward auctions.

GMR Chhattisgarh Energy, for instance, won the Talabira I at the centre of so much controversy outbidding Adani and Essar; it will pay ₹478 per metric tonne of coal to Odisha government. These high prices paid by the coal miners cannot, however, be loaded on to the electricity they will produce from the coal, since those rates are tied under long-term power purchase agreements they have signed on earlier.

As things stand, GMR will extract the coal incurring all costs including state levies, taxes and transportation charges without adding a paisa to the cost of producing electricity from its plant. The coal ministry had estimated that if CIL had mined the coal, it would have cost it ₹450 MT. The bidding war among the companies had begun from this ceiling price; each undercutting the other's bid until prices reached zero and then moved to a premium payable to the state government where the mine is located, explained Nitin Zamre, managing director of ICF International, a consultancy company in energy sector.

The entire auctions earned for Goyal and Swarup some sort of celebrity status. Experts from the industry tried to figure out how this could have happened, some like the former power secretary Anil Razdan said that the bids defied logic. 'The companies are gambling on huge improvements in their efficiencies to make this bidding work, as I see it', he said. But Goyal exclaimed in an interview soon thereafter, 'We got honest value of coal through auctions'.

There were other surprises in the auctions. Naveen Jindal's bid for three blocks, Gare Palma IV/2 and 3 plus Tara and Anil Agarwal's Vedanta group firm Balco's for Gare Palma IV/1 were cancelled. It was a difficult decision. Swarup described their final prices as evidence of 'outliers' instead of bracketing them as evidence of cartelisation but the charges stuck. In the same hill range in Mand Raigarh in Chhattisgarh, where Hindalco had paid ₹3,502 for Gare Palma IV/5, Balco paid half the price or ₹1,585 for a similar coal block. How come? Of course, it did not escape attention that Jindal was a Congress MP and so his moves would be suspect in the NDA government. Anil Agarwal's political links were less clear, though the former finance minister P Chidambaram had been a non-executive director at his company before becoming finance minister in 2004. The bids for both were demonstrably lower.

Despite the cancellation of these four, the auctions attracted a lot of positive attention in India and abroad for their gigantic scale of operation and the sum of money raised for the exchequer. As a Twitter feed said, 'coal was generating white money instead of black'. The telecom spectrum auction conducted just a month earlier in February was far low-key in comparison.

Goyal told the Parliament later that the six states Chhattisgarh, Jharkhand, Madhya Pradesh, Maharashtra, Odisha and West Bengal would earn ₹193,512 crore as auction and royalty from the exercise. These were big numbers. Jharkhand, for instance, is expected to get about ₹1,672 crore every year just from these mines (assuming a thirty-year life for the mines). He had made his mark in Prime Minister Modi's team as a minister who had changed the business climate in India in a sector that had refused to be transparent for decades.

There were more goodies. 'An estimated amount of ₹141,854 crore would accrue to coal bearing states from allotment of 38 coal mines to Central and State government run companies', he told the Parliament.

The Narendra Modi government had found a winner soon after coming to power. Its plan for the sector was evident. In exchange for the money going to the states, the Centre would be able to assure companies in the manufacturing sector certainty of supply of coal. It was an energy security programme as promised in the BJP manifesto. Swarup ambitiously said that the government anticipated that by the financial year 2019, auctions of the 204 coal blocks would add about 500 million tonnes to the national pool in addition to the 1 billion that CIL would extract from its own mines.

The environment around coal had clearly changed. There was a CAG report on the auctions tabled again in the month of August like the report of Vinod Rai. The report raised some questions on whether some of the bids were rigged. It barely created a stir. Now in opposition, the Congress party also did not find them strong enough to talk about.

Bare-knuckled Negotiations

There is a story from the union–management discussions of public sector banks in the 1980s. The trade union leaders would do something curious when they would troop in to conference rooms to negotiate with managements. They would ceremonially throw the reports into the dustbins to tell the management that they did not believe a word of what was printed as financial disclosure in the reports.

Coal economy is a sector where someone would easily feel justified in tossing numbers into the dustbins in dismay. On one hand, CIL sat on a net profit of ₹13,383 crore as on 31 March 2015. Its annual report counted its cash reserve and bank balances at ₹52,389.53 crore. On the other hand, banks and financial institutions which had financed the power plants to run on coal instead drowned in humungous losses. Until recently, few promoters of coal-related enterprises in India got into financial trouble for reneging on their loans.

Crony capitalism sat well with coal. 'Public sector banks had handed out ₹96,484 crore to coal mining companies by 2013', minister of state for finance Jayant Sinha told the Parliament. It is far more than what most other sectors got from the banks over the years. There were good reasons why the banks were liberal with the loans. They understood the political affiliations of the coal miners. So, the bank managements were at peace assuming that all the risks were accounted for since coal entrepreneurs were all politically connected. The promoters, they reasoned, would be able to secure government support to stay in the black.

Few in the Indian financial sector consequently anticipated the extent of hit that would soon accrue. On the morning of 25 September 2014, the day after the SC order cancelled 204 coal block allocations, that sense of serenity was smashed. Bank stocks dived. State Bank of India (SBI) stock fell 2.68 per cent, PNB 4.28 per cent, ICICI 1.42 per cent, Bank of Baroda 2.50 per cent and Union Bank 1.94 per cent at the Bombay Stock Exchange (BSE). The cancellation 'Leaves (₹) 1 lakh crore, 30,000 MW question', screamed an *Indian Express* headline.

Outright, the cancellations meant that 42 mining companies would have to pay ₹9,427 crore to the government by 31 March 2015. JSPL was the hardest hit among them with a bill of ₹2,999 crore. Companies like Jaiprakash Associates, a part of the Jaypee Group, could escape with a token knock since their mine Mandla North had just been opened. But CESC was not so lucky. Sarisatolli mine was operating since 2003 and so their penalty was estimated at

₹947 crore; Hindalco could thank its stars that the mine clearances for Talabira I took so long. Its penalty was ₹602 crore. There are some like BLA Industries running a coal mine that CIL had abandoned as too small to be commercially viable. Still the company was asked to pay ₹68 crore. All the EMTA joint ventures had to pay good money too as penalty. BLA and others have gone to court challenging the amount payable as penalty.

A UBS India analysis of the company-wise impact ran as follows:

- JSPL: Entire domestic coal block assets taken away with a heavy penalty—financial year 2015 earnings per share (EPS) impact of –107 per cent with valuation impact of –35 per cent
- Reliance Power: Excess coal usage from Sasan block still poses a risk
- Adani Power: Replacement of captive coal block is at risk
- Tata Power: Captive coal blocks with production potential of ~5 MT per annum are at risk
- BHEL: Projects of Jaiprakash Associates and Monnet Ispat are at risk—financial year 2015 EPS impact of –8 per cent with valuation impact of –7 per cent
- Furthermore, downstream companies like Crompton Greaves, Thermax India and ABB India would be affected as Capex cycle recovery could get delayed
- It is worse for smaller companies (sponge iron particularly) who got these blocks. They (listed and unlisted both) would have to actually tweak their entire business model.

Even the 2G telecom crisis or the Satyam scam had not impacted such a large segment of India Inc. and at this scale. The impact on the banks was the most dreadful. The coal price rise of 2011 against which several of these companies had rushed to New Delhi to remonstrate with Prime Minister Singh was chicken feed in comparison. Of all the state-owned banks that crashed on 25 September 2014, the day after the SC verdict, Allahabad Bank fared the worst. The Kolkata-headquartered bank's scrip went down almost 13 per cent that day. In two days, it sank almost 17 per cent. The bank set up in Allahabad in 1865 by a group of British agents has practically co-existed with India's coal economy. All of its initial branches in the nineteenth century at Jhansi, Kanpur, Lucknow and Kolkata straddled the coal trade. Its office in Kolkata on the Netaji Subhas

Bose Road was just next to that of CIL headquarters and the jostle of coal traders all around. Few chairmen of Allahabad Bank went through their paces in the early decades without learning the details of the coal business. In next door coal-rich Jharkhand state, it was the convenor of the RBI-mandated state-level bankers' committee.

A year earlier, the RBI was forced to order what it called a special audit of the books of Allahabad Bank along with a forensic audit of its neighbour, United Bank of India. Auditors from Ernst & Young asked to conduct the special audit would not have been aware then, but as the heat from the coal fires spread, the linkage became clear. A report by India Ratings and Research noted, 'the risk is much higher for the mid-sized banks', in which it included Allahabad Bank right at the top.

Why did coal-based projects acquire such a dubious reputation for the banking sector? For that, we would have to retrace the past a bit.

Banks were collateral damage from the energy business from the 1990s. They were hit when entrepreneurs took out loans to begin power generation based on government promise. They were also hit when projects were stalled because of environmental or land acquisition problems.

Those happened in every phase. From 1993, when Rao's cabinet handed out coal mines to power generation companies, it also nudged the RBI to push banks to cut the interest rates. RBI governors baulked. Those differences intensified in the United Front government. In fact, the first differences between New Delhi and the RBI in setting interest rates date from this period. Without a warning, C Rangarajan suddenly handed in his papers as the governor of RBI in November 1997 and proceeded to become the governor of Andhra Pradesh without completing his term.

Earlier, to get some of those initiatives through, Rao got new officers in the finance ministry. *India Today* in its April 1993 issue reported that the economic affairs secretary Montek Singh Ahluwalia was made the new finance secretary, replacing KP Geethakrishnan. 'Backed by finance minister Manmohan Singh, (Ahluwalia's) appointment was cleared despite protests by IAS officers, annoyed that such a post was given to a non-IAS officer'. When Rangarajan stepped down from the RBI, Montek was considered a certainty for the post but was beaten to the post by member secretary of the Planning Commission, Bimal Jalan. His grandfather, Mr Ishwar Das Jalan, was a speaker of the West Bengal Assembly and later a cabinet minister under Bidhan Chandra Roy. The Bengal influence especially that of its chief minister Jyoti Basu in the national politics was again unmistakable. The United Front government counted CPIM as its most important ally.

As the pressure to lower rates intensified, banks like Allahabad Bank brought their card rate for infra projects down to 14 per cent. Although Rao had packaged a free coal mine for fuel supply to the plants, as coal prices remained sluggish, it was not very exciting except for politically supported calls like those for two coal blocks in West Bengal that were won by its state electricity boards, Tara East and West, and then handed over to a private company to provide coal supply for the state-run Bakreswar Thermal Power Project.

Rao also made an offer for a sovereign guarantee, especially for covering the foreign exchange component of the costs of a power project. This attracted even more attention, particularly in the subsequent 13-day government under Atal Bihari Vajpayee and also in the United Front government which sported two prime ministers in the space of less than a year. In the second half of the 1990s, as elected governments came and disappeared from Raisina Hill, decisions were being taken in a hurry. Among those which took up the offer from the government was US-based Enron Corporation to set up a power plant at Dabhol in Maharashtra. The project was unique in that it planned to tide over India's shortage of coal mines by importing naphtha as feedstock.

The Indian financing came from IDBI which was not yet a bank but a development financial institution, the leader among the four such created by the government in the 1950s and 1960s to do long-term lending. Its chairman was Serajul Haq Khan, who was an unlikely candidate there. Khan had graduated from Patna University in Bihar more famous for sending up civil servants than bankers. Soft spoken, with a love of Urdu literature, Khan was described as an aristocrat in his bearings by a foreign journal. Despite lobbying from a candidate supported by one of the Mumbai-based industrial houses, Rao picked him to lead India's charge into the power sector in 1993. One of those files related to the Dabhol power project.

The project though has forever got linked with the lady on the other side of the table from Khan, Rebecca Mark, and her 'bare-knuckled negotiations' that almost shut down political careers.

At her height, Mark epitomized all that was good about Enron: the brains, the verve—and yes, even the sex appeal. Lithe and stylish, she was often photographed in Central Asia, India, and South America, entourage in tow, making her way to another 'Mark the Shark' like negotiations with some government official like Khan over a new Enron power plant or pipeline project.

But as Swaminathan S Anklesaria Aiyar wrote, that gain she won for Enron was illusory. 'I think it is ridiculous to view the Dabhol deal through Mark's sex appeal. If (Indian) politicians and bureaucrats were suckers for a good-looking woman, the neta–babu raj would have been subverted long ago'. He argued that instead, 'India took Enron's money (the investment in the project). Then it reneged on the favour it was supposed to grant (the guarantee). Then it drove Dabhol to closure'.

The impact of the exposure ended IDBI's innings as a development financial institution. Khan was tasked by the RBI to plan a road map for converting it and others into banks. One of the members of that committee was KV Kamath, chairman of ICICI. It too went the IBDI way to become a bank. By 2004, when the government merged IDBI with the newly minted IDBI Bank, it had to transfer ₹1,200 crore run-up from the Dabhol exposure to a Stressed Assets Stabilisation Fund, a precursor to the current Asset Reconstruction Companies.

Among the domestic company-led consortiums to come up in the power sector was the $4.5-billion 3,960 MW Hirma project in Orissa, promoted by Reliance Power, a subsidiary of the then undivided Reliance Group. It tied up with a foreign partner Southern Electric Asia Pacific. So was the 1,850 MW Ennore project in Tamil Nadu, a consortium of developers with Aditya Birla's Grasim Industries Ltd that included CMS Energy Corp., Siemens and others.

In the case of Enron's Dabhol project, the Centre was saved by one officer in the finance ministry—Gajendra Haldea—who rewrote the contract to make Maharashtra government offer a guarantee instead of New Delhi. Several careers were made and hurt by these projects, none so spectacularly as that of EAS Sarma. He had moved in as economic affairs secretary in the finance ministry in the year 2000. Sarma arrived at economic affairs with a formidable reputation after writing India's first Fiscal Responsibility Bill, the precursor to the Fiscal Responsibility and Budget Management (FRBM)

Act, as expenditure secretary. For plenty of years before that, he had worked in the Planning Commission as adviser (power), so he knew the sector well. He resigned when he was abruptly transferred one evening, ironically to the Ministry of Coal, just four months before the annual general budget was to be presented by the then finance minister Yashwant Sinha next February. Sarma's department had baulked at providing the guarantee for one of those projects to raise finance on easier terms instead of preferring to offer a letter of comfort to the financial institution involved.

The evening when the orders for Sarma's transfer came through, I went to meet him at his Pandara Park residence. He was sitting in the lawn, and he courteously introduced us to his wife. He was keen to talk about everything happening in the finance ministry but was firm about not commenting at all on his transfer. 'It is the government's prerogative', he repeated to all the visitors who were rapidly filling up the lawn on the order which one media outlet described as 'late night massacre'. He never made public his reasons for quitting. His boss, Finance Minister Yashwant Sinha, made his personal unease about the departure clear in his autobiography: 'We were not fair to Sarma. He was an extremely competent officer. The government did not do justice to him when it transferred him from economic affairs to coal. He left the service in a huff'.

Essentially, the government was short-circuiting reforms in the sector by offering to share its revenues with the power generation companies to allow them to borrow at easier rates from banks. The political leaders worked on the premise that the companies had a cast iron case for their business. They reckoned that the economy needed power and steel. The generation companies armed with the foreign technology players had the wherewithal to set up the plants to produce power and steel quickly. The banks also had the money to finance them. The only thing Khan and his brotherhood in the banks needed to do were to ask the government to provide a guarantee. It would ensure that in the event of a default, the loans from the banks would be protected. It was a particularly useful device to get back-up funds from abroad by the banks since India did not have a strong credit profile. A guarantee could shave off some of the cost of those funds.

But as officers such as Sarma and Haldea pointed out, there was a fatal loophole in the argument. The political leaders sort of hoped that if they kept their eyes shut long enough, the problems at two ends of the power sector would get sorted. At one end, they promised a free supply of coal for the power and steel plants as fuel to reduce costs and make the plants come on stream quickly. At the other end, the political expectation was that the health of the state electricity boards would improve as they would find the self-discipline to make the consumers of power pay for the electricity they bought. The money realised would allow the distribution companies run by the state governments to buy electricity from the generation companies. None of those happened, not at least at the pace they were needed to. The loans were consequently risky and the sovereign guarantees would in all likelihood have to be invoked. In other words, a private risk would become a public risk.

Suresh Prabhu noted about his first term as power minister,

> These half-baked measures failed. It led to an exodus of investors from the power sector. So, my first few months (2000–02) as the minister for power were spent not in celebrating a new birth in the family but in attending several and unending funerals of stillborn projects.

Prabhu arrived at the ministry as the risks from these projects began to unravel as the growth rate of the economy began to dip in the wake of the East Asian crisis.

Incidentally, the post of secretary (banking), who was the face of the government for all the state-owned banks, kept on revolving through these years. Between 1999 and August 2001, it did not even get a full secretary. Mr Devi Dayal got the post of a secretary just a month before his retirement.

Meanwhile, wise after the wretched experience of guarantees, the NDA government under Vajpayee as the prime minister rewrote the norms for power projects next year. Prabhu as the power minister steered the first of those through the Parliament. The Electricity Act was passed in 2003; predictably, the left parties opposed it.

The passage of the act attracted attention. Newspapers were awash with dire stories from the power sector despite a decade of attempted reforms. One of those was carried on the same day the Parliament passed the act.

> Punjab State Electricity Board is over-burdened with a surplus of around 15,000 employees, said KS Kang, member (administrative) of the board, while talking to TNN here on Monday. Ironically, more energetic and young people were required at the fulcrum level (sic) to

deliver the goods in the best possible manner but these people were not being inducted because the establishment cost was very high, he added.

A new set of companies in the power generation, sponge iron and cement reckoned; there was strength in the government's renewed offer. Coal blocks were there for the asking. Even those who could not and so had to buy them also assumed that as prices had been flat, it would pan out similarly in future too. Between 1993 and 2015, coal prices increased at a cumulative growth rate of only 7.97 per cent. Within that too, the steeper corrections happened post 2006.

Vinayak Mavinkurve, group head, project finance and principal investments, IDFC, who has seen through the heady days of power project finance in the second phase, was willing to give credence that some serious work happened in the sector at that time. Bank consortiums often led by SBI along with officers from the power ministry would rustle up meetings with project developers to iron out their problems. These meetings often held at the local head office of SBI in New Delhi saw detailed evaluation of those projects to get them on steam. Smaller public sector banks like Allahabad Bank simply took those papers and attached them to their loan books.

IDFC came up at about the same time when the first phase of power sector shenanigans took down IDBI. The finance ministry again felt that it needed a project appraisal institution. So IDFC was formed as a public–private partnership in 1997 based on a report by Rakesh Mohan who later served both as secretary, economic affairs, in the finance ministry and as deputy governor in the RBI.

'The environment was bullish. In the rush to get projects off the ground some of the basic project finance rules were possibly left behind', Vinayak added. The UPA government which arrived after the NDA in 2004 on Raisina Hill followed up on the Electricity Act to issue a National Tariff Policy for distribution companies to buy power in 2005. The policy scrapped the older system under which the distribution companies offered an assured 16 per cent return on power generation projects. Instead, they were asked to sign power purchase agreements on a case-by-case basis to keep their costs low.

These case-by-case rules came to be known as the case 1 and 2 bidding plans. In other words, for case 2, the generation companies would be assured of a coal linkage (in case 1, the builder of the power plant figures out a line of coal supply himself). For the private sector companies, obviously there is no prize for guessing which one of these they would plump for. Until 2012, there was only one stand-alone case 1 bid—from Reliance Infrastructure for a 320 MW project. The rush was for case 2 bids.

The companies sort of assumed that the path to set up a power plant was then on an auto mode. And they were not wrong. The eleventh Five- Year Plan added 54,963 MW of power capacity within which coal and lignite made up 43,384 MW. India had added more power capacity than in the three previous five-year plans. It was a fantastic achievement. The target was to generate 100,000 MW of power by 2012.

The speed at which projects would be set up through the plan accelerated. By the terminal year, it had reached 20,501 MW, just short of the total capacity added in the previous block of 5 years.

Flush from that success, the Central Electricity Authority assumed that the twelfth plan would add another 72,340 MW based on coal. It looked possible. In 6 months, the coal-based power capacity leapt up another 8,081 MW.

Since the National Tariff Policy also offered a five-year exemption to the state-run companies to sign contracts with any power distribution companies without the need to go through a competitive bid process, another level of incentives were added to the spread. And this one played out in case 1 arena to bring in interesting partners.

The most prolific among those partners was EMTA. There were nine such bids from state government-led joint ventures to bid for case 1 projects. Of them, seven involved EMTA. Since the coal supply was not guaranteed for the projects, the price of electricity for case 1 bid were in each case higher than what the private sector case 2 bidders offered to sell electricity for.

'The party was going on full blast. It was a government sponsored private sector programme' was how another banker put it. Manning the bar was Singh's team handing out free blocks and expecting the RBI to keep rates soft for companies to borrow plenty. It ended when the SC verdict of 25 September 2014 woke them up. Sajjid Chinoy, Indian economist at JP Morgan, explained to me that the party was over even before that, as early as 2012 when the RBI refused to cut rates. 'What really caused growth and investment to slowdown was a lot of policy and regulatory uncertainty;

land acquisition, environment clearances, availability of coal for the power sectors' —as the government froze in the middle of the dance, once Rai read out his riot act.

As the party ended in chaos, the costs of mopping up thereafter became clear. IDFC's restructured loans, for instance, jumped 53.5 per cent in 1 year to ₹4,270 crore. Of its total loan book, 41 per cent is accounted for by the energy sector. One can see how exposure to the sector hurt. If this could happen to IDFC with possibly India's best credit appraisal system, the state-run banks were bound to flounder. By March 2016, the cumulative loss of the public sector banks had reached ₹18,000 crore. It is India's largest-ever banking crisis. And it grew each year from 2014. The day after the order from the two-judge bench of the SC, *Indian Express* reported that it would cost ₹100,000 lakh crore. 'Our judgment highlighted the illegality and arbitrariness in the allotment of coal blocks and these consequence proceedings are intended to correct the wrong done by the Union of India'. The judgement actually defined what it felt was crony capitalism, 'It is expected that the government *will not deal with the natural resources that belong to the country as if they belong to a few individuals*'[italics mine].

Within days, the Indian Banks' Association (IBA), the apex body of all banks in the country, convened an urgent meeting of its management committee to chalk out steps to safeguard their exposure.

'The IBA managing committee will be meeting later this week to work out a strategy. We have to protect our money', said an IBA official. Bank sources were still hoping that the total exposure of the sector to the affected projects would be much lower than the figure of 1 lakh crore. While the lenders claimed that the SC order would not give a 'hard knock', Credit Suisse estimated that the crackdown would put ₹60,000–₹72,000 crore of loans at risk.

All the foreign brokerage houses, however, agreed that the orders opened the way for structural reforms in the sector. There was also stoicism that none of the coal blocks to be auctioned anew would come into production before three years. As a CRISIL report put it, 'On a pan-India level the impact will be negligible as these power plants account for less than 5 per cent share of total generation', but metals players will be hit hard. Coal production was back to CIL again. Industry chamber FICCI which had led sharp attacks on the government decades ago on coal could only say,

(It) hopes that Hon'ble Supreme Court's decision of cancellation of coal blocks allocation is quickly followed by the Government action of constituting a framework to reallocate these blocks on the principles of transparent allocation and competitive bidding to restore investor confidence in India's coal industry.

Where most of the analysts went wrong was in their assessment of the cost on the banking sector for repair of the balance sheets of metals and mining companies and then, to finance them again for the subsequent auctions. The pain was not about to leave the banking sector; fresh exposure was about to dry up. RBI data shows that in the financial year 2015, additional credit for mining and quarrying was almost nil at 0.5 per cent. In the power sector, the largest draw for credit in industrial sector, growth was a dismal 14.2 per cent.

The auctions consequently only brought those companies to the table which had deep pockets. The smaller ones fled. Even among the larger ones, those like the steel industry were now keen to check out details they had never bothered to do so earlier. Like how much of coking coal would a block hold? Since there was no avenue yet to sell the non-coking coal in a free market, the companies were unwilling to engage in a bruising battle. As the coal miners read the rules for operating the mines, they realised that there would be a blanket of regulations to surround their mines. It was not a free-for-all anymore. 'The power sector has hardly any assets today which operate without regulatory or fuel issues', said Vinayak.

His boss Vikram Limaye, managing director and chief executive of IDFC, was even more frank. 'We were in fact expecting that both coal and gas risks would come down. It might well be the case that the risk has not come down, it has in fact gone up'. Limaye has never been reluctant to speak candidly, one of the reasons investors and media have come to instinctively believe what he says, a rarity among bankers.

Essar's 1,200 MW power plant at Mahan was conceived for running on domestic coal. Sushil Maroo, its executive vice chairman, was livid describing its travails. 'When the plant was designed and location was planned, only two costs were kept in mind—coal pithead and evacuation of power by laying transmission lines. But the plant is shut for the past three years as coal was not available'. The company bid for Tokisud North mines in Jharkhand at a 'record price of ₹1,100 per MT' in the auctions. They have some reasons to feel cheated. Australian coal was running at AUS$51.16 as on 31 May 2014. That converts into ₹2,537.37 per tonne. When the cost of transporting a tonne of coal from Jharkhand to Chhattisgarh is added in, the difference looks pretty less. Without a committed buyer for the power from the plant, the numbers look difficult to patch up. 'It's time to look up after three years of nightmare', he told *Business Standard*.

The prospects for domestic coal finally soured, as demand conditions in the world economy for energy collapsed with that of China. It is hard to blame the Indian companies for misreading the trend. Price of Indian crude in December 2014 was $70.08 for a barrel; Australian coal price was at $62.44 per MT when the financial bosses at companies like Essar made a pitch with the banks for loans to get in the auctions. Both oil and coal prices collapsed by over 23 per cent in three months.

Since there were fewer regulatory hassles plus the inferior quality of most Indian coal and the transport bottlenecks to contend with, promoters figured out it was a better option to source coal from abroad. Companies are now free to arrange for themselves a regular supply from abroad. It was possible earlier too; in fact, it was a possibility right from 1993 when the imports of the mineral were freed since it was put under open general licence. The difference now is that they have begun to sense the contours of the global energy business and step up to the plate accordingly. Companies can now take a geopolitical risk like not only contract supplies from abroad but also own a mine overseas and hope to survive. As a report of February 2016 by Brookings India puts it, 'Non-power imports of coal are not expected to end any time soon—we do not have prime coking coal—are we then targeting an unrealistic objective of eliminating imports?'

All of them thus had reasons to hedge their bets against Indian coal. When the same blocks were available for free in an earlier era, these considerations made no sense. Once the government began to demand a price for the blocks however, the cost benefit analysis became rigorous in the company boardrooms. High costs for coal and oil had to be set against the expected returns from the investments made in thermal power, steel and cement production units. The fossil fuel order in the economy has changed.

Both are compelling reasons for a fundamental transformation of the energy economics in India. Energy resources are best mined in India when they are imported.

Coalfield Express

.

Chingiriguda village in Ib Valley of Odisha sits on top of some of the best mines of MCL, the most profitable subsidiary of CIL. A little further ahead are the ones of private sector companies such as Talabira and Hirma. For twenty years, the government miners and the people of this village have pushed back at each other. In 1995, MCL had invoked both the Coal Bearing Act, 1957 for those areas of the village that sat on coal and the Land Acquisition Act for the rest to acquire rights over the area. The notifications were issued in March of that year, but the case for relocation has stretched out making the resettlement package extremely complex by this stage.

Minutes of the meeting held in December 2013 between MCL officials, the villagers and the district administration acknowledge that the disputes are now pending for eighteen years or more. The disputes span three strands—employment, terms of rehabilitation, amount of compensation.

For villagers like Dulamani Pradhan, the president of the village committee, the wait has meant that family sizes have expanded. 'The families have extended their house structures to accommodate their needs. Hence a fresh family census may be carried out and resettlement benefits to the extended family may be given'.

For Shanti Hati, Tikeswar Bag and other residents of the village, resettlement primarily meant expectation of employment offers from the coal company. As Lalit Pradhan, ex councillor from the village, put it, 'after a wait of twenty years the village is going to be shifted and the children are now grown up. MCL may take care of their employment'.

The villagers wanted a fresh census with the cut-off date brought forward to 2010 to ascertain the number of displaced people. For MCL, this was a tough call to handle. Fresh census could open a fresh set of demands as in families like that of Dulamani. The company would naturally want an assurance that any such census would be the final one, so that people agree to the compensation awarded and leave for a new colony that would not sit astride a coal block. On their part, the villagers wanted to push the employment packet as much as possible before they left. Considering that the land was their only card, it was only fair that they would drive a hard bargain. This was one of the reasons why arriving at a compromise was so elusive.

For instance, two years ago, the village people had agreed that they would revert in a few 'days' about a proposed rehabilitation site. This was recorded in the minutes of a similar meeting held in January 2012. That revert did not happen.

It is a scene that is being played out in hundreds of villages across India facing the spectre of being uprooted. But as the people have become more aware and the pitch against land acquisition has got raised, the tone of the demand has become shrill.

So companies have softened their pitch. For instance, the venue of this meeting has changed. Instead of the offices of MCL, the latest meeting was held in the primary school of Chingiriguda. The closeted venues in offices allowed for only a few people to be present, while this one was in presence of all villagers who wished to be present.

On the issue of rehab while earlier the company had told them that the site chosen by MCL and the district administration was better than another site, the villagers wanted that since it was further from the mines, the officers were now emphasising the attractiveness of the proposed relocation site. 'Dense afforestation to be done in the site ... boundary wall and all other facilities as provided in the MCL colony shall be provided in the R&R site' in addition to the compensation of ₹578,000 to each family with a bonus of ₹100,000 for those who move in early. 'This shifting will be (just) from one municipal area to another municipal area', argued the general manager of the company.

But in a sign of assertiveness, the villagers refused the calculation for compensation. While the company representatives had recommended paying of interest until 2012, the board of MCL had said that the interest would be grandfathered as on the date of notification which is March 1995. The issues do not look headed for an early settlement.

Land problems that have blighted India's mining and manufacturing sector owe their origin to mainly legal challenges.

Each one of them is swaddled in legalities that defy the efforts of the best of state and district administrations to unravel, as is happening in Chingiriguda. It not only affects issues of resettlement but is also a big hassle if companies want to return unused land. For quite some time, the coal ministry has plans to return unused land lying with CIL to the families of original owners. Land acquisition for coal mining was never an easy exercise, but it is proving tougher to return the land. In 1957, when most of Indian coal mines were in the private sector, the central government had brought in the Coal Bearing Areas (Acquisition and Development) Act (CBA Act). This act was more wall to wall in its scope than the Land Acquisition Act (1894), but the compensation calculation was virtually the same for both. It allowed government companies to get land but strictly only for coal mining. If the company needed space to build offices or residential quarters for miners, then those would have to come through by the operation of the latter. So in Chingiriguda, the villages that sat on mines were acquired under the Coal Bearing Act; nearby villages got acquired under the Land Acquisition Act.

At first sight, return of land lying fallow should seem easy enough. Since there are big swathes of land acquired under the provisions of the former act for coal mining, those patches lying unused for various reasons should sensibly be returned. There are various reasons why those lands are fallow. In some cases, the mining of the land is over; more frequently, the envisaged projects have got shelved or the land acquired just happens to be far more than was needed to mine coal from underneath it.

What is the size of the unused land bank with CIL and its subsidiaries? The coal ministry's Central Mine Planning and Design Institute (CMPDIL) using remote sensing data had calculated it at 603.82 sq km in the financial year 2013. This is 43 sq km more than the size of all special economic zones (SEZs) in India (560.67 sq km). Of this, just about 20 per cent is under active mining as per its latest data. Laid out end to end, it would be roughly the size of Coimbatore, India's ninth largest city by area.

In densely populated areas of ECL, WCL and BCCL, these unused tracts of land are often encroached upon. To prevent encroachments, CIL and its subsidiaries have to raise security forces to police the turf. Land owners have begun to ask for the return of their plots since the price of those tracts of land has shot up. This demand is often supported by state governments, either to return the plots to the owners or else to the governments for their own use. So of the 603 sq km, the coal companies are policing an unnecessarily massive segment.

It is clear until here. The problems arise hereon. Since the CBA Act is administered by the central government, CIL or its constituents have no right to give them back to the ultimate owners for any purpose, say forestry or agriculture. Not even the central government can do so. So when a piece of land is no longer required, it remains fallow unless CIL tries to convert it into forests or let encroachers set upon it. 'Yet if a piece of land is not required anymore by the centre it needs to go back to the state government since it is the custodian for all land falling within its jurisdiction', an official said.

An amendment could sort out the mess as it would allow for recreation of rights that had been extinguished. Except that, a well-meaning change in the land laws has made this one difficult to go ahead with.

The UPA-II government in 2013 got the Right to Fair Compensation and Transparency in Land Acquisition, Rehabilitation and Resettlement Act cleared by the Parliament.

Once this act had come into force, the more-than-a-century-old Land Acquisition Act got repealed. And while the 2013 act provided for the CBA Act to continue, it did not decide what would happen to land that was not required for mining any more. For instance, there is no retrospective provision in the 2013 act to deal with them. As matters stand, the ownership of the acquired land cannot be transferred back to the original owners. A trenchant criticism of the act came from Indira Rajaraman, professor at the National Institute of Public Finance and Policy. In one of her newspaper columns, she pointed out,

> By trying to bring in transparency, (the act) introduces new rigidities. With its provision for overlapping layers of diligence by committee, it will markedly slow down the pace of land acquisition and lead to further choking of supply and escalation in the price of land.

Partha Bhattacharya estimates that about 60 per cent of the land CIL is saddled with was acquired under the CBA.

The Parliament has meanwhile passed the amended Coal Mines (Nationalisation) Act to bring some order in the chaotic sector. It settles one of the land acquisition issues. For instance, it makes clear that the companies which get land to mine coal underneath will get the surface rights too. But this too does not specify what would be the fate of surplus land with coal companies and it does not reconcile the conflict between the Coal Bearing Act and the new land act.

The dilemma over land required for coal or the episodes surrounding the SEZs in India shows how land has become a catechism for industrial development.

In fact, land issues flared up big time as a public policy debate for the first time in the wake of the passage of the SEZ Act in 2006. But since then, the compelling aspect to note is that land issues drowned not only the SEZ policy but having done it has not ended there. Instead, it has swamped even older policies like the one on coal. In the process, it has forced a rethink on the role of coal as the fuel of choice for the energy economy of India. This is a challenge which the Indian public policy practitioners were not prepared for.

SEZs obviously needed land to be set up. Once the states began approving multi-product SEZs, the land dimension became apparent. Since most of those were to be situated close to ports or mega cities, the visibility of scale of land sought to be acquired became apparent. Since the developers of these SEZs were often companies involved in real estate development whose reputation as corporate citizens were not great, the process acquired an unsavoury reputation. It became difficult for governments to convince the people that it was not a land grab. It led to some major agitations in states ranging from West Bengal to Maharashtra. Once the leftist party-led government in West Bengal lost power in the polls dominated by these issues, the appetite for SEZ-led development plans evaporated among the political parties.

What it also demonstrated is that land issues unless handled well can turf out a political party, no matter how well it conceptualises any policy for economic development. This holds particularly true for the manufacturing sector. It is the new political rejection slip.

And even on SEZs, the last word has not been said. In the last week of August 2016, the SC asked for return of land at Singur in West Bengal to the original owners. The judgement could open several cases of land acquisition carried out before 2009. But fortunately, it will have no impact on land being acquired for Smart Cities projects.

'The judgment again tosses in the air the concept of public interest', said Suhaan Mukherjee, partner at PLR Chambers, which specialises in public policy. The two judges have differed on whether the land acquired for the Tata Nano project in Singur was in public interest.

The two-judge bench ruled invalid the acquisition of land in Singur by the West Bengal government for a Tata Motors' project made in 2006. The judges asked the state to return the 997 acres of land to the farmers, since the acquisition made under the Land Acquisition Act of 1894 was 'perverse and illegal' by the then state government. The Singur land acquisition has been a watershed for land disputes in India that kick-started protests against many SEZ projects. All political parties scurried to include their opposition for land alienation in their manifestos, which resulted in the passage of the Land Act of 2013. Just as in the case of coal, once the act was written in the books, states began to try intermediate methods to take over land for construction projects. In Andhra Pradesh, for instance, the government had used a land lease model to build the new state capital Amaravati.

Speaking about the change in the philosophy of land acquisition under the NDA government, Amitabh Kant, CEO of Niti Aayog, said that it was critical to understand that the 'upside' of the rise in value of land should not be captured by only those who were powerful, like the political parties in power. 'Urbanisation cannot happen without monetisation of the value of land. But, this monetisation has to be put back in the cities', he said at a Brookings India event on Smart Cities. Using the same line of argument, the SC judges also held that it was 'completely understandable' for the government to acquire land to set up industrial units. But, the impact of the 'brunt of development' should not 'fall on the weakest sections of the society'. It is the same argument that Kant had offered about the perils of upside being captured by those in power and real estate companies.

In 2014, I was a part of a team that did possibly India's largest-ever survey on land records. The team trawled through data for sale of land in rural areas for 30 years across India's 4 districts to see what the factors that move land prices. The four districts are the undivided Faridabad and rural Ambala in Haryana and Singrauli and Mandla in Madhya Pradesh. They form a continuum with Faridabad, the most urbanised and closest to Delhi, having evolved from a semi-rural area in this period. Ambala is a great snapshot of India's tier-III town with its vast rural belt, while Mandla is a tribal district and as per Government of India records, also one of India's poorest fifty. Singrauli has seen the largest number of land acquisition cases in India in the past 30 years and so provided a fantastic counterfactual to our evolving hypothesis.

Until then, there was no study in India that had attempted to understand the factors which guide land sales in rural India as seen through the actual sales records. It was a different exercise from the anecdotal evidences, like those in Haryana or around Mumbai like Raigarh where there are claims about people having often sold land in distress to SEZs or other urban projects.

The survey was commissioned by GIZ India, the German government's aid agency (the Deutsche Gesellschaft für Internationale Zusammenarbeit [GIZ] GmbH). It was executed by Thought Arbitrage Research Institute (TARI), a young think tank based in Delhi. Kaushik Dutta, its director, is always gunning for new studies to explore and when I told him about my idea to understand what moves land prices, he was immediately game.

One of the key members of the team we rounded up was Rita Sinha. She was secretary, Department of Land Resources, in the central government until 2011 and proved a treasure trove of knowledge on land regulations besides possessing an inexhaustible fund of anecdotes from India's IAS land.

With her help, we were able to decipher the language of land records, as those in Madhya Pradesh which had remained unchanged in their use of Persian words until the 1980s. Rita explained that in a perverse logic, the states which had kept up collection of land revenue were able to keep their records better. This has also helped to keep their land-related litigation cases down.

Collection of land revenue had acquired a lot of stigma in colonial India, so after Independence, it was one of the first taxes the Government of India encouraged the states to abolish. But once that source of revenue was scrapped, it became difficult for cash-strapped state governments to justify why the department and its records need to be maintained. For government acquisition of land, those records were useless under the Land Acquisition Act of 1894. The governments looked dimly at the need to maintain the department to facilitate the sale and purchase of agricultural land between private persons.

Haryana (then under undivided Punjab), for instance, had abolished land revenue but Central Provinces or Madhya Pradesh did not, even though it cut the rate to 50 paise per acre per annum. I saw the validity of Rita's observation in the land record rooms of the two states. In Faridabad, just 30 km away from Delhi, the land records for the period before they were computerised in early 2000s were in shambles—the dust-filled rooms were piled up to the rafters with registers of land sales whose covers often held nothing between them.

When we arrived at one of the minor forts of Gwalior town, where the land revenue department is housed, we saw the reverse. Land records from even the nineteenth century were kept neatly rolled up in red bundles numbered and dusted, on shelves in long snaking rooms at whose entrance the doors were so low that one had to duck. Maps of old kingdoms with ancient names were stacked in steel trunks and all of them were in good condition, a historians' delight!

She explained,

> Transactions on land in India are based on deeds, rather than titles to the land. So a piece of land is accepted as good for sale because there is no other record to reject it. It is the deed system and depends heavily on the presence or absence of land revenue records.

A plot sold in Faridabad or Ambala in the absence of a land revenue deed going back into the past could therefore be hoary. But there is little which can be done to bring back to life the records of government which have got destroyed.

For agricultural land, this could be a larger problem. For determining the value of tracts of agricultural land where the frequency of sale is less frequent than in urban areas, a deed-based system divorced from title is obviously risky for the states to contemplate. Although the land revenue records provide only a tangential proof of ownership, yet they have become the sole arbiter in absence of titles to the land.

The study threw up two statistically significant results. Prices of land in any region were mostly guided by market considerations and this was agnostic of the decade considered. The other one was that fertility of the soil counted for much less in determining the price; instead, geographical factors like proximity to road or a railway link impacted prices far more. This held true in districts as diverse as Ambala and Mandla. Tribal people it would seem were not economically illiterate but were hamstrung as there were few price signposts to guide them along when they sold land.

To get around these rigidities, the Modi government just a day after the winter session of the Parliament brought in an amendment to the UPA government's Land Act of 2013. The changes were made through a slim ordinance peppered with mostly semantic changes. The two substantive changes in the act were as follows:

It excluded five types of projects from the need to get at least 80 per cent of the project-affected persons (PAP) to support the project.

It also did away with a provision introduced in the 2013 act to provide for a social impact assessment of the proposed project.

The basic difference between the ordinance of 2014 and the act of 2013 is as follows: The latter considers land alienation as an avoidable exercise that should be an exception than the norm; the former seeks to bring back land as a tradable commodity.

The opposition parties attacked the government saying that the ordinance was akin to surrender to the industry captains. The critical theme highlighted was that good quality crop land was being surrendered for projects and for which the farmers were not able to get decent prices. As the TARI study showed, there was a reason to believe that information on latest prices often reached the tillers late. But there was no reason to believe that soil fertility had anything to do with the prices that were offered for land. It was the geographical proximity to the cities, the rail links, that determined how high prices would go. The study showed that land parcels in a contiguous geographical area fetched the same price growing northwards as inflation and economic development proceed. So the argument that there is an extortion of land from the 'poor' farmers is facile. What is instead required is to develop a nationwide system of information exchange on land prices.

This is something that the Indian political class has often not digested. The ordinance had to be finally jettisoned.

In coal bearing areas of states which have let their land revenue records crumble, paying compensation for the land acquired is becoming a nightmare. How can a company planning to pay compensation distinguish between those who owned the land and those who did not? The absence of older land revenue records has swelled the number of families which demand compensation from the companies. It has not helped, as the UPA government has introduced the term PAP instead of depending on land records, in the land act of 2013. This nomenclature simply depends on a certificate from the panchayats to make any person eligible.

Coal industry has an additional problem regarding land. Since mining is a site-specific industry, it cannot be shifted anywhere else. Open cast mining, which is the chief way India extracts coal, affects the land topography too.

To buy some degree of freedom, CIL has dived into its cash reserves. Successive chairmen of each of its subsidiaries knew that the coal ministry was always keen that there should be no disturbance. So whenever a land acquisition problem threatened to go out of control, they offered a job in their company as a trade-off to the leaders of the agitation. A government committee discovered that a major reason for addition of unskilled workforce to its rolls 'is the continuing policy of providing employment liberally against acquisition of land despite the lack of avenues for gainful deployment'.

> It was noted that the company had recently introduced a scheme of recruiting young sons as the replacement for old unskilled women employees. In most cases the young son will also join as an unskilled worker & become a liability for a far longer period. CIL was advised to revisit the scheme & restrict such employment only to cases where the son is technically qualified & (can) be gainfully deployable. (sic)

The practice impacts other companies that set up shop for coal mining. They cannot offer similar benefits. One of the members of the Prabhu committee said that CIL's practice has to be terminated and instead replaced with a suitable long-term annuity payment scheme as the principal benefit.

The coal companies now realise that there is an urgent need to reclaim and restore the mined-out land for productive use. This would not only restore environmental degradation but also make it easier for land acquisition to go through. This is the reason why the ministry is pushing for amending the CBA Act.

The amendment would hopefully show that the companies are not out for land grab. It could also create a groundswell of support in other areas for land acquisition for fresh deposits and reduce the problem of the entire population of the area coming up as PAP to demand compensation. But there are several regions under the coal mining companies where the debris from the acquisition process is not yet over.

Taken together, these land issues have developed as flash points around coal mining areas and brought work to a halt. It could do so in future too.

Within the ECL-run coal belt is the town of Salanpur in West Bengal. Nothing much happens there except for coal business; like most Indian towns, the size of its urban population has expanded fast since the agricultural land surrounding the town barely yields one crop per year. Just like in Singur, the Left Front government in 2010 had planned to develop an industrial park where a steel plant by Bhushan Steel would come up. It predictably ran into acquisition troubles when the villagers opposed the project and refused to give up their land. They now sit on the land that has no agricultural value and no industry to beckon. The only sizable industry in and around the city and of nearby ones like Rupnarayanpur is coal pilferage.

It is not the kind of choice a welfare state should be imposing on citizens.

8

A Promise to Keep

Few saw it coming. The mood in Paris was sombre like the winter frost which set in late that year. A fortnight before, 130 people had been killed in the city by terrorists from the Islamic State of Iraq and Syria (ISIS) spraying gunfire on the streets and at Bataclan theatre. At the Conference of Parties (CoP), the annual stocktaking by the nations of the world on where they stood on environment pledges, the assembly of national heads was clearly rattled by the visible remains from the event. The mood was decidedly downbeat.

There was not any particular reason to expect anything particularly cheerful when Indian Prime Minister Narendra Modi took the stage at the plenary session on 30 November 2015. In most international work programmes including those on trade and finance, India has opted for 'reluctant engagement', as Chief Economic Adviser Arvind Subramanian puts it, offering few commitments of its own but hectoring those around for larger offers.

Instead, Modi straightaway made an offer to raise the footprint of renewable energy to 175 GW in the Indian energy matrix by 2022. The offer surprised even those within government circles. It was big. As in 2014, this amounted to 10 per cent of the total renewable energy capacity put up worldwide. Modi prefaced it by adding that by 2040, '40 per cent of our installed capacity will be from non-fossil fuels'. The Paris Declaration from CoP 21 had acquired substance with India taking on powerful responsibilities along with the USA and China, the top two greenhouse gas emitters. As a report by *New York Times* summing up the CoP noted,

> (US) Secretary of State John Kerry, who has spent the past year negotiating behind the scenes with his Chinese and Indian counterparts in order to help broker the deal, said, 'The world has come together around an agreement that will empower us to chart a new path for our planet'.

'Kerry finds India positive at Paris climate conference', described another newspaper headline from the conference.

'We had planned to make this CoP take note of India', said Ashok Lavasa, who as secretary, environment, forests and climate change was negotiating those numbers at Paris. 'Our homework showed we could take a risk of going very high', he told me when we met after the event.

Environment Tigers

In the summer of 2015, nearly 2,500 people in India were killed in the heat wave. The summer's hot spell had been the second deadliest one since 1998. These two are in the roll call of the ten most intense heat waves to have scorched the globe in the last two decades.

Temperatures had already risen in the winter before when on a cool January evening in 2014, volunteers from Greenpeace hung a banner on the facade of the Essar Group's head office in Mumbai, protesting its investment in a coal block in the Mahan area of Madhya Pradesh. The effort was dramatic. It was novel for India's largely staid world of environment activism. The stunned company retorted with a police case against the protestors. An Essar Group spokesperson described the protest as 'a blatant and anarchic act of trespassing'.

The Indian Express newspaper reported next day that the Greenpeace activists who scaled the company's 180 ft tall headquarters were dressed in tiger costumes and hung on with the giant 36 × 72 ft banner for some hours. Embarrassingly, for the UPA government, the banner also featured photographs of the then environment minister M Veerappa Moily and Prime Minister Singh.

They were protesting possible destruction of the forest and also takeover of land for mining. The stitching together of both of these causes highlighted how coal mining had the potential to be a public policy nightmare for any Indian government. In the subsequent round of coal auctions, the NDA government took care to keep Mahan coal blocks out of those which went under the hammer. Essar had to instead buy Tokisud North, the costliest mine on offer.

There are several areas of the Indian economy where land or environment poses difficult questions; urban areas like Delhi, for instance, have grappled with air pollution problem with intermittent success. Agricultural zones around mega cities are on the other hand grappling with land issues.

The coal economy is a marquee zone where both have come together. The earlier challenges of political–criminal nexus which has wrecked the sector to create the coalgate scam, for instance, have ceded space to these subjects. There is also a paradigm shift. Criminalisation and so on were the outcome of badly run coal economy. The land and environment issues question the very raison d'être of the coal economy.

Ninan noted pithily, 'India is caught in an ecological crisis that is rolling out in many directions'.

Although from the public policy perspective they raise different issues, the civil society movements have clubbed the two. This has complicated the resolution of the land problems while also raising the cost of these wars for the Indian financial sector.

Of the 289 companies that got their nose into at least one block since 1993, the overwhelming majority with un-worked mines claimed that it was either of these which had stopped them from making their leases operational. The list includes even those arraigned by the CBI in thirty-nine criminal cases.

The mess has got worse as the globe has turned up its nose on coal. Coal is not the only reason why the planet has heated up. But it is one of the reasons. About 44 per cent of the global carbon dioxide emissions come from coal. Bloomberg News reported in April 2016 that Norway's $860 billion sovereign wealth fund—the world's largest wealth fund—had released its first list of miners and power producers to be excluded from its portfolio following a ban on coal investments.

Of the fifty-two companies on the list was India's Tata Power. Others included American Electric Power Co. Inc., China Shenhua Energy Co. Ltd, Whitehaven Coal Ltd and Peabody Energy Corp., according to a statement from Norges Bank Investment Management. 'The exclusions are based on new criteria introduced by the government in February impacting companies that base at least 30 per cent of their activities or revenues on coal', Bloomberg quoted Marthe Skaar, Norges Bank Investment Management's spokeswoman to say. There were others coming.

Environmental challenge for coal arrived fairly early in India. There were concerns going back to the 1980s about the footprint of coal. There is no stage at which coal does not damage environment—even during mining, it releases methane. The US-based Centre for Climate and Energy Solutions notes, 'mining can result in the direct release of methane (which has a global warming potential twenty-three times higher than CO_2, but only persists in the atmosphere for 12–17 years), particularly from underground mines'.

From there on, it is downhill all the way. Despite that understanding, however, there was little evidence that mining companies in private or public sector thought deeply about it. A government report from the 1990s blandly noted that CIL needed to focus on improving its environmental practices,

> [P]articularly in the area of controlling air pollution as well as land restoration & reclamation & align it to global best practices. This is imperative to enable the company achieve & sustain the desired high rates of growth in coal production in the longer term.

Navroz Dubash, senior fellow at the Centre for Policy Research has a succinct explanation of the long-term impact of coal on the economy. He says that when gauging the impact of coal, the conventional logic about doing ameliorative works on its environmental footprint is not relevant. According to him, India has missed the chance to use coal when it could. 'We are ramping up production from coal when pretty soon the cost of renewable energy will be lower'.

The decision to ramp up the production of coal has to be consequently understood within this transition. If coal production is ramped up now to peak at say in the year 2025, then the impact of that would be there with the economy for a far longer period as a high cost energy option until about 2065, when the rest of the world would have moved to renewable energy.

Of the 260 GW of energy India now produces, more than 171 GW (171,376 MW as on 31 May 2014) comes from coal. Of this, the Central Electricity Authority estimates that about 30 GW would need to be scrapped soon since the plants have become fuel guzzlers. But investments in renewable energy would not be able to fill in this gap so early. The alternative is to bring to steam the power plants already close to commissioning but languishing because they cannot be assured of coal supply.

Those plants are necessary as Goyal says that his government has a plan to provide 24 × 7 electricity to all Indians within its current five-year term. Even assuming for some leeway on what would constitute a round-the-clock electricity supply across India, it would still need an additional 66 GW of coal-based power to meet this level of demand. As Dubash points out, the economy may get locked into a suboptimal level of production for a long time. A government estimate puts the demand for power in India by 2030 at 562 GW of which renewable is expected to be 32 per cent.

Also, to finance the coal economy, the options from abroad have become limited. The Norwegian Wealth Fund is setting a trail which is likely to be picked up by others too. A report by *Time Magazine* notes that Goldman Sachs sees long-term coal prices at $42.50 per tonne. 'Unlike most other commodities, thermal coal is unlikely to experience another period of tightness ever again because investment in new coal-fired generation is becoming less common and the implied decline in long-term demand appears to be irreversible', Goldman Sachs' analysts concluded. It added that even India would fail to make up for the shrinking thermal coal market in the rest of the world and concluded, 'This is horrific news for coal mining companies. It also ensures that the list of coal companies that have declared bankruptcy—at least several dozen in the last four years—will continue to grow'. If not several dozen, an assessment by the Carbon Tracker Initiative (CTI), a non-profit initiative, puts their number in the last five years at 26, while it calculates that US coal equities are down over 76 per cent in value in the same period.

In spite of those efforts, the companies listed in the Norwegian initiative make up less than 30per cent of the world fuel suppliers by volume. Mega coal and oil companies in the world are now government owned like CIL and Oil and Natural Gas Corporation (ONGC) in India and Sinopec or China National Petroleum in China. They do not figure in this list since they finance themselves from the domestic market. How they would change their act will be determined by what the states decide on as its policy on fossil fuels.

This is where the Geneva-based International Institute for Sustainable Development is working with an international group of civil societies to put pressure on the G20 nations to include a commitment 'to phase out and rationalize fossil fuel subsidies by 2020'.

Their draft declaration argues that fossil fuel subsidies 'encourage wasteful consumption, reduce our energy security, impede investment in clean energy sources and undermine efforts to deal with the threat of climate change'.

Yet before New Delhi can be limited by these concerns, it would want to ensure that its concerns about domestic energy security like those of providing round-the-clock electricity supply, which Goyal has articulated, are met.

(So) When the Modi government swept to power in the summer of 2014, its priorities were clear: get stalled projects moving so that investment could be revived and the economy nudged to pick up speed. The new environment minister, Prakash Javadekar, showed very quickly that he was no Jairam Ramesh clone. The rules were modified to reduce the scope for public hearings (required before projects got cleared); more powers were given to states to clear projects; and a committee of former bureaucrats, armed with loose terms of reference, recommended rewriting the country's environment protection laws. The signs were that environmental clearance requirements for projects would be diluted, decentralized and rendered less effective. Javadekar quoted Indira Gandhi and declared that poverty was the 'biggest polluter'. (Ninan, 2015)

International Energy Agency (IEA), the world's primary intergovernmental energy tracker since the first oil crisis, estimates that these concerns will propel the demand for coal in India to increase by 23 per cent globally up to the year 2030. Organisations such as CTI, however, insist that this need not happen. Reid Capalino, the lead author of the report writes,

Providing universal energy access does not significantly increase coal demand. The extra coal demand in the IEA Energy for All scenario is equivalent to 1.8% of global coal use, and could be offset by India and sub-Saharan Africa reducing electricity distribution losses by a third.... If energy efficiency improvements also outpace projections this will further erode demand requirements. For these reasons it is clear that providing 'energy' does not automatically mean more demand for coal.

The key takeaway from that report is the need to cut back losses in electricity distribution. India has tried it two times already in the past fifteen years and is in the middle of Uday, its third iteration of the effort. State electricity boards have found it fiendishly difficult to make consumers pay for their electricity, especially as state elections approach. Even prosperous cities like Delhi or Jaipur are not immune as an IISD survey showed: 'Citizens expect (state) to maintain electricity subsidies'.

Every revision of electricity prices in Delhi has become a political football. Subsidiaries of Tata Power and Reliance Power run the two distribution companies catering to the city state. Those companies cannot raise prices on their own, however. Under the Electricity Act of 2003, those have to be accepted by an independent regulator, the Delhi Electricity Regulatory Commission. But any such jump runs afoul of the Aam Aadmi Party which runs the state government. Since power tariff was hiked seven times for various categories of consumers since 2011, it would seem that the electricity regulator has had its way.

Since 2015 when the Aam Aadmi Party led by Arvind Kejriwal won the state elections, there has been no rise. Instead, the party has asked for an audit by the national auditor of the finances of the distribution companies to trace alleged inefficiencies in the investments made by the two which could be checked instead. The party won a decisive victory at the polls promising to roll back current power tariffs and pushing the private distribution companies from out of their business.

The party's victory reinforces the theme among the political parties that free or at least subsidised power is a powerful poll promise. Deep South in another prosperous state Tamil Nadu, both the leading contenders had promised electricity sops. Post the elections, the then chief minister J Jayalalitha announced that the state would provide 100 units of electricity free to all households each month. Each of those subsidies encourages industries which have to pay a higher price to game the distribution system, raising the costs all round.

CTI has argued that cutting back on distribution losses can make the cost of power cheaper ringing in renewable energy. The other element of the discourse is to raise energy efficiencies. Mohua Mukherjee of the World Bank has argued for it too.

> One may well ask why the burden for high levels of inefficiency and losses should be borne by the end users ... how can anyone be sure the a higher price paid by the customer would not lead to a bigger governance problems—that is more of the customer's finding its way into the leak?

As urbanisation spreads in India, the demand for power eclipses that of most items the governments can provide. Off-grid renewable energy is often seen as the means to shunt the poor to limited usage levels of electricity. Political parties can and do support renewable energy but not at the cost of large grid-based electricity networks. In India, that means support for coal-fired plants.

For instance, asking for easing up on those needs means that the government has to make a choice about who gets the priority. Those who have the means to spend on the generator-based electricity production will be willing to pay their way out. Diesel-based generators are now common phenomena in Indian cities and offer more of a pollution hazard than from coal burnt at power stations. Yet the urban middle class now heavily dependent on diesel-based generation of electricity is also the one who is the most vocal about environmental footprint of coal-fired power plants.

So limiting domestic production of coal will hurt those at the lowest rung of the energy chain. They will be hurt more if the government substitutes domestic with costlier coal imports as those would raise power tariffs even more. It has happened at Tata Power's Mundra project which has got the electricity regulator's nod to raise tariffs. Any move to subsidise the need of the poorer segments can run only for a limited time until there is fiscal space. So, the choice could be deeply divisive.

What these efforts often do not answer is who will pick up human capital cost of switching off investment in the fossil fuel sector. CIL, for instance, employs over 350,000 employees. Of them, nearly 315,000 are non-executives with very little skill set to migrate elsewhere. They are also drawn from India's most-populated states of Bihar, Jharkhand and West Bengal where alternative employment is awfully short. CIL records one of the highest numbers of charge sheets every year served on employees who demand bribe for recruitment as miners. Tapas Kumar Lahiry, the former BCCL chairman, told me that on his very first day in the corner room, he was confronted with a political leader who demanded the right to recruit his own people. The stakes are immense. The company's profit is equivalent to 3.3 per cent of the total annual budget of Jharkhand. BCCL over the years has ploughed back most of that money into Dhanbad town. Without the coal company, there is hardly any economic activity for the densely populated town and its huge semi-urban hinterland to look forward to. Turning off the investment tap would be catastrophic.

It is akin to the larger problem from turning off the tap of fossil fuel-led economy in the world.

'For a few hours on the first Sunday of May 2016, Germany went full "green". Its power grid had surplus, and for a few hours residents actually earned money from using electricity, rather than paying for it', noted tech webzine *Alphr*.

As Germany shifted to one whole day of renewable energy-fed consumption cycle, it has dawned on most analysts that fossil fuel-led energy cycle may close out far sooner than expected. It could extract a terrible cost as Ninan pointed out at a public lecture organised by the Indian Council for Research on International Economic Relations (ICRIER) in New Delhi in May 2016 on the prospects for the global economy by 2050. There is a perspective to it. Most of the remittances of $68.9 billion received by India in 2015 are from the Middle East. It is 3.4 per cent of India's GDP for the year.

'Germany is the sixth largest total energy consumer in the world. If USA, China and India rapidly follow its path of green energy, imagine what would happen to some of the remittance flows to the economies of the subcontinent', Ninan pointed out. The shutdown of the petro-based economies of the Middle East would be colossal. It does not improve matters that such a shutdown will bring neighbouring Pakistan and Bangladesh to their knees. World Bank data show that remittances account for 7 per cent of the former and 8.7 per cent of the latter's economy.

Behind the big banner headlines, these problems often get obliterated. It is these nuts and bolts working of the economy which needs closer inspection. There has been some convergence of thoughts between the government and environment tigers; the Mahan coal block project for which Greenpeace staged its dramatic protest has been scratched.

While the debate was on, Greenpeace India campaigner Priya Pillai was offloaded in New Delhi from a London-bound flight where she planned to raise the issue. While New Delhi did not obviously approve of the way the environment group had gone about raising a din, it responded with alacrity to the problem, scratching the Mahan project.

Kaushik Bandyopadhyay, professor at The Energy and Resources Institute (TERI), is one of India's deep-dive scholars in the energy sector. He is clear that coal has to play a large role with a rising rural population demanding access to electricity.

Even when making a controversial argument, Kaushik has a disarming way of going about it. 'It would be worth exploring if the new power plants could be made carbon capture ready by retrofitting with the capture technology'. After years of dithering by the Indian government to invest in this costly technology, the US government has decided to push it from its own end. It has made a rare appointment of a specialist from its department of energy in New Delhi. In the last century, all such appointments used to be in the oil-rich countries.

Elizabeth Sherwood-Randall, deputy secretary in the US Department of Energy told as much to *The Economic Times*:

> We are doing a tremendous amount of research in Department of Energy labs on carbon capture utilisation and storage and on coal technologies that are more efficient. Indeed our leading expert on that topic has accompanied me here because we want to expand our collaboration on coal and on how it can be used in a way that is not damaging from a climate perspective. We have just signed an MoU with our leading laboratory on fossil fuel use—the National Energy Technology Lab—and an Indian counterpart.

Making coal deliver a clean result has become necessary, as despite Modi's promise—the National Action Plan on Climate Change promises that by 2019–2020, at least 15 per cent of the electricity generation has to come from renewable energy—there are clogs.

One of those clogs is the unequal ability of the twenty-eight state electricity regulatory commissions to enforce their rules. They have to set year-wise targets and within those distinguish between solar and non-solar sources. And then they have to bring the actual level of compliance closer to the targets.

In the past 2–3 years, except for states such as Karnataka, others have not met their targets to purchase renewable energy. After achieving compliance of 5.78 per cent in Rajasthan in 2011–2012, the state regulatory commission reduced the target from 8.5 per cent to 6 per cent. Similarly, Tamil Nadu lowered the target from 14 per cent to 9 per cent (actual compliance 9.59 per cent). Gujarat Electricity Regulatory Commission allowed its distribution licensees to carry forward the shortfall for the financial year 2012 to be met in the financial year 2013.

The usual problems of the state electricity boards are their large debt load. When they buy power from NTPC, they get a long line of credit. There is no comparable company in the renewable energy space which can do likewise, and the government with its limited fiscal room does not have the money to set up one with a similar strong financial muscle.

NTPC officials told me about their colleagues in the commercial division who coax and cajole the distribution utilities to pay up regularly for the power they buy from the company. 'It is only a long established relationship, which makes them pay', one of them said. When that does not work, notices like this one go out.

> Subsequent to the issue of Regulation of power supply notice to BSES Delhi discoms by NTPC … (they) have agreed to pay NTPC dues as per the action plan given to NTPC/DERC/GoNCTD/MoP and have indicated to pay all NTPC dues by Sept 2016. From Sept/Oct 2016 onwards, they will maintain outstanding limited to 60 days. The outstanding dues from these two discoms (i.e., BRPL & BYPL) is amounting to ₹1,534 Cr for NTPC as on 14.06.2016.

Anil Sardana said that one of the options for the central government could be to use the space created by Uday to improve transmission and distribution efficiencies. He said, 'That would be like creating additional supply but without having to depend on new generation. It would also be stable and will cajole some downstream manufacturers to expand their production'.

There are lots of options being considered to make the renewable energy options become more alive such as stricter enforcement, fixing of long-term targets to create visibility about solar power requirement, say a ten-year horizon instead of the current 3–5 years one and making those tradable and bankable. The government has also imposed a cess on coal to finance solar power. It has risen to ₹400 a tonne and one can be sure that like cigarettes, the rate of this one will climb further.

Senior government officials feel that organisations such as Greenpeace International do not appreciate the scope of the challenges the energy makeover entails. They claim that when organisations such as Greenpeace see it as a binary problem of coal or no coal, the complex choices are drowned in the din.

The campaigners would disagree. At the same time as Priya's case grabbed attention, ahead of the Paris CoP, Kumi Naidoo, executive director of Greenpeace, made a strong pitch for support from Modi.

Naidoo requested Modi to make India use only renewable energy by the year 2050. The letter cannily made no reference to what Indian Intelligence Bureau had accused it of a year before and which landed her Indian colleague in trouble. The bureau argued that the environment campaigner was undercutting Indian efforts to achieve self-sufficiency in energy through its campaigns in the coal sector. Naidoo ducked it: 'Greenpeace and civil society stands with India in demanding accountability from the major polluters.... Could you, the political leader of nearly one fifth of humanity, make history by securing a deal for the world?'

In the event, it was a smart bit of positioning by Modi at the conference. He had made a trade-off. India needs to keep its coal fires burning for a long time even as a lot of nations have begun to switch off fossil fuels. If the fossil fuels have to burn, India can only escape global censure if it also picks up a large basket of renewable energy commitment.

Coal Puff

Just as it is difficult to kick the habit of a cigarette puff, coal seems to be a long-drawn puff for the Indian economy. A special report on India by IEA issued around the Paris event noted that India would soon be the second-largest coal producer in the world. But there is more to it. The same IEA report said that in another 4 years, India would become 'the world's largest coal importer, overtaking Japan, the European Union and China'. At the same time, India's demand for oil would grow more than any country in the globe, and 90 per cent of that supply would be through imports. As industries found domestic coal progressively difficult to mine, imports rose in importance. Modi's trade-off was necessary for the companies to keep moving overseas to dig for coal.

This has implications for how India views questions of energy security. In a perceptive analysis for Niti Aayog, the successor organisation to the Planning Commission, Atul Jain, one of the finest analysts of India's energy options noted, 'The creeping growth of the share of imported energy in our demand, threatens our energy security'. His estimates showed that by the end of the financial year 2016, India would depend on imports for 46 per cent of its total requirement of energy. It was 38 per cent in the financial year 2012. The tab includes coal, oil and gas.

India, it seems, would drive quite a bit of the global trade in coal and oil for the next two decades. While a report by Goldman Sachs on global coal and gas trade issued in February 2016 said, 'India is set to ramp up its own domestic production of coal, cutting out the need to import more', a report by Brookings India supported the alternative IEA position. 'Imports of coal would rise in the next few years', it argued, 'Imports cannot be wished away'.

Driving a large fuel trade over the high seas opens up a lot of questions, however. Those questions concern market access, safety of shipments, policing of the routes and the impact on the economy when a supply line from overseas develops 'cramps'. Those lines thus need friendly ports to start from and ports to disembark the cargo at. One of those ports is coming up at Chabahar being built with Indian investment at the mouth of the Persian Gulf. And there is more in offing.

The 'creeping growth' of imports, as Jain describes it, is the challenge for India that has also totally altered its foreign policy strategy, especially in the Indian Ocean region. Elements of those are only now falling into place. These involve questions of geo-political strategy on high seas, questions that India had diligently striven to stay away from since Independence.

Oil on Sherwani

India has had difficulty reconciling its pacifist worldview with the obvious felt need, energy security. Independent India's first government under Nehru including the newly set up Planning Commission tried to keep aside these difficult questions on energy strategy. The country instead slipped out of the global trade in energy commodities as it considered those trades to be vestiges of imperialism. Post-colonial India was about to 'undermine the three planks that had sustained (globalization) thus far, namely, commodity export, global firms and private banking-cum-moneylending'.

In the absence of a strategy, there were hardly any efforts made to stitch together an energy patina. It disregarded history that showed that rights over fuel have rarely led to good feelings among nations. Post the spread of the Industrial Revolution, the demands for fuel security made nations which had ambitions to grow fast become eager hunters for sources of energy. Since the distribution of fossil fuel resources often does not respect national borders, the hunt became even more fractious. None of the developed countries of today escaped the script. Japan's assault on the Pearl Harbour during the Second World War was meant to neutralise the role of the US Navy when Tokyo would muzzle into the oil reserves of Borneo and Sumatra.

The external markets for coal were allowed to go dry without anyone taking a conscious decision to do so. At the same time, it never got clear how New Delhi would if at all steer a higher production of coal and oil. For instance, Prasanta Chandra Mahalanobis, Indian government's first statistical adviser and author of the second Five-Year Plan, argued that it made no sense to fill up the ballast of the railway engines with coal to then lug more coal by wagons across the country to fuel other industries. Imported oil could do the work better.

The man who could secure the oil security for India was Gamal Abdel Nasser, the president of Egypt from 1956 until his death in 1970. Nasser and Nehru came famously close but only politically. Egypt had hardly any oil to sell and Nasser was not exactly popular with the oil sheikhs of Saudi Arabia, Oman or Kuwait, especially after he began nationalisation of foreign oil companies. There was also a little economic hitch. Egypt's staple export was cotton; India also produced cotton. No one needed the other's products. And as Nasser remained bogged down through the Suez Canal crisis and more in the 1950s, India did not really get going with the oil-rich kingdoms who were scared of both Nehru and Nasser.

All the time, India remained sure that it did not need to replicate the spheres of influence to procure oil, unlike what UK and the USA had created in the desert. Nehru was sure that he would not only get oil, but he would get that at the same price that UK got it for. After all, Mumbai and London were broadly the same distance from Abadan in Iran. When international oil companies such as Burmah Oil raised the price of Indian petrol by an anna in 1957, Nehru described it as 'loot' and speeded up the construction of state-run oil refinery at Barauni in Bihar. Before the revision, the price of a gallon of oil imported from the Middle East by India cost just six pence more than the cost in UK.

A couple of years later in May 1960, the prime minister ran to Ankleshwar in Gujarat when India struck its first oil well beyond Assam. As he stood beaming at the site, a gusher began spouting oil, spraying some on him too. Even as the engineers ran to switch it off, Nehru said that 'I shall address the Parliament in this *sherwani*. Let everybody know that we now have our own oil'. He named the well Vasundhara.

These were naïve expectations and worse, piecemeal. Naturally, they were a series of hits and misses. In the early 1960s, ONGC's first chairman KD Malaviya notched up a big success when Iran offered it four offshore exploration blocks. In a joint venture with ENI and Phillips Petroleum, India found oil in two of them Rostum and Raksh; the oil was also brought to Cochin. But soon thereafter, India was forced to surrender those two blocks in 1979 when the Shah of Iran was deposed. A decade later, ONGC set up its sub-sidiary ONGC Videsh Limited (OVL) in 1989 to prospect for oil abroad. But of course it did not have the balance sheet to purchase anything worthwhile for a long time.

It is rather curious that India bade goodbye to the US-dominated oil companies in the 1970s, again through nationalisation of their Indian assets, but ended up in a hug with the oil oligarchs of Russia post 2000. OVL's success has been patchy with Rosneft, or with Venezuela managing to generate equity returns but no oil supply for back home.

The impact of this inability to organise the foray into a cred-ible import policy hit me, as I stood at Diamond Harbour in West Bengal. The Hooghly river, Ganga's biggest distributary flows into the Bay of Bengal just beyond Diamond Harbour. Coal laden barges can be seen streaming in from the sea, inland.

Coal on Barges, Again

About a couple of hours ride further down from Diamond Harbour is Sagar Island in Bay of Bengal. The island hosts a huge annual pilgrimage in winter. Thanks to the coal trade, it is swiftly becoming a new pilgrimage centre for coal—a new market for coal on the high seas. From hesitant beginnings around the same time as domestic coal supplies became scarce post 2000s, 'coal devotees' arrive there for their supply. These devotees are the same small units whose demand for coal is often unmet. This is from where the coal barges sail inland to Diamond Harbour and further inland to Kolkata.

I got to see a sample of the working method of this new market with Indronil Roychowdhury of *The Financial Express*. Indronil has possibly the most extensive Rolodex for the mineral sectors in all of Eastern India. One of his extensive contacts is Pritam Dutta, an entrepreneur for this market of high seas coal. Dutta's office in Dhakuria, Kolkata, is like scores of nondescript offices that dot the port city. His company UCDS proudly describes itself as a procurer of coal from all corners of India. A brochure at his office says, 'We are a prominent supplier and exporter of Meghalaya coal, Jharia coal, Kharsiang coal, Ranigunj coal, Nangal coal, quartz stone, iron ore and limestone. Our products are of highest quality and accessible as per the exact specifications of the clients'. The latest addition to his list is the consignments from Indonesia.

Traders running small sponge iron units, lime factories, smoke-less fuel plants, coke oven units, tea gardens and even brick kilns contact him for their supplies. Dutta aggregated those demand just as the coal suppliers in the Varanasi markets used to do in their heyday. He explained that his customers were those who had no assured promise of coal linkage with CIL; they fell below the 4,200 tonne per annum limit to qualify for it. Their options so far were to buy from nominated state agencies, from CIL's e-auction coal or from the Varanasi markets which in turn sourced their supplies from the rat-hole mines of Nagaland and Meghalaya.

The prices of coal from CIL are now relatively high, while the supply at the illegal markets have got difficult. When the SC clamped down on private mining, the supplies from Dhanbad and Singrauli also dried up. Companies which have bought coal min-ing rights are reluctant to feed the illegal markets as they used to do earlier for fear of having their mines snatched away again. The supplies from Meghalaya or Nagaland have also dried up.

'In such a situation, the best option is Indonesian coal. With prices of Indonesian coal falling and government imposing zero duty on coal, Indonesian coal has become a cheaper option for small consumers', Dutta said. Since the big Indian consumers are already flush with coal, miners in Indonesia are unable to strike any long-term contract. In such a scenario, aggregators like Dutta spell boon for the overseas suppliers too and they wait for his call.

Dutta makes life simple for the coal buyers by removing from them the hassle of handling the bulk cargo at the ports—he makes the high sea purchases on their behalf. The miners, mostly from Indonesia, bring their consignment to the mouth of Bay of Bengal where Dutta unloads those for his clients. Prince Dwarkanath Tagore would have been delighted with the return of high sea-based coal trade to his city of birth.

'It is absolutely legal', said Debashis Dutta, chairman of the Federation of Freight Forwarders' Association in India. The traders lift coal after paying a 2 per cent Central Value Added Tax (CENVAT). Once the payment is made, the buyers generally lift the coal in small barges carrying it from the seas to their point of consumption inland. 'Many traders both from India and Bangladesh are trying to make an entry into the new space tying up with the miners of Indonesia', Pritam added. He is a computer engineer who had begun his career with the IT sector. Coal came up as an alternative as it has been to generations of businessmen before him in this port city.

Indronil introduced me to another such trader—Assadullah Choudhury from Dhaka. The trader confirmed Pritam's story from the other side of the border. There had been a lot of interest generated about Indonesian coal in Northeast India and Bangladesh, Assadullah said. Transporting coal to Northeast through Bangladesh has become an easy affair because of increased navigability of Brahmaputra after the establishment of a new port and creation of national waterways between Sadiya and Dhupri. It is crazy again how traders in Meghalaya now use imported coal instead of sourcing it from their own state. But then it is only fair that movement of international prices should benefit all even if it seems surprising at first sight. The domestic markets have shifted to the high seas. But the continuous wash of the coal barges through the seas around India has raised the stakes to keep them under surveillance.

At the other end of the country, the coal trade on high seas is more organised, though often lethal, environmentally!

Haji Bunder at Sewri in Mumbai is the largest site for import of coal in India. Coal is imported there by the Mumbai Port Trust for the state electricity board's plants at Nasik from Mozambique and South Africa; some of the big buyers are Tata Power feeding its Trombay power plant and others, further inland.

It is fine grade coal, the sort which is a rarity in India and so is highly prized. This is also what creates trouble. Indian coal is rocky; it is rarely possible to grind it down to fine dust before transportation. The imported–fine-coal-dust travels by air for phenomenal distances from the open railway wagons blackening everything in its way. The 19 acres of coal deposit at Haji Bunder has proved lethal for its hinterland where property prices have dipped and respiratory diseases have soared as India imports more coal. For instance, one of the reasons why Tata Power imports coal is its Trombay plant located in a high population density area which is mandated to use only fine coal to keep its environmental footprint low. But the same coal creates havoc at Sewri making the area more soot-stained than any inland coal town in India like Kustaur or Dhanbad. Until a decade ago, the company used Daramtar Port about 170 km from Mumbai as its coal import base. The shift to Mumbai apparently saved the company about ₹50 crore a year on transport costs, said a report by *Business Standard*.

The state pollution board had recently asked for the Haji Bunder facility to be shut down. But the state environment minister Ramdas Kadam had promised to make the necessary changes to keep it going submitting a list of fourteen steps he proposed to undertake. Key among those was that the 19 acres of coal storage area should be covered, transportation should be via covered trucks and wagons and there should be a closed coal-handling terminal. These are new challenges which threaten the fresh imports. The earlier challenges of a decade ago emerged as the government back-pedalled on the support it should have offered to companies when they prospected for coal and gas resources abroad. The energy foray of the government has been somewhat like that of the Indian Olympics foray where the news of the preparations have seldom been paired with medals at the competitions.

From Ganga to Zambezi

One of such forays revolved around the former minister of state for external affairs, Shashi Tharoor. In January 2010, Tharoor led an Indian delegation to Addis Ababa to participate in an African

Union summit. In an interview, the minister had already made his preference for Africa clear in his usual candid way, 'we have an opportunity to enjoy a privileged position in many African countries that we would be foolish not to develop'. Ethiopian prime minister Meles Zanawi accordingly buttonholed Tharoor to finance a railway line project to connect the port city of Djibouti with Addis Ababa. The single-line 781 km railway then 'ran' on standard gauge, most of it through Ethiopian territory and about 100 km in neighbouring Djibouti. The fortune of the railway company went almost bankrupt after France went out of Ethiopia ceding its colonial control. The century-old station at the Ethiopian capital lies overgrown with weeds. 'So to reach Djibouti from Addis, passengers have to travel more than 470 kilometres on extremely difficult roads to Dire Daoua to pick up the train'.

Addis Ababa asked for interests from four foreign entities to build the railways again. A new Indian entity Overseas Infrastructure Alliance bid for the project with the backing of the Indian government. The company picks up a smorgasbord of orders from the various African states to connect with specialised entities back home. There are several of these entities in the continent, each decorated with at least one former civil service officer in its board of directors. The Ethiopian railway order was one of those.

Sachin Chaturvedi, director general of Delhi-based think tank Research and Information System for Developing Countries, had an interesting story recalling the misadventure. Investment in the rail route made a lot of sense for India. At the hinterland, it would have connected to a clutch of sugar factories in Ethiopia. Zanawi was trying to accommodate political interests which wanted the line to be nearest to their plants. As time and plans expanded, so did the costs. India's Exim Bank which until recently ran on shoestring budget found the cost more than it could underwrite; the line of credit was allowed to lapse.

Within a few months of the order coming its way, Tharoor's glamorous wife Sunanda Pushkar's financial role in the Cochin-based T-20 league cricket team rocked political connections back in India. The minister had to resign because of the perceived scandal and in the din, nobody in the Indian government remembered to pick up the project which at one stage was considered a done deal.

'So even though it was a complete value chain and would have given us an impressive foothold in the region, we stepped back', added Sachin.

Zanawi waited for some time and then handed over the project to China. 'According to Hailemariam Desalegn, the chairman of the Ethiopian Railway Corporation (ERC), the Indian Government too(k) long to respond to the request for funds.' The IPL fiasco cost India a lot more than fun on the cricket field.

All these happened even when India had supposedly woken up to the need for imports by 2008. 'It was at this time we decided to set up Coal Videsh', said Partha Bhattacharya, former CIL chairman. He set it up as a division within CIL to prospect for thermal coal abroad.

For five years thereafter, the government dithered about the guidelines for the venture. And as the former coal ministers Santosh Bagrodia and Sriprakash Jaiswal pondered deeply, the steel ministry next door had a brainwave. As steel was also facing a shortage of domestic coking coal, the SAIL chairman SK Rungta nudged the steel minister Beni Prasad Verma to form another overseas exploration body. International Coal Ventures Private Limited (ICVL) was set up under the administrative control of steel ministry as a consortium of top public sector firms, SAIL, NTPC, Rashtriya Ispat Nigam Limited (RINL), CIL and NMDC. It was a checkmate.

Coal Videsh wanted to get thermal coal, while the five-company joint venture, ICVL, wanted coking coal. No one could expect the two entities to perform with such contradictions and they did not. Even though CIL held a 28 per cent share of the capital in the company, the same as SAIL, it was represented in the board by its director while the SAIL chairman became the ex-officio chairman of ICVL.

Most of these shenanigans happened in the same year when CIL ran headless. Beni Prasad Verma, the steel minister, used his clout as the senior political man to carve out another inconsequential empire in a progressively dysfunctional government.

Coal Videsh was stillborn, and ICVL since its inception in 2008 had just one project to show in Mozambique, Coal India Africana Limitada. The prospecting licences it got have been scraps of paper since it has run into difficulties over the setting up of an Apex Planning Organization and an Apex Training Organization for coal sector in that country. The Mozambique government is not willing to provide the cost of land and building for the institutions and so CIL offered to bear this cost as part of their commitment while obtaining coal from there. The process has eaten up six years. Meanwhile, right from inception, there were questions if CIL should retain the stake. Yet it took six years of bureaucratic work for the company to surrender its stake. With decisions made at this clip, it was obvious that buying of assets abroad was never going to be a priority for ICVL.

So, just as domestic coal remained underground wrapped in environmental and legal hurdles, efforts of the Government of India to get coal from abroad too did not help. Instead, they gave time for the coal entrepreneurs to explore their options.

One of the most bizarre proposals in this environment was for the public and private sector companies to form a joint venture to scout for coal abroad.

'SAIL, RINL, JSW and JSPL are discussing together to bid for good quality coking coal assets overseas…. This will be a JV company', JSW vice chairman and managing director Sajjan Jindal told reporters while exiting an ASSOCHAM Steel Summit in New Delhi in 2010. He claimed that the public–private partnership model would dip below the regulatory hurdles which the public sector companies cannot handle.

For instance, in 2013, ONGC and Oil India signed a deal for the acquisition of a 10 per cent stake in a gas field in Mozambique. The $2.5 billion transaction was for the Rovuma Area 1 Offshore Block in Mozambique which is supposed to be the largest gas discovery in East Asia. When the area first went up for exploration, none of these two companies could, however, join in. The cost for joining the exploration was a measly US$300 million to finance their share. Executives of these companies found the petroleum ministry reluctant to spare the money. The stake was instead picked up by Venugopal Dhoot, owner of the Videocon group, with interests ranging from Fast-moving consumer goods (FMCG) to oil. When the gas was stuck, he could realise $2.5 billion from his investment Videocon Mauritius in the sale of the newly incorporated entity to ONGC. The state-owned oil explorer will hold a 60 per cent stake with the buyout.

Like him, the wins were notched up by the non-state actors or the Indian private sector companies. By the beginning of the 1990s, the number of Indian companies which had figured out that they would need to import coal than depend on domestic sources had reached a critical mass. The Rao government obliged putting import of coal under open general licence which meant that anyone who needed it could import it. One of the first companies to tap the route was Tata Chemicals. It sourced coal from South Africa. A hardy band of traders who had earlier dabbled in ferrying CIL coal across the country came up to exploit the opportunities this threw up.

Just when the Jindals were moving into domestic coal-based power and steel production, another new-generation entrepreneur Gautam Adani moved into the business of importing coal. Adani was also one of the men present at the meeting with Singh. His rise to the eleventh richest Indian as per Forbes list of 2015 has been one of the most documented episodes; it also showed the power of India's coal economy to generate wealth. As of now, Adani's Mundra Port has begun supplying coal to the UMPP of 4,000 MW, Coastal Gujarat Power run by Tata Power and another 2,640 MW built under its own umbrella.

Adani and other smaller players realised that India's peninsular structure provided a long coastline which was wonderfully placed to offer an opportunity to import from the east or from the west. While Adani moved eastwards tapping the Indonesian coal, Naveen Jindal and then the Tatas tapped into Africa. Public sector CIL sat on the sidelines. Even though they have been far smaller than the state-owned companies, they have been more nimble to pick up victories.

I got to see an example of the nimbleness on display at Johannesburg in South Africa with Ashish Kumar, CEO of Jindal Africa. He runs the operations from his office in one of the tony suburbs of the city as the overseas subsidiary of JSPL. The office reception is plastered with quotes from OP Jindal, the group patriarch, making it seem rather unreal, as outside the tall windows the African city lies uncoiled.

Ashish met me just after the coalgate episode had begun to wind down in India in August 2014. He was confident that with the increasing level of difficulty for Indian companies to source coal from within India, their investments in Africa would be more valuable. They were!

In 2009, Jindal Africa had stepped into Mozambique, starting development of an estimated 10 billion MT Chirdozi coal mine in the Moatize district. The mine had an expected lifespan of twenty-five years. Moatize had excellent coal deposits. Six years later, in the same flight from New Delhi with me were the officials of government-owned ICVL. They were travelling to Moatize to seal their buy of a $50 million mine from Rio Tinto. By the time they sealed up their investment, global coal prices had begun to crash and ICVL was now sitting on a dud investment.

Meanwhile, elaborating on the company's expansion plans in Mozambique, Kumar said that Jindal Africa planned to transport coal from the mine to the port through either the development of a rail line between Moatize and the Port of Beira or the construction of a coal slurry pipeline.

As the scale of these investments became big, the Indian government came to realise that it had to dip into energy politics. The realisation came in bits and pieces. An early example of that was the politics over the Mozambique rail link.

The link has been in the works since 2004. As Mozambique politics hemmed and hawed, the project kept on getting delayed. Indian government companies RITES and IRCON got the contract for the project forming a joint venture, Companhia Dos Caminhos De Ferro Da Beira, SARL, for the $230 million project. Unlike the Ethiopian misadventure, the consortium had outbid their Chinese rivals. But just after they completed the project in 2011, the Mozambique government expropriated it. Expropriation was not new to this country. The man who ordered it President Armando Guebuza had in 1975 ordered all Portuguese residents of Mozambique to leave the country within twenty-four hours. The two Indian companies have begun arbitration proceedings against the country. Although Guebuza's successor, the current head of state Filipe Nyusi, received his management degree from India, he has not helped their cause by taking off the arbitration from the table.

Bibek Debroy had once told me,

> In a country that should have been desperate in trying to get investment into energy production at home, estimates are that nearly $ 53 billion of capital earned in India has left its shores in the past decade chasing energy deals abroad in oil, coal and gas sector.

One has to keep pace with Debroy when he talks—he does not suffer fools easily. It was a massive figure—as a comparison, the size of the Indian telecom sector in 2016 was about so much. Moreover, he pointed out, most of the actual benefit of that investment went to China which had the market and the network to buy from those production sources.

Geopolitical Lessons, Finally

Never has an Indian prime minister reached the USA so soon after being sworn in as Modi did when he reached the US President Barack Obama within months after stepping into South Block in New Delhi. The US–India Joint Statement of 30 September 2014 mentioned the role of navy just once, but it was a telling comment. Deep into the statement was a clear message, '(The two leaders) also agreed to upgrade their existing bilateral exercise MALABAR'.

Modi and Obama had pulled out a more-than–a-decade-old mutual drill that the two countries had begun on the high seas. The Malabar exercises were conceived during the term of the first BJP-led government in 2002 as a means of making up from the frosty relations India and the USA had swung into after India's nuclear tests. But since then, in a long desultory decade, the exercises had achieved little of tangible value to act as force multiplier for the Indian Navy.

In fact, it came close to being called off in 2007. Flush with the success of the signing of the India–US civil nuclear deal, Prime Minister Singh agreed to expand the scope of the exercise to include Australia, Japan and even Singapore. One leg of it was to be held near the Japanese coast for the first time.

China immediately made its annoyance clear at the enthusiasm of the drill. It plainly saw it as an anti-Beijing stance and sent de-marches to all the nations involved. India's defence minister AK Antony immediately moved to water down the scope of the exercise because of his 'morbid fear of irritating China', noted Ravi Velloor, associate editor of *The Straits Times*. Antony demanded to know from Admiral Suresh Mehta how an exercise code-named Malabar referring to the coast of Kerala was being held on the other side of the peninsula in Bay of Bengal.

'Left parties led by the CPM, always sympathetic to China, were supporting the Manmohan government.... CPM chief Prakash Karat was threatening to march from Kolkata to Vishakhapatnam, port city that is home to the Eastern Fleet, if Exercise Malabar went through. Anthony was shaken', wrote Velloor in his book *India Rising*. Later in the same year, when the USS Nimitz docked off the Chennai coast, there was again an outcry from the left, this time over the possibility of nuclear radiation from the ship. No such fear had come stalking when vessels from Russia or China had come to port. Naturally, they did not forget to paint the visit as a sign of deepening collaboration of the Indian government with the USA, something which they opposed strongly.

After such high-pitched opposition, Malabar slipped into inconsequence. Noting India's timid response to the Chinese demarches, the US Navy substantially scaled down its involvement in the annual drill. Only frigates, corvettes and submarines came along every year from the USA. Naval build-up was forgotten. Indian mandarins while happy to note that the name Indian Ocean for the waters off the coast of Kanyakumari conveyed the sense of an Indian backyard were happy to let the US Navy police those waters.

Meanwhile, events had moved forward rapidly in the Ocean. The guys moving them were 'non-state actors'. These was the band of pirates from Somalia who woke up New Delhi to the scale of the challenges. Simultaneously, as the demands on the US Navy increased in the Pacific Theatre, its aircraft carriers and other heavy ships moved out there leaving the Indian Ocean pretty much open to the Somali pirates who started threatening coal import vessels from Madagascar and South Africa to India, big time.

And just as the worried Indian businessmen watched the US Navy disappear over the straits of Malacca into the Pacific, they found the Chinese navy sailing into the Indian Ocean. Beijing's excuse was that 40 per cent of their imports of coal and oil used the Ocean and the Indian Navy was far too weak to do anything about the pirates.

Just as UK needed naval supremacy in the Atlantic to keep its oil supply lines open in the last century, India realised that it now needed to police the Indian Ocean. Effectively!

A total of 30 ships from various nations and more than 660 people were taken hostages by the pirates by February 2011. Among them were a British couple Paul and Rachel Chandler, who were freed after being held captive for 13 months. Indian Ocean was turning into a dirty un-policed zone like the gang wars of Mumbai in the 1980s. Those pirates could move deeper to play havoc with the coal barges queuing up in Bay of Bengal; they could also encourage other desperadoes from other destitute nations to storm the shipments from southern Africa. And once those disturbances became a big enough nuisance, a nation with a strong navy could demand setting up of a base in the Indian Ocean to police the area.

As a part of the Malabar exercises, one of the skills the US Navy taught the Indian Navy was to deal with piracy operations. It was to prove useful now. In the space of 3 months, Indian Navy leant heavily on the pirates. It struck three times to capture first fifteen of them, then twenty-eight and finally sixty-one pirates in those months until March. The pirates were brought to Mumbai to be prosecuted for 'attacking Indian ships'. New Delhi had never taken such a tough action on the high seas against foreign nationals of any country in its post-Independence history, not even during the India–Pakistan wars. 'Indian Navy succeeds in pushing back pirates', reported a newspaper headline in 2012. It went on to describe that Somali pirates had backed off from the Indian coastlines, making the zone a safe passage for merchant ships.

Pramit Pal Chaudhuri, one of India's best commentators on energy issues, said that the naval action was precipitated by the sight of Chinese navy taking up a pole position in the Indian Ocean. The eulogistic reports in the world press post the Indian Navy action would have been replaced with paeans to the Chinese navy if they had been given the chance to take the initiative instead.

India had learnt an economic lesson on the high seas. High levels of trade need a high level of policing of the lanes, not only to keep its supply lines free for the coal lines back home but also its oil economy steady. But pirates were thus only a catalyst to begin the battle for the shipping lanes. The key decisions still needed to be acted upon, and quite a few of them were with respect to China.

The Chinese have always complained of an unequal position in the Indian Ocean. It stems from a geographical bottleneck, the Straits of Malacca. The narrow mouth of the ocean just off the coast of Singapore means that the entire flotilla of Chinese merchant ships bound for Asia and Europe can be held up à la the Suez Canal in the Middle East unless they take the option of a long costly voyage across the Pacific. India has no such problem.

As the volume of China's engagement with the world has expanded, the need to secure the trading lines in the Indian Ocean has become important for Beijing. Pramit points out that the Somali pirates gave Beijing a valid reason to establish a permanent naval presence in the Indian Ocean.

Since 2008, 19 Chinese naval task forces have rotated in and out of the ocean. Beijing clearly has greater ambitions. Since 2014, Chinese

intelligence-gathering ships and submersibles have begun making regular forays into the Indian Ocean. To these have now been
added submarines. None can have anything to do with pirates. In
2014 China also held its first military exercise encompassing the
eastern Indian Ocean—until now such exercises were confined to
only the Pacific.

In the last year of the UPA government, the Planning Commission
was tasked with projecting India's energy mix until 2030. The
scope of the work changed as the government changed in New
Delhi the next year. The NDA government not only expanded
the mandate for the new organisation Niti Aayog that succeeded
the Commission but also asked the Aayog to stretch the forecast
deeper into the future until 2047, the year when India would
have completed 100 years of its Independence. The Niti Aayog
document 'Using India Energy Security Scenarios, 2047' is only
the second time since 1971 when Sukhamoy Chakravarty did a
similar exercise as member Planning Commission when Indian
energy demand in all its aspects has sought to be projected so far
out into the future.

The conclusion from the new report is clear. Despite the hoopla
about renewable energy, fossil fuel will dominate Indian energy
mix making up 68 per cent of the supply until then. Of this, coal
will account for more than a half. It means a lot of it will have to be
imported. Since imported coal is of superior quality than domestic
coal, these 'fuels would be higher priced than coal based power,
but once adopted in moderate measures in the electricity grid the
strategy would be irreversible and would find acceptance in the
market'. Add in the demand for imports of oil and gas. The report
estimates India's dependency on fossil fuel imports to 'rise from a
level of 32% in the base year to 45% of the primary energy supply
in the year 2030'.

And the IEA special report notes that as India's reliance on oil
imports climbs, it would 'require constant vigilance as to the implications for energy security'. It is among the first international
reports to explicitly state this position. The report was prepared
after consultations with the two Indian energy ministers, Piyush
Goyal, minister for power, coal, mines and renewable energy, and
the oil minister Dharmendra Pradhan.

Where UK moved from coal to oil in the twentieth century which made it scout for energy security abroad, India is doing it to secure more coal from abroad.

The Indian Ocean in the twenty-first century thus has a critical presence in the world energy matrix. Of the thirteen largest energy import- or export-dependent states of the world according to IEA statistics, six littoral states of Indian Ocean figure in the list. These are Australia, Iran, UAE, India, Indonesia and Singapore. Just off it are Saudi Arabia and Kuwait. Add China and Taiwan to the mixture, both of which source 40 per cent of their oil imports from the Middle East via the lanes of the Indian Ocean and then factor the rising presence of Thailand and Bangladesh as new consumers; it becomes obvious that these waters are the current energy pipelines of the world.

Yet an acknowledgment of importance can only go so far. Least of all because it is rather difficult to chart an aggressive maritime agenda when India neither has a navy that can operate independently off the Indian coast, a blue water navy as it is called, nor can it afford to build one for some time. The other is the risks involved in making such an objective public enough to hang out for every nation to inspect. Especially, when one of those nations is a large neighbour with the same energy needs and also uses the same geographical lines to feed its manufacturing base, China!

Still, when these two neighbours ply their ships so close to each other through the same channel from the same countries if not the same ports, points of irritation are bound to emerge.

The Modi–Obama signature to upgrade Malabar was thus an affirmation that India will pursue its maritime expansion to secure its energy interests. The upgrade meant that other navies in the littoral region will join in. In 2016, as Japan came into the exercise, and the US aircraft carriers returned, China sensed trouble and sent in a naval reconnaissance vessel to check out the developments.

On 15 June 2016, a Chinese naval ship broke in upon a three nation naval exercise conducted near the Japanese island of Okinawa.

As *Hindustan Times* reported quoting wire agencies, 'The Chinese ship shadowed the US aircraft carrier John C Stennis in the Western Pacific, the carrier's commander said, as it joined warships from India and Japan for drills close to waters Beijing considers its backyard'. Along with the 100,000-tonne Stennis, there are nine other naval ships including a Japanese helicopter carrier and the Indian frigates in the seas off the Okinawa island chain.

Chinese ships are routinely entering Japanese territorial waters. In June itself, Tokyo had voiced concern over another Beijing 'intrusion' near the Senkaku Islands in the East China Sea.

The former foreign secretary Shyam Saran agrees that India has reasons to reach out to the US Navy. Writing in *Business Standard*, he notes,

> It is in the maritime domain that India and the US appear to have the most significant alignment of interests. This is mainly with respect to the Indian Ocean and the Western Pacific, including the South China Sea, a region now better known collectively as the Indo-Pacific. The China factor is clearly a shared concern.

It is not surprising that India and the USA have signed a logistics treaty. Behind the usual verbiage is a clear understanding that if necessary, India can use the US Navy as a force multiplier.

As C Raja Mohan, possibly India's most trenchant observer of the world order, through his delightful Raja Mandala columns in *The Indian Express* put it, the risk of a possible military clash between India and China over energy transport corridors 'cannot be entirely dismissed. India straddles the sea lanes through which most of China's imported oil passes and segments of the Chinese strategic and military community are concerned with the potential of the Indian navy to interdict China's maritime oil lifeline'.

Still, to be the policeman for this busy network, a stronger long-term action plan needs something more. Access to ports!

The way New Delhi has begun to react to China in the great energy game has a parallel with the way UK and Russia squared off in Persia, now Iran from the nineteenth century onwards. The Russians needed a warm water port and access to Iranian oil. The British were equally determined to deny them both. The formation of the Anglo-Persian oil company and that of Burmah Shell were steps to block those moves. The subsequent amalgamation of the former into the latter was also a means to keep the finance flowing for the expansion of the oil explorations in the desert which took a long time to bear a fruit.

There is a key difference though. The European powers and the USA played the game through their private companies keeping the state power just a step behind. It did not fool anyone but as Rockefeller, Nobel and Rothschilds fought for their prize, the countries kept up an element of deniability at times of crisis.

In the energy folio of the twenty-first century, among the Asian countries that fig leaf is absent. This difference is crucial as the skirmishes are clearly state led from the start.

This is where New Delhi plays from not one but more than one weakness. Of these, the first is the size of the state-run corporations. While China has built up Sinopec or China Petroleum and Chemical Corp. followed by China National Petroleum Corporation as the two biggest oil and gas companies in the world, India has lagged behind. Compared to the annual revenue of $440 billion for Sinopec in 2014, ONGC stands at a measly $13 billion.

China Shenhua, the coal company, is comparatively much smaller than these oil giants at $38.8 billion in 2014. It is of course also a power-generating company. India's CIL earned revenue of $11.4 billion in the financial year 2014. It is these differences in scale that have made it difficult for the Indian companies even though all of them are state owned to tap global energy resources abroad effectively. These differences matter, and as we saw in the case of African forays in Mozambique and Ethiopia, without the deep pockets to strew goodies like investment in infrastructure facilities along with core investment in the mines in the countries, they spell the difference between success and failure.

A key stratagem to make up for this weakness would be to invest in ports along the shipping lanes. India has delayed this investment for far too long. In the list of top ports of the world, fourteen are from China. Only one Indian port, Jawaharlal New Port Trust (JNPT), figures in the list and that too at number thirty-three. The list unlike airports does not look at facilities etc. but is a brute ranking of tonnage handled by the ports.

Comparisons of naval powers are more lopsided in favour of China. It has sixty-eight submarines against fourteen that India can deploy. Numbers however do not tell the extent of the difference. When the Malaysian Airlines flight MH370 disappeared over the Indian Ocean, Kuala Lumpur had asked for radar readings from India's air force posts at the Andaman and Nicobar Islands. Sandeep Unnithan in his column wrote about the embarrassment in New Delhi when it was discovered that the ageing radars to prolong their working life had been switched off at that time of the day. He wrote, 'The islands lack the radar coverage for India to be even able to monitor civilian traffic, leave alone declare an Air Defence Identification Zone (ADIZ) as China is contemplating over the South China Sea'.

In fact, the defiant build-up of presence by China in the South China Sea is not just a political statement. Beijing needs the oil and gas reserves of the seas and is not willing to share with anyone else. India's foray into the sea at the invitation of Vietnam has, therefore, landed it in direct conflict with China. As Saran wrote in another piece in *Business Standard*,

> A Chinese scholar, when asked where India fitted in the hierarchical order that China envisaged, said for China, India was a 'swing State' which ought to be kept from leaning too close to the United States or straying too far from its traditional non-alignment. This may require China, he acknowledged, to make greater efforts to woo India and this is what its leaders were committed to.

The former finance secretary S Narayan, now a visiting senior research fellow at the National University of Singapore, agrees with the impression. Addressing a select session of foreign policy experts at Mumbai this year, he wondered, 'Did we miss an opportunity to secure the Indian Ocean sometime ago?' According to him, how China uses the Indian Ocean would be 'very important' for India to assess going ahead.

It is this context which makes the heads of the Indian Ocean islands valuable guests in New Delhi, Canberra and Beijing. A telling photograph from the visit by Abdul Gayoom to New Delhi in April is him seated at a desk signing on a visitors' book with Modi standing right behind him looking over his shoulder. It was the only visual evidence of how they worked together during the visit. 'The Prime Minister's Office decided not to conduct a press conference by the two leaders, a norm when a foreign dignitary visits India and holds talks with the Prime Minister'.

Indian analysts have long held on to a position that it will be a matter of concern if Beijing begins to own some of those ports it is building for foreign governments in the Indian Ocean. So far it has not. But China has begun to pump in inducements to make the large number of small Indian Ocean-based island states agree to do so.

It was partly for this reason that Prime Minister Modi decided to attend the funeral of Lee Kuan Yew in March 2015. There was a personal reason too. Lee was 'a torchbearer of hope, not just for Singapore, but for all of Asia', wrote Modi in the condolence book, but the timing of the visit just after a three-nation tour of Seychelles, Mauritius and Sri Lanka was noticed. The *Nikkei Asian Review* said, 'Modi trips mark sea change in India's foreign policy' punning on the word sea. It explained that despite all of its oil imports using the Indian Ocean

> For more than six decades since independence, New Delhi has been preoccupied with defending long and disputed land borders with Pakistan and China, neglecting the Indian Ocean in spite of its strategic importance. Modi's visits signalled that initiatives to forge new regional partnerships with littoral countries are now under way, replacing India's former focus on regional groupings confined to the Asian continent.

It was the first time in thirty-four years that an Indian prime minister visited Seychelles.

It could not be otherwise. Of the 1.5 billion MT of coal India expects to provide its manufacturing industries by 2020, a third will come from abroad. That means securing the mines abroad and getting the coal from them safely back to the shores.

As the *Nikkei Asian Review* went on to note, the flurry of visits just after taking over was driven by one concern—to outflank China.

> In all three Indian Ocean countries that Modi visited, China has taken economic and strategic initiatives over the last few years, in line with its view of the oceans as an increasingly important arena of political, economic, military and technological competition, and its aspirations to become a maritime power. The Seychelles offered refuelling and docking facilities to Chinese warships involved in anti-piracy operations. In Mauritius, China's state-led investment in a special economic zone muscled India aside. And in Sri Lanka, China has invested billions of dollars in loans and infrastructure ventures. Much to New Delhi's annoyance, a Chinese warship and two submarines visited Colombo port last year.

Modi has left behind a permanent relic as a reminder of his visit to the islands. In both Seychelles and Mauritius, he inaugurated

India-built coastal surveillance radar systems. 'These will eventually be integrated with India's coastal monitoring network with the aim of tracking what a senior Indian diplomat referred to as the moves of unsavoury elements in the region.' In the 1970s, the USA had offered a similar facility to New Delhi from its base in Diego Garcia. India had rebuffed the offer at that time. In addition, it offered a $500 million concessional line of credit to Mauritius for 'key infrastructure projects' as the two nations signed five pacts. In the island, the key infrastructure is obviously port. 'I consider our security cooperation to be a cornerstone of our strategic partnership. We intend to quickly build the petroleum storage and bunkering facility in Mauritius', Modi said at the signing of the pacts with Mauritian prime minister Anerood Jugnauth.

One of the islands the prime minister did not visit was the Maldives, where Indian business GMR saw its airport project expropriated in 2011. For long, India has been squeamish about even acknowledging its role vis-à-vis these nations, though Seychelles enjoys the same relation with India as nearer home Bhutan does.

To patch up the differences in April 2016, as Gayoom winged in to India, strategic affairs analyst Rajeev Sharma wrote that India and Maldives had signed on to defence cooperation. He wrote, 'A key feature of the defence pact based on sources-based information is that India will supply critical defence equipment and hardware to the Maldives and will train Maldives defence personnel'.

Few of them are as valuable as the footprint India has secured at Chabahar, the Iranian port. India will build two docks at the port, one for containers and another for oil. The journey to Chabahar from the coal trade at the mouth of the Hooghly has taken more than a hundred years.

It is a part of India's Spice Route Initiative. 'The Spice Route Initiative is both important and timely with India seeking to once again emerge as a major centre of international trade and transport as well as a maritime power', President Pranab Mukherjee noted in Kerala this year. The setting of the speech though was incongruous. Mukherjee declared the initiative at the launch of a heritage project in the coastal state for conservation of maritime museums along with a number of other archaeological monuments to be implemented by the Kerala tourism department.

The Chabahar Port project sits in the middle of the gradual build-up by India to have a dominant say in the maritime business of

Indian Ocean. While there has been fair amount of attention paid to the prospect of what one would call the second rung of business, namely export of manufactured goods, India would seek to market in Central Asia including Afghanistan and in turn import mostly textile and agro products through Chabahar, the key to the importance of this Iranian port lies in its possible role in the commodity trade in minerals that India sees as essential to subserve its energy needs. There are other ports that are expected to be part of this ambitious agenda. It is not surprising that at the commemoration event for the Chabahar Port, Modi flagged this context when he said, 'In the Indo-Pacific, a rise (of) a mix of political competition and economic opportunities is putting pressure on the existing Asian order'. Unlike Pranab, he did not choose a backwater to make sure that the right audience heard him.

It is in this context that one should examine the projected role of the special purpose vehicle New Delhi has floated to run the port project, the Indian Ports Global Private Limited. It will be a holding company with equity participation by JNPT and Kandla Port Trust. As per the MoU signed with Iran, India will equip and operate two berths in the first phase of the project with a capital investment of $85.21 million and a projected annual revenue expenditure of $22.95 million on a ten-year lease. 'Ownership of equipment will be transferred to Iranian side on completion of 10 year period or for an extended period, based on mutual agreement. The Iranian side had requested for provision of a credit of $150 million', India's largest ever financial outlay to a foreign government so far. Kandla will run the general berth and JNPT the container berth. For Europe, coal is out of the door and oil is drawing closer to the door. For India, and even for China, the investments will run for at least two more decades. So, the money on developing the ports will be well spent.

Indian Ports Global will invest not only in Tehran, but it has also already signed a MoU for another port closer home at Payra in Bangladesh. More than any of the other Indian state-owned entities set up to secure its economic interests abroad, this is the one which could consequently occupy the pole position soon. Just as Chabahar will provide an alternative to Bandar Abbas in Iran, Payra will seek to do the same with Chittagong port in neighbouring Bangladesh. Both are deep sea ports, a rarity for India struggling to find anchorage for its deep-draught vessels. None of them are meant to be anchorages for military vessels at this stage though. And plans to add to them at Mozambique, Seychelles and Mauritius are already in the works, say government officials at New Delhi. There is no doubt that the race for building ports in the Indian Ocean to secure friends in the busiest energy sea-borne lanes has begun in earnest.

Just as Chabahar sits next to the port, China is building for Pakistan at Gwadar—it is incidentally an 'insurance against supply disruptions through the narrow Strait of Malacca'—similarly Payra will have a Chinese investment in a 1,320 MW thermal power plant sitting next door to keep a watch on India's maritime foray.

9

Energy Ambitions

In his second cabinet reshuffle since he came to power at the Centre, Prime Minister Narendra Modi made a change which pretty much demonstrates the direction he thinks the Indian energy economy is headed for. He clubbed the portfolio of mines within the domain of his ebullient colleague Piyush Goyal who was already in charge of the ministries of power, coal and renewable energy. It is quite on the cards that in another few months, the coal and mines ministries would be merged into a single entity.

Does it mean the end of India's love affair with coal? It is a bit more complicated.

For the first time in India since the 1950s, all the energy ministries are now held between just two ministers. Even more, since neither Pradhan nor Goyal holds a cabinet rank, the overarching control of India's energy policy rests with the prime minister.

Modi is likely to know it well. How India plays its energy card matters a lot to the world in 2016. It is the third-largest consumer of coal behind China and the USA. On the basis of IMF World Economic Outlook report of April 2016, the world economy was then on the equivalent of a wing and a prayer. Only one and a half economies show any reasonable sign of sustained growth to make a significant impact on the global stage for the rest of this decade. They are India and China, in that order.

In a paper written for Nature Geoscience in 2016, Qi Ye, Nicolas Stern, Tong Wu, Jiaqi Lu and Fergus Green estimated that China's coal consumption decreased by 2.9 per cent in 2014 and 3.6 per cent in 2015, though 'the economy has maintained a moderate speed of growth. This indicates that there is a decoupling of economic growth from the growth in coal consumption. China's coal consumption might have in fact already peaked'.

That sort of decoupling would send shivers down the Indian energy complex. For India, coal is far more than a fuel. Coal companies contribute both as employers and as powerful GDP force multipliers. A shutdown of this economy with a shift to renewable energy is not an easy choice. India is still, in the words of

Daniel Yergin, the author of *The Prize*, the most definitive history of global oil economy, 'a hydrocarbon man'.

The pressure is rising though. In early September 2016, the US President, Barack Obama, travelled to China where the two countries formally announced their ratification of the Paris Agreement. *The Guardian* reported that the move was 'the result of weeks of intense negotiations'. Patched against the time table for ratification of global treaties, the coming into force of the climate action was done at lightning speed—the commitment by the two largest emitters was made in less than a year after Paris. They add to 38 per cent of global emissions; India is at 4.1 per cent. India too has followed soon after offering the Paris Accord the record for the fastest-ever global commitment. That could unravel though once the Trump administration decides on its priorities. Unravelling of those gives India a window it badly needs to reorder its energy landscape.

Elements of Reorder

One of those has already gone through. Unimaginable some years ago, the coal ministry has been reduced to relative insignificance. It is a huge success as Swarup himself pointed out. With its emasculated role, India has managed to wipe off a large embedded economy of privileged access to natural resources stretching from land to telecom airwaves. For any future Indian government to regress into an era where ministers or officers can again hand out a piece of government property without opting for transparent bidding for the resource is impossible to countenance. Not many countries can claim this piece of distinction.

Among the range of government actions since the liberalisation of 1991, the auctions of coal block appear more significant than possibly any other in the past twenty-five years. In any public discussion of black money, coal has always found a ready recall. All reports that dwelt on the Indian business–political–black money nexus had coal as a reference point. Since the industry also straddled the poorest geographical areas of India, the activities surrounding them also had an outsized demonstration effect. The Congress discovered this to its cost in the 2014 general elections.

The risks from the sector have not been smoked away. The privately run mines may have fallen quiet. Changes at a larger scale are happening in the mines run by CIL. They are getting taken over by mine development operator, essentially getting mechanised. It is an area of potential governance risk, given CIL's spotty record in handling of tenders. Former CIL Chairman Narsing Rao described it graphically to me, 'It was amazing how keen some of my directors (at CIL) were, to join as chairman of the subsidiary companies. As chairmen they could be like maharajahs, dole out favours. These companies for example, even buy explosives for hundreds of crore of rupees'.

Beyond the immediate political risks of reordering the energy economy is an even more sizable one. Shutting the coal shop too soon will release an unemployment hurricane.

The size of the coal economy is massive. CIL itself employs close to 350,000 people directly, of them over half are employed in West Bengal, Bihar and Jharkhand—each densely populated and highly unemployed state where these are the most-prized jobs. It provides indirect employment to close to double that number.

Those trends are already changing disconcertingly. Deep inside Shyamsundarpur Colliery in West Bengal, run by ECL which is the weakest subsidiary of CIL, within the ghostly white-painted long rows of coal tunnels it is rare to find a worker even as the noisy machines cut through the coal layers. Shyamsundarpur is one of the largest of the collieries of ECL that is on the verge of becoming totally mechanised. As coal companies are handed stiff targets, they are shifting to machines. Instead of 2,000 odd men employed per shift in this colliery next to Durgapur industrial town, the numbers are now about a tenth per shift. Since the output per man shift is abysmal in CIL mines, the result of the switchover to total mechanisation has been awesome. To ensure that it stays that way, the mining companies have begun to lease out their mines to mine development operators in the private sectors. Those are entirely mechanised operations.

As the perennial coal shortage turns to oversupply across mines like Shyamsundarpur, the unions are livid. The 'unions, with a history of hostility towards management, are pushing back on Coal India's plans, fearing modernisation and outsourcing will hit jobs', noted a report by Reuters in May 2016. 'High-tech mining will mean fewer job opportunities for labourers and no job guarantee for existing employees', Baijnath Rai, president of BMS, which claims to represent 100,000 CIL employees and contractors, told the wire agency.

As of now, from the seventy-five mines handed out via auctions and allocations post the SC order, only 8.49 million tonnes of coal has been dug out. Most of these mines are in the equivalent of mothballed conditions. At the private companies-run mines at Singrauli, Mahan and Mand Raigarh, sites of pitched battles for control until 2014, idle machineries can be seen lined up for acres.

At the sites of these closed private sector mines, unemployment is thus rising. Entire communities like those of Singrauli town in Madhya Pradesh which is pretty much dependant on coal economy face deep trouble. By district-wise employment register, the number of unemployed in the district is 31,237 in 2016 or over 7 per cent of the working age population. This is way above the national average of 3.6 per cent calculated by the Government of India's National Sample Survey Organisation. Reckoning through a thirty-day moving average statistic which the BSE has launched with the Centre for Monitoring Indian Economy (CMIE) this year might provide more accurate answers, but the data as of now is in beta stage. This statistic shows the national average at about 9 per cent since it was launched. Because of the difficulty of collecting data, actual unemployment statistics from districts in the deep interior such as Singrauli would not show up soon. When it does so, the chances are that it will be correspondingly higher. In fact, the initiative by BSE is a response to lack of timely data on employment trends in the economy which successive governments are naturally reluctant to hang out in the public. Local newspapers such as *Rajasthan Patrika* in Singrauli frequently carry banner headline making fun of the employment fairs the district administration puts up: *rozgaar ke naam par berozgaron se thuggi* (looting the unemployed by offers of employment). It is like a powder keg waiting to explode.

As CIL mines get mechanised and private mines stay mothballed, this pile-up of unemployed population will have a profoundly unsettling effect on the choices available for a switchover to cleaner energy. The 2016 global employment report card of International Renewable Energy Agency (IRENA) estimates that currently there are just 416,000 Indians employed in the sector. With the best of effort, this number will reach only 1.1 million by

2022. And remember, estimates by international agencies are often a bit exaggerated. 'However, meeting skills requirements (30% of these jobs would be highly skilled) requires stepping up training and educational initiatives'. Of more worry is the emerging trend in the sector. Solar panels, liquid bio-fuels and wind power are the three largest sources of employment in the renewable sector, and each have begun to displace labour big time. 'Employment in liquid bio-fuels declined by 6% in 2015 to reach 1.7 million. This was mainly due to continued mechanisation in countries such as the United States and Brazil and falling production in others like Indonesia'. These three countries account for the bulk of bio-fuel production in the world.

Yet globally respected organisations like Geneva-based International Institute for Sustainable Development is pushing the G-20 nations to switch off public funding for fossil fuel companies with a deadline of 2020. Swarup said that it made no sense, 'In my discussions with some of them I said show me the alternative'.

There are really few. One of those is to decarbonise the transport sector by carting a larger share of freight traffic on railways instead of roads! While greenhouse gas emissions have stabilised over most sectors by the 2000s, the share of transport in emissions of carbon dioxide has risen. The share of transport in worldwide carbon dioxide emissions is now one-fourth compared with one-sixth in the 1980s.

Most of the rise now comes from non-OECD (the Organisation for Economic Co-operation and Development) countries, typically China and India. Within transport sector, the biggest jump comes from road transport. The Intergovernmental Panel on Climate Change data show that its carbon footprint outdistances other forms of transport in the ratio 3:1. The volume is expected to double by the year 2050. Within road transport, the largest share of these gases will come from freight transport. It thus makes enormous sense to plan a shift away from road to rail for freight transport.

The catch! There is no global success for the model to lean on.

Suresh Prabhu's rail ministry wants to capture at least 45 per cent of the total freight traffic by 2046–2047 from the current share of less than 30 per cent. International experience shows that this will be a first of sorts if it happens. Over the past 15 years, the share of freight on railways as compared with roads has declined in every key rail network of the world.

Whether it is the mega railway networks of the USA, China or Russia or the small but efficient rail networks of Japan and Switzerland, the railroads have lost out to roads.

The success or failure of the shift of freight traffic to rail is, however, quite pivotal to India's chance to meet the Intended Nationally Determined Contributions (INDC) targets to reduce its energy intensity by 33–35 per cent by the year 2030 from the level of 2005. A lower intensity means higher efficiency in powering GDP growth.

The railways strategy aims to lower its own energy footprint from the current levels by shifting from diesel to electric traction. At the same time, it wishes to capture more share of the freight business from the roadways.

Professor Dinesh Mohan, India's leading authority on transport sector, said that the Indian Railways was flying in the face of international experience in assuming that such a large volume of freight traffic would gravitate towards it.

Data from the European Union (EU) countries showed that he was right. Rail freight traffic as percentage of total surface transport had declined to just 23 per cent by 2014 from close to 37 per cent in 2001. In the USA, it had dipped from 42 per cent to 39.5 per cent in the same period. Canada had also followed the same route and so had China.

This has implications.

In 2015, Prabhu's ministry set up a dedicated directorate of environment to lead the challenge. Typical of government functioning, the rail bureaucracy moved to scuttle it, saddling it with additional responsibilities too like housekeeping of the giant rail machinery. Also, typical of the government, it does not have much of powers to enforce a change in business practices within the railway empire. Chief of the department, K Swaminathan, advisor, environment, however, exuded an air of confidence, 'We are confident of a phase change once the work on the Western and Eastern Dedicated Freight Corridors gets completed'. The work should be largely over by 2020 according to railway estimates. By then, the railways estimates that it will carry 1,117 billion traffic kilometres at a compounded average growth rate or CAGR of 9 per cent. This is a huge level of expectations.

Saon Ray, senior fellow at ICRIER, is sceptical about the numbers. She has authored a recent report on decarbonisation of Indian Railways; her calculation shows that railway freight traffic has grown at a CAGR of much lower 5.43 per cent between 2003 and 2015. 'The trend of low growth in freight transport is expected to continue till (railways) improves the speed and quality of freight service'. She does not see that happening for the next five years.

To come anywhere close to even retain the current share of goods traffic business, the railways has to double the single-line tracks at the rate of 2,000 km every year until 2020. This is in addition to the 400 km of new track it must lay out at the same time.

To begin to wean freight traffic from the road sector, the railways must depend on the addition in route length which will come from the dedicated freight corridor. The target is 3,376 km.

There are further complications. By the year 2030, the railways as part of INDC plans to move 80 per cent of its passenger traffic and 100 per cent of its freight traffic to electric haulage. That is just fifteen years away, yet the current railway electric traction is just 40 per cent of its total route length. Ray points out that since electric engines are 10 per cent less effective to start a train and also when pulling the wagons along, the railways will have to invest correspondingly much more on electric locomotives. So the transformation to a less carbon footprint can actually mean loss of freight traffic share by the railways.

To bring so many moving pieces together, you need the PMO to stay in the loop. And one of those which need a top-level intervention is privatisation.

Privatisation

Commercial coal mining companies need to be allowed into the sector. Goyal has allowed state-owned companies to sell their coal on commercial basis. Allowing private sector miners like Rio Tinto or BHP Billiton to do the same needs a sanction from the Parliament. It could even be an Indian company, but the law needs to be changed. Unlike auctions of coal mines mandated by SC order, does the government have the stomach for the legislative change?

Swarup and Goyal have a thin window to pass the law to unwound 40 years of nationalisation. Just like Goods and Services Tax (GST), this will necessitate deep dialogue with the state parties. The year 2017–2018 is the last effective year of governance for the

NDA's five-year term. If it does not happen now, there is no way such an explosive plan can run in an election year. It will then have to wait for a new government to come in.

Goyal has managed to bring in several changes in the hoary rules on how companies use the coal they mine. All of these have used the window offered by the SC verdict and so are based on executive orders. In other words, it is not yet tested if these will hold if some disgruntled parties contest them in a court. India does not lack in such pro bono spirit. It is for these reasons companies find more reassurance in the minister's presence than in constructs like coal portal.

As of now, the government is replicating the way it circumvented the role of Bharat Sanchar Nigam Limited (BSNL) and Mahanagar Telephone Nigam Limited (MTNL) when opening up the telecom sector or that of Air India when doing so for civil aviation sector. CIL is more difficult as the Coal Mines (Nationalisation) Act of 1973 fuses the role of the company with that of the sector as a monopoly producer. One of the ways forward could be to make CIL also bid for mines in the auctions instead of allotments made to it. The other is, of course, to split CIL into its constituent companies.

Swarup says that this may not help since the companies are almost independent in their operations. One would, however, feel that it is easy to split them and offer competition among them. Each company would bid to run the mines better bringing in their expertise. Currently, the better-run ones like MCL operate tougher mines, while loss-making BCCL and ECL sit on rich ones.

Rajiv Kumar, senior fellow at the Centre for Policy Research and director, Pahle India Foundation, is emphatic about privatisation. According to him, it is a given that CIL will not be able to produce clean coal or even ramp up production significantly.

> We may not like it, but the fact is CIL cannot ramp up production to the level we all would want them to. Like China, we should also be producing three billion tonnes of coal every year. This makes the case much stronger for getting on to commercial mining.

Privatisation is also a key assumption on the basis of which the US government's International Energy Outlook 2016 has estimated that India's coal production will expand strongly from 2015 to 2020 and eventually surpass that of the USA, 'making India the world's second-largest coal producer'.

Clean Coal

Saran met me at his office in India Habitat Centre attired in his trademark kurta and pyjama. The former foreign secretary, now chairman of the Research and Information Systems for Developing Countries, has espoused the role of clean coal for India to solve its energy riddle for a long time.

'Globally, I don't see the role of coal coming down much in the next two decades', he said. More so, in the Indian energy mix! The option he said to try out was clean coal.

Clean coal takes its name from application of super critical technology in the production of power. When water is used to produce steam at very high temperatures, the coal burning becomes far more efficient giving off less toxic fumes into the environment. That water in turn can move the turbines to produce far higher megawatts of power than what sub-critical technology can provide. But this requires engineering of the plant with a quality of metal that few countries possess or are willing to give.

Post the signing of the civil nuclear deal with the USA, the Manmohan Singh government got interested in getting this technology. Saran said that the Indian atomic energy establishment began to provide valuable support at that stage. He said, 'When I had called the first meetings with all agencies they were not enthusiastic as several attempts to soak in frontier technology into Indian industry had run aground. But as I kept pushing in subsequent meetings, they got very interested'.

By 2013, Saran's team was successful. He said, 'Under the Clean Coal Mission and we have already witnessed success in developing a prototype for a 880 MW supercritical plant'. Again, for no good reason, it was mothballed for two years thereafter. In August 2015, the Modi government offered a cabinet approval for a proposal to fund the 'research and development of AUSC technology for thermal power plants at an estimated cost of ₹1,554 crore (over $230 million)'. In terms of spending power, it is not much but it assures that the final prototype could be ready by 2019. A report by *Economic Times* said, 'The timeline for the *actual* construction of an actual 800 MW power plant with AUSC boiler would depend on the regulatory approvals for the plant design and the funding of the plant construction'. No country has reached there, but then no country needs the technology as badly as India, not even the

USA which still runs 40 per cent of its power plants on coal. But then India can also procrastinate. The possibility of supercritical technology was introduced in the Indian policy circle in 2006—it has been a decade since then to the approval for a prototype.

Clean coal meanwhile will have to be imported. Along with the technology! One of those places from where it could come is Japan. 'The sustainable coal fired power plant in Yokohama has a tennis court and a park inside. No carbon footprint!', tweeted the member secretary of Niti Aayog Amitabh Kant after a visit there. Under him, Niti Aayog is working to decide if it can be fitted to India too.

A news report said that in two of Japan's infamous nuclear sites Hiroshima and Fukushima, the Japanese government and industry are backing emerging coal technologies which 'they say are less damaging to the environment'.

Japan has backed continued financing of investment in the coal sector, making it one of the rare allies of India in the G-20. A government-backed demonstration project uses a technology called integrated gasification fuel cell combined cycle (IGFC) in two stages. In the first stage, it heats or cooks coal to produce gas to be burned in a turbine. The waste heat from there drives a steam turbine to produce electricity. In the next stage, some of the captured emissions are used to power a fuel cell to generate more electricity.

These is still a long way from being commercially viable. Meanwhile, a similar project in the USA at Kemper in Mississippi has run into cost and time trouble. A report in *The New York Times* describes it as follows:.

> The Kemper coal plant is more than two years behind schedule and more than $4 billion over its initial budget, $2.4 billion, and it is still not operational. The plant and its owner, Southern Company, are the focus of a Securities and Exchange Commission investigation, and ratepayers, alleging fraud, are suing the company. Members of Congress have described the project as more boondoggle than boon.

Even with such technology, India will need to import plain superior grade coal. This means India will have to keep its supply lines from abroad intact, as well as keep room within its foreign exchange reserves to buy space for these imports. 'We will look for technologies for clean coal as this will be the mainstay in India's fuel mix even as we strive to address climate concerns', Goyal said last year to the Japanese minister of economy, trade and industry,

Yoichi Miyazawa. On a visit to New Delhi, Miyazawa agreed with the assessment. He said, 'Coal is geographically available and will remain an important energy source'.

So, will India keep on adding to the demand for coal for some more years but expect progressively more of it to be bought from abroad? Since the prices abroad are unlikely to shoot up significantly, even the smaller companies will join the queue.

The scare for the coal and the larger energy economy at this stage is the global slump in manufacturing.

Post-manufacturing Society

Quite on cue with global trends, the Indian manufacturing sector too is slipping up. No country has managed to push up the share of manufacturing as a share of total employment to above 45 per cent. This was the level achieved by UK before the First World War. It has gone down since then to less than 10 per cent. No other country has come close.

India has peaked at close to 13 per cent and is in a decline since. The trends are visible all round. Industrial cities such as Rourkela, Bhilai and Tuticorin are giving up their population in the core areas to the suburbs where self-employment and service sector employment have sprung up. As the data from the renewable sector show, the additional numbers from there are unlikely to change this trend till 2030.

As ballast for the manufacturing sector coal, has played a major role until now. Does it still have some years to go before its usage peaks? Kant's Niti Aayog had estimated that the demand for coal would peak at 1.5 billion MT as India pushes its manufacturing output to about 24 per cent of the GDP. China, as the article by Qi Ye et al. showed, may have already crossed the peak.

What if this scenario for higher import does not play out taking cue from global trends or even if it plays out, ends up with a huge spike in energy efficiency, that is, larger carbon footprint? Both have implications for the energy sector and none of them are promising.

The first of the scenarios follow from Dani Rodrik's de-industrialisation thesis. The Harvard professor made two (now) famous postulates. According to him, countries on an average specialise less in manufacturing the closer they are to the recent decades and this is true for all nations irrespective of where they stand on the scale of development. His next hypothesis is that this process of de-industrialisation or giving up on manufacturing is happening earlier in the development process for more countries.

Taking the argument further, Arvind Subramanian in a 2014 piece argued that the hypotheses tallied with the development record of all Indian states. With Amrit Amirapu of Boston University, Subramanian studied the data of how much of each states' GDP was attributable to the manufacturing sector. According to him, no Indian state had been immune to both of Rodrik's hypotheses.

> Gujarat has been the only state in which registered manufacturing as a share of GDP surpassed 20% and came anywhere close to levels achieved by the major manufacturing successes in East Asia. Even in Maharashtra and Tamil Nadu, manufacturing at its peak accounted for only about 18 to 19 per cent of state GDP.

> Second, in nearly all states (with the possible exception of Himachal Pradesh), manufacturing is now declining and has been doing so for a long time…. Third, and this is perhaps the most sobering of facts, manufacturing has even been declining in the poorer states: states that never effectively industrialised (West Bengal, Uttar Pradesh and Rajasthan) have started de-industrialising.

In an article for *Business Standard*, the two authors showed that Uttar Pradesh had reached its peak share of manufacturing at about 10 per cent of GDP in 1996, at a per capita state domestic product of about $1,200 (PPP dollars). In comparison, Brazil attained its peak share of 31 per cent at a per capita GDP of $7,100.

The implications are severe. There is scarce possibility in the face of the Rodrik hypotheses for aggregate manufacturing in India to reach 24 per cent or even 20 per cent at any point in the future. In which case, there is even less possibility that the demand for coal to power the sector will reach anywhere close to 1.5 billion MT. Less manufacturing means less demand for coal and other fuels. By the middle of 2016, government officials were coming around to this view.

In a recent dialogue with *Swarajya* magazine editorial director, R Jagannathan, Nandan Nilekani made this apprehension open. He said that it was impossible for the manufacturing economy of India as it was evolving to be a magnet for attracting employment.

He said, 'Only a few categories of work in the formal sector will stand up to the onslaught. Most people will become self employed'.

A pretty important requirement for the phalanx of self-employed would be power. Experiments in deployment of off-grid technology become vital in this context.

Kaushik Bandyopadhyay and Debajit Palit, both professors at TERI University, pointed this out. In Sagardweep Island in the Sunderbans region in West Bengal in India,

> [W]ithin a short spell of time of four years, there have been noticeable improvements and significant impact on education, trade and commerce, entertainment, health etc. as a result of the supply of power from solar power plants. The power supply at night has helped the shopkeepers, tailors, betel leaf cultivators to continue their night time activities for a longer period. Similarly, another study in the same region observes that the supply of solar power has helped, though on a small scale, to run the video hall, battery charging centre, etc.

Depending on which model you would prefer, the contours of India's energy economy spread out accordingly. On the plus side in a span of less than three years, a century and more of uncertainty on energy supply has been largely sorted. Already, the memories of coal shortages and the terrible attendant cost of pilferage, purchase of political power and overall cost to the economy seem to be an echo from a long way off. The Indian population as every demographer points out is a young one—the corollary to that is that attention span moves on. For instance, the massive uproar around the scams that swept them up in 2011–2013, with coal occupying centre stage, has become the past.

At the same time, the future has become uncertain, thanks to the geopolitical turbulences. They make any plausible estimate for the years ahead maddeningly difficult. In a softer era, an event like Brexit or the pause in China would itself have pushed the global economy into a meltdown. In the case of India, add to it the effect of two successive droughts and a public policy crisis, it was a given that the economy would hiccup badly.

Instead, the Indian economy as former RBI Governor Raghuram Rajan has pointed out is holding steady and growing amazingly fast. The economy has calibrated to expectations that inflation will remain low. These adjustments as he pointed out were initially 'difficult and painful in the short run. (But) We must not get diverted as we build the institutions necessary to secure a low inflation future'. He picked out for attention the possibility that India will have a 'low inflation future'. In the past when inflation went spiralling upwards, scare around coal and energy economics in Indian economy happened.

A low inflationary trend makes a return of such episodes of scandals unlikely in the future. This offers space for new ideas in public life. In few towns of India, youngsters do want to invest in a future that is a throwback to one based on shortages of fossil fuel, which only produced decades of poverty.

Digital India and Startup India Initiatives in the coal cities of Dhanbad, Rourkela or Bhilai find little reason to share public space with the old-world feel of carbon economy.

There is of course no way that a carbonless footprint will emerge immediately. That would be a ridiculous expectation at this stage. But instead of setting the agenda for the economy, it is fair to assume that coal and the larger fuel economies have receded to the background to do best what they are meant to do—power the economy without glitches.

Bibliography

Chapter 1

1. Suresh Chandra, 'India: Flood Management—Damodar River Basin'. In *Integrated Flood Management—Case Study*, edited by Technical Support Unit, December 2003. Available at: http://www.apfm.info/publications/casestudies/cs_india_full.pdf (Accessed on 29 December 2016).
2. Ranjan Borra. *Subhas Chandra Bose, The Indian National Army, and The War of India's Liberation*, Institute for Historical Review. Available at: http://www.ihr.org/jhr/v03/v03p407_borra.html (Accessed on 29 December 2016).
3. Christopher Bayly and Tim Harper. *Forgotten Armies: Britain's Asian Empire and the War with Japan.*UK: Penguin, 2005.
4. 'Second Five Year Plan', Chapter 18, para 15. Planning Commission of India. Available at: http://planningcommission.nic.in/plans/planrel/fiveyr/2nd/2planch18.html (Accessed on 29 December 2016).
5. Nandan Nilekani. *Imagining India*, 452. New Delhi: Penguin, 2008.
6. Ravi Velloor. *India Rising*, 228. New Delhi: Konark Publishers, 2016.

Chapter 2

1. Tathagata Roy. *Life and Times of Shyama Prasad Mookerjee*. New Delhi: Prabhat Prakashan, 2012.
2. Narendra Jadhav. *Industrial Policy Since 1956*. Available at: http://www.drnarendrajadhav.info/drnjadhav_web_files/Published%20papers/Indian%20Industrial%20Policy%20Since%201956.pdf (Accessed on 29 December 2016).
3. Frank Moraes. *Jawaharlal Nehru*, 125, 235. New Delhi: Jaico Publishing, 2007.
4. Amal Sanyal. 'The Curious Case of the Bombay Plan'. *Contemporary Issues and Ideas in Social Sciences*, (June 2010). Available at: http://citeseerx.ist.psu.edu/viewdoc/download?doi=10.1.1.680.334&rep=rep1&type=pdf (Accessed on 29 December 2016).
5. Nitish Sengupta. *Bengal Divided—The Unmaking of a Nation*, 479. New Delhi: Penguin, 2011.
6. Bakhtiar Dadabhoy. *Barons of Banking*. Gurugram: Random House India, 2013.
7. 'Speech of Shri R.K. Shanmukham Chetty, Minister of Finance Introducing the Budget for the Year 1947–1948'. Available at: indiabudget.nic.in/bspeech/bs194748.pdf (Accessed on 29 December 2016).

8. Sumit K Majumdar. 'Finance and Commerce Pool: An Old-is-gold Idea'. *The Hindu—Business Line*, 2 December 2006. Available at: http://www.thehindu-businessline.com/todays-paper/tp-opinion/article1753620.ece (Accessed on 29 December 2016).

9. 'Industrial Policy Resolution 1948'. Ministry of Micro, Small, & Medium Enterprises. Available at: http://www.dcmsme.gov.in/policies/iip.htm (Accessed on 29 December 2016).

10. Tirthankar Roy. *Trading Firms in Colonial India*. Harvard Business Studies, 2014. Available at: http://www.hbs.edu/businesshistory/Documents/roy-trading-firms-colonial-india.pdf (Accessed on 29 December 2016).

11. Geoffrey Jones. *Merchants to Multinationals: British Trading Companies in the Nineteenth and Twentieth Centuries*. New York: Oxford University Press, 2000.

12. Rajat Kanta Ray, ed. *Entrepreneurship and Industry in India, 1800–1947*. New Delhi: 1994.

13. 'Keshub Mahindra'. Available at: http://www.mahindra.com/about-us/history (Accessed on 29 December 2016).

14. Ranjan Borra. 'Subhas Chandra Bose, The Indian National Army, and The War of India's Liberation'. Institute for Historical Review. Available at: http://www.ihr.org/jhr/v03/v03p407_borra.html (Accessed on 29 December 2016).

15. Nasir Tyabji. 'Private Industry and the Second Five Year Plan: The Mundhra Episode as Exemplar of Capitalist Myopia'. Working Paper No. 2010/04, Institute for Studies in Industrial Development, May 2010. Available at: http://isidev.nic.in/pdf/WP1004.PDF (Accessed on 29 December 2016).

16. Blair B Kling. *Partner in Empire: Dwarkanath Tagore and the Age of Enterprise in Eastern India*. California: University of California Press, 1976.

17. John F Riddick. *The History of British India: A Chronology*. Connecticut: Greenwood Publishing Group, 2006.

18. 'Guru Jones and Bengal Coal'. Available at: http://shodhganga.inflibnet.ac.in:8080/jspui/bitstream/10603/22094/11/11_chapter%206.pdf

19. 'Coal after Carr Tagore incl Indian Entrepreneurship'. Available at: http://shodhganga.inflibnet.ac.in/bitstream/10603/22196/10/10_chapter%205.pdf

20. Kuntala Lahiri Dutt. *The Coal Nation: Histories, Ecologies and Politics of Coal in India*. New Delhi: Routledge, 2016.

21. Amitabha Ghosh. 'Guru Jones—A Private Engineer in the Colonial Trap'. *Indian Journal of History of Science* 32, no. 2 (1997): 139.

22. Amalesh Tripathi. 'Trade and Investments in the Bengal Presidency, Calcutta 1979'. In *Entrepreneurship and Industry in India 1800–1947*, edited by Rajat Kanta Ray, 220. New Delhi, 1994.

23. Famine Inquiry Commission. *Report of the Indian Famine Commission, 1880–1885, India*. Agricole Publishing Academy, 1989.

24. Raja Shiva Prasad of Jharia, https://indiankanoon.org/doc/321281/

25. Anubhuti Ranjan Prasad. *Coal Industry of India*. APH Publishing, 1986.

26. RM Lala. *The Creation of Wealth: The Tatas from the 19th to the 21st Century*. New Delhi: Penguin, 2006.

27. Sir Dorabji Tata—Tata Central Archives; http://www.tatacentralarchives.com/history/biographies/04%20djtata.htm (Accessed in October 2016).

Chapter 3

1. Ranbir Singh and Kushal Pal. 'Changing Roles of the Presidents of India'. *Mainstream Weekly* L, no. 34 (11 August 2012).
2. http://shodhganga.inflibnet.ac.in:8080/jspui/bitstream/10603/13974/12/12_chapter%2007.pdf
3. Michael Kidron. *Foreign Investments in India*, 133. London: Routledge, 2001.
4. Amal Sanyal. 'The Curious Case of the Bombay Plan'. *Contemporary Issues and Ideas in Social Sciences*, June 2010. Available at: http://citeseerx.ist.psu.edu/viewdoc/download?doi=10.1.1.680.334&rep=rep1&type=pdf (Accessed on 29 December 2016).
5. Gulzarilal Nanda. 'FICCI Letter to Deputy Chairman of Planning Commission'. FICCI, vol. II, 261, 6 November 1952.
6. AK Dasgupta. 'Socialistic Pattern of Society and the Second Five Year Plan'. *The Economic Weekly Annual* (January), 1957.
7. Vangal Thiruvenkatachari Krishnamachari. *Letter to Financial Times*, reproduced in Planning in India. New Delhi: Orient Longman, 1961.
8. Philip John Eldridge and London School of Economics and Political Science. *The Politics of Foreign Aid in India*. Weidenfeld & Nicolson, 1969.
9. 'Nehru on Oil'. *The Economic Weekly*, 1957. Available at: http://www.epw.in/system/files/pdf/1957_9/24/nehru_on_oil.pdf (Accessed on 29 December 2016).
10. Anubhuti Ranjan Prasad. *Coal Industry of India*. New Delhi: APH Publishing, 1986.
11. Cheryl Payer. *World Bank: A Critical Analysis*, 202. New York: NYU Press, 1982.
12. 'Post War Stream'. *Indian Steam Pages*. Available at: http://www.irfca.org/steam/postwar.html (Accessed on 29 December 2016).
13. 'Landmarks in CLW's History' Available at: http://elocos.railnet.gov.in/CLW/Landmarks.htm (Accessed on 29 December 2016).
14. Terushi Hara. 'Reflections on Postwar Technical Exchanges Between Japanese and French Railways'. *Japan Railway & Transport Review*, no. 27 (June 2001): 32–39.
15. Sumit Mitra. 'Close Call: The Mining and Allied Machinery Corporation, a Product of the Cold War, is in Doldrums'. 2000. Available at: http://indiatoday.intoday.in/story/mining-and-allied-machinery-corporation-a-product-of-the-cold-war-in-doldrums/1/245446.html (Accessed on 29 December 2016).
16. Shankkar Aiyar. *Accidental India*, 110. New Delhi: Aleph Book Company, 2012.
17. Gopa Sabharwal. 'Price of Cars' In *India Since 1947: The Independent Years*, 143. New Delhi: Penguin, 2007.
18. Vijay Joshi and Ian Malcolm David Little. *India: Macroeconomics and Political Economy, 1964–1991*. Washington, DC: World Bank Publications, 1994.
19. 'Cooking Fuel and Lighting'. Available at: http://censusmp.nic.in/censusmp/All-PDF/7.%20Chapter-5%20%20Cooking%20fuel%20and%20lighting.pdf (Accessed on 2 January 2017).
20. PN Dhar. *Indira Gandhi, the 'Emergency' and Indian Democracy*. New Delhi: Oxford University Press, 2000. Available at: http://rbidocs.rbi.org.in/rdocs/content/PDFs/90069.pdf (Accessed on 2 January 2017) [footnote on page 36 where a meeting with KN Raj is discussed].
21. Kaushik Basu and Annemie Martens. *Oxford Companion to Economics in India*. New Delhi: Oxford University Press, 2012.

22. Sukhamoy Chakravarty. *Report of the Fuel Policy Committee, India.* Planning Commission, 1974.

23. AM. 'A Forgotten Brilliance: An Explorer in the World of Ideas'. *The Telegraph,* 1 July 2013. Available at: http://www.telegraphindia.com/1130701/jsp/opinion/story_17025206.jsp#.V-kT5vl97IV (Accessed on 29 December 2016).

24. Rajiv Kumar. 'Nationalisation by Default: The Case of Coal in India'. *Economic and Political Weekly* 16, no. 18 (2 May 1981): 824–830. Available at: http://www.jstor.org/stable/4369782

25. 'Coking Coal Nationalisation Gazette'. Available at: http://coal.nic.in/sites/upload_files/coal/files/curentnotices/ca4_0_0.pdf (Accessed on 6 February 2017).

26. Arpita Asha Khanna. 'Governance in Coal Mining: Issues and Challenges'. Available at: http://www.teriin.org/projects/nfa/pdf/nfa-WkP9-coal-governance.pdf (Accessed on 29 December 2016).

27. 'Worker Condition in Coal Mines'. Available at: http://shodhganga.inflibnet.ac.in:8080/jspui/bitstream/10603/22094/11/11_chapter%206.pdf

28. 'The World's Worst Coal Mining Disasters'. 2014. Available at: http://www.mining-technology.com/features/feature-world-worst-coal-mining-disasters-china/ (Accessed on 29 December 2016).

29. Dilip Bobb. 'A Tragedy of Errors'. 2011. Available at: http://indiatoday.intoday.in/story/a-tragedy-of-errors/1/127286.html (Accessed on 29 December 2016).

Chapter 4

1. Rajesh Kumar Singh, Debjit Chakraborty and Rakteem Katakey. 'Stolen Coal Fuelling Varanasi's Underground Economy'. *The Mint,* 31 July 2014. Available at: http://www.livemint.com/Industry/FnNRBxuvtaRIXcbi5Od74M/Stolen-coal-fuelling-Varanasis-underground-economy.html (Accessed on 29 December 2016).

2. Alka Pande. 'A Slice of Sicily'. *Outlook* (19 December 2005). Available at: http://www.outlookindia.com/magazine/story/a-slice-of-sicily/229602 (Accessed on 29 December 2016).

3. Delwar Hussain. *Boundaries Undermined the Ruins of Progress on the Bangladesh–India Border.* New Delhi: Oxford University Press, 2013.

4. Special Correspondent. 'Abandoned Miners of Santhal Parganas'. *Economic and Political Weekly* 18, no. 40 (1 October 1983): 1690–1692. Available at: http://www.jstor.org/stable/4372550 (Accessed on 6 February 2017).

5. Shantanu Dutta and Praduman Choubey. 'Political Apathy Fans Jharia Fire'. *The Telegraph,* Friday, 12 December 2014. Available at: https://www.telegraph-india.com/1141212/jsp/frontpage/story_3335.jsp#.WGocDlN97IU (Accessed on 2 January 2017).

6. Prashant Pandey. 'Russian Consulate Writes to Jharkhand CM: BJP MLA Blocking Work, Seeking Money, Jobs' *The Indian Express,* 17 February 2016. Available at: http://indianexpress.com/article/india/india-news-india/russian-consulate-writes-to-jharkhand-cm-bjp-mla-blocking-work-seeking-money-jobs/ (Accessed on 30 December 2016).

7. Makarand Gadgil, Aniek Paul and Cordelia Jenkins. 'Manoj Jayaswal—The Man Who Fell to Earth'. *The Mint*, 7 September 2012. Available at: http://www.livemint.com/Politics/1XLKrsNKMztWUOmgjQ9CKN/The-man-who-fell-to-earth.html (Accessed on 30 December 2016).

8. Mukesh Bhardwaj. 'Political Fortunes of Jindals Set to Take a Hit'. *The Indian Express*, 11 April 2014. Available at: http://indianexpress.com/article/india/india-others/political-fortunes-of-jindals-set-to-take-a-hit/ (Accessed on 30 December 2016).

9. M Sabarinath and V Balasubramanian. 'Billion-dollar Couples: How Business Families in India Often Come Together Through Weddings'. *The Economic Times*, 3 January 2013. Available at: http://economictimes.indiatimes.com/industry/billion-dollar-couples-how-business-families-in-india-often-come-together-through-weddings/articleshow/17863726.cms (Accessed on 2 January 2017).

10. Govind Daga. 'CBI to Probe Central Collieries Action of Selling Captive Block Coal in Open Market'. *The Hitavada*. Available at: http://www.thehitavada.com/news-details/cbi-to-probe-central-collieries-action-of-selling-captive-block-coal-in-open-market (Accessed in June 2016).

11. *The Hindu*. 'Chargesheet Against Congress MP Vijay Darda, Son in Coal Scam'. *The Hindu*, 27 March 2014. Available at: http://www.thehindu.com/news/national/chargesheet-against-congress-mp-vijay-darda-son-in-coal-scam/article5839607.ece (Accessed on 30 December 2016).

12. Prayas (Energy Group). 'Comments and Feedback Regarding the Draft Documents for Auctioning Coal Mines under the Coal Mines (Special Provisions) Ordinance, 2014'. Available at: http://www.prayaspune.org/peg/publications/item/288-comments-and-feedback-regarding-the-draft-rules-proposed-to-be-notified-under-the-coal-mines-special-provisions-ordinance,-2014.html (Accessed on 30 December 2016).

13. *The Times of India*. 'Income Tax Sleuths Raid Aryan Coal Ltd'. *The Times of India*, 13 April 2012. Available at: http://timesofindia.indiatimes.com/city/nagpur/Income-tax-sleuths-raid-Aryan-Coal-Ltd/articleshow/12643974.cms (Accessed on 30 December 2016).

14. Shishir Arya. 'CBI Books Padmesh Gupta for Fraud, Conspiracy in Coal Washing'. *The Times of India*, 20 March 2015. Available at: http://timesofindia.indiatimes.com/city/nagpur/CBI-books-Padmesh-Gupta-for-fraud-conspiracy-in-coal-washing/articleshow/46627657.cms (Accessed on 30 December 2016).

15. Shishir Arya. 'Gupta Group's Closed Washery Business Gets Debt Recast'. *The Times of India*, 17 September 2014. Available at: http://timesofindia.indiatimes.com/city/nagpur/Gupta-groups-closed-washery-business-gets-debt-recast/articleshow/42653679.cms (Accessed on 30 December 2016).

16. M Rajshekhar. 'Ujjal Upadhyay: The Man Who Controls 14 Coal Blocks'. *The Economic Times*, 6 September 2012. Available at: http://economictimes.indiatimes.com/industry/indl-goods/svs/metals-mining/ujjal-upadhyay-the-man-who-controls-14-coal-blocks/articleshow/16275258.cms (Accessed on 2 January 2017).

17. Sumit Moitra. 'Supreme Court order on coal blocks puts EMTA under rating watch'. *Daily News & Analysis*, 13 October 2014. Available at: http://www.dnaindia.com/money/report-supreme-court-order-on-coal-blocks-puts-emta-under-rating-watch-2025491 (Accessed on 6 February 2017).

18. Shreya Jai and Vijay C Roy. 'EMTA Takes Punjab and Karnataka to Court on Coal Mining Rights'. *Business Standard.* Available at: http://www.business-standard.com/article/economy-policy/emta-takes-punjab-and-karnataka-to-court-on-coal-mining-rights-116020900442_1.html (Accessed on 2 January 2017).

19. *The Telegraph.* 'Jharkhand Diary'. *The Telegraph.* Available at: http://www.telegraph-india.com/1030120/asp/jharkhand/story_1589189.asp (Accessed on 2 January 2017).

20. Shyamlal Yadav. 'MoS with Coal "Ties" is Top Frequent Flyer'. 8 September 2012. Available at: http://indianexpress.com/article/news-archive/web/mos-with-coal-ties-is-top-frequent-flyer/ (Accessed on 30 December 2016).

21. Maulik Pathak, Utpal Bhaskar and Ruchira Singh. 'KSK Comes under Renewed Scrutiny'. *The Mint,* 13 September 2012. Available at: http://www.livemint.com/Politics/FLZAOttlK95ylKCWtsa4SI/KSK-under-renewed-scrutiny-over-coalfield-allocations.html (Accessed on 30 December 2016).

22. *The Financial Express.* 'Santosh Bagrodia, H C Gupta Prima Facie Committed Misconduct in Coal Scam'. *The Financial Express,* 30 January 2015. Available at: http://www.financialexpress.com/economy/santosh-bagrodia-h-c-gupta-prima-facie-committed-misconduct-in-coalscam/37022/ (Accessed on 30 December 2016).

23. 'Report No. 6 of 2012–13—Performance Audit of Ultra Mega Power Projects under Special Purpose Vehicles, Ministry of Power'. Comptroller and Auditor General of India. Available at: http://cag.gov.in/content/report-no-6-2012-13 -%E2%80%93-performance-audit-ultra-mega-power-projects-under-special-purpose (Accessed on 30 December 2016).

24. *The Financial Express.* 'Govt Aborts UMPP Bidding over Tepid Private Sector Response'. *The Financial Express,* 8 January 2015. Available at: http://www.financialexpress.com/economy/govt-aborts-umpp-bidding-over-tepid-private-sector-response/27586/ (Accessed on 30 December 2016).

Chapter 5

1. Press Information Bureau. 'Talabira Coal Block Allocation Matter'. 19 October 2013. Available at: http://www.pib.nic.in/newsite/erelease.aspx?relid=100125 (Accessed on 30 December 2016).

2. *The Indian Express.* 'Accused No. 6 Manmohan Singh: Court Summons Former PM over Hindalco Coal Block'. *The Indian Express,* 12 March 2015. Available at: http://indianexpress.com/article/india/india-others/coal-block-case-manmohan-singh-ex-coal-secy-parakh-hindalco-officials-summoned-as-accused/ (Accessed on 30 December 2016).

3. Archis Mohan. 'Judge Bharat Parashar: Man of Integrity Who Doesn't Spare the Guilty'. *Business Standard,* 11 March 2015. Available at: http://www.business-standard.com/article/current-affairs/judge-bharat-parashar-man-of-integrity-who-doesn-t-spare-the-guilty-115031101156_1.html (Accessed on 30 December 2016).

4. Harsh V Nair. 'CBI Chief's Lawyer Bursts into Coalgate Hearing with Anti-diary Argument'. *India Today,* 20 September 2014. Available at: http://indiatoday.intoday.in/story/2 g-scam-cbi-ranjit-sinha-supreme-court-vikas-singh-prashant-bhushan-diary-row-rm-lodha/1/383961.html (Accessed on 30 December 2016).

5. 'Manohar Lal Sharma vs the Principle Secretary & Ors. on 25 August 2014'. Available at: http://supremecourtofindia.nic.in/outtoday/wr120.pdf (Accessed on 2 January 2017).
6. Jairam Ramesh. *To the Brink and Back, India's 1991 Story*, 22. New Delhi: Rupa, 2015.
7. Kaushik Basu. *An Economist's Miscellany*. New Delhi: Oxford University Press.
8. Shankkar Aiyar. *Accidental India*: A History of The Nation's Passage through Crisis and Change. New Delhi: Aleph Book Company, 2012.
9. 'Eighth Five Year Plan'. Planning Commission. New Delhi Available at: http://planningcommission.nic.in/plans/planrel/fiveyr/8th/default.htm (Accessed on 30 December 2016).
10. RV Shahi. *Indian Power Sector: Challenge and Response: Compilation of Papers Presented during 1991–2001*. New Delhi: Excel Books India, 2006.
11. Kirit Parikh. *Integrated Energy Policy: Report of the Expert Committee*. Planning Commission, October 2006. Available at: http://planningcommission.nic.in/reports/genrep/rep_intengy.pdf (Accessed on 30 December 2016).
12. Subhomoy Bhattacharjee. 'Wheres the Bank Now'. *The Financial Express*, 19 September 2010. Available at: http://archive.financialexpress.com/news/column-where-s-the-bank-now-/683145/0 (Accessed on 30 December 2016).
13. Sunil Jain and Shefali Bhimal. 'Still Fighting Shy: Multinational Companies Continue to be Wary of India Despite Steps Like a More Open-door Policy to Foreign Investment'. *India Today*, 15 December 1991. Available at: http://indiatoday.intoday.in/story/low-returns-despite-new-open-door-policy/1/319208.html (Accessed on 30 December 2016).
14. *The Hindu Business Line*. 'Spotlight on Reforms'. *The Hindu Business Line*, 11 December 2014. Available at: http://www.thehindubusinessline.com/opinion/spotlight-on-reforms/article6683247.ece (Accessed on 30 December 2016).
15. Sameer Kochhar, ed. *An Agenda for Growth; Essays in Honour of P Chidambaram*, Chapter 15. New Delhi: Academic Foundation, 2013.
16. 'Open Casting'. *India Today*, 31 March 1993. Available at: http://indiatoday.intoday.in/story/coleman-associates-likely-to-be-awarded-contract-for-mining-rajasthans-barsingar-mine/1/303894.html (Accessed on 30 December 2016).
17. T Ramakrishnan. 'Will Jayamkondam Project See the Light of the Day?' *The Hindu*, Chennai, 24 January 2013. Available at: http://www.thehindu.com/news/national/tamil-nadu/will-jayamkondam-project-see-the-light-of-the-day/article4336976.ece (Accessed on 30 December 2016).
18. *Tharawat Magazine*. 'RPG Group: An Indian Family Business of 50,000 Employees'. *Tharawat Magazine*, 1 July 2010. Available at: http://www.tharawat-magazine.com/family-business-succession/rama-prasad-goenka-group-india-rpg/#gs.kmMjvf4 (Accessed on 30 December 2016).
19. *The Telegraph*. 'Takeover Ace Who Bet on Bengal'. *The Telegraph*, 15 April 2013. Available at: http://www.telegraphindia.com/1130415/jsp/frontpage/story_16786958.jsp#.VLp94UeUeK8 (Accessed on 30 December 2016).
20. 'CESC Investor Presentation'. October 2014. Available at: https://www.cesc.co.in/wp-content/uploads/invpresent/CESCInvestorPresentation-Oct2014.pdf (Accessed on 2 January 2017).
21. Jharkhand Finance Mischief; CAG Report, Jharkhand, 2013. Available at: http://saiindia.gov.in/english/home/Our_Products/Audit_Report/Government_Wise/

state_audit/recent_reports/Jharkhand/2013/Report_1/Chap_3.pdf & http://saiindia.gov.in/english/home/Our_Products/Audit_Report/Government_Wise/state_audit/recent_reports/Jharkhand/2014/SF/Chap_1.pdf

22. Raman Kirpal. 'Madhu Koda Connection Emerges in Coalgate Scam'. *Firstpost*, 6 September 2012. Available at: http://www.firstpost.com/india/madhu-koda-connection-emerges-in-coalgate-scam-446127.html (Accessed on 30 December 2016).

23. PC Parakh. *Crusader or Conspirator? Coalgate and Other Truths*. New Delhi: Manas, 2014.

24. Surjit Bhalla. 'CAG, Credit and Credibility'. *The Indian Express*, 22 August 2012. Available at: http://archive.indianexpress.com/news/cag-credit-and-credibility/991197/0 (Accessed on 30 December 2016).

25. Indira Rajaraman. *Economically Speaking*, 75. New Delhi: Academic Foundation, 2016.

26. *The Hindu*. 'Never Said "Zero Loss": Chidambaram on Coal Block Issue'. *The Hindu*, 27 August 2012. Available at: http://www.thehindu.com/news/national/never-said-zero-loss-chidambaram-on-coal-block-issue/article3827736.ece (Accessed on 30 December 2016).

27. *Zee News*. 'CAG Overstepping Its Constitutional Mandate' *Zee News*, 18 August 2012. Available at: http://zeenews.india.com/news/nation/cag-overstepping-its-constitutional-mandate-govt_794521.html (Accessed on 30 December 2016).

28. Vinayak Chatterjee. *Getting it Right: India's Unfolding Infrastructure Agenda*. New Delhi: Lucid Solutions, 2011.

29. Vinod Rai. *Not Just an Accountant: The Diary of the Nation's Conscience Keeper*. New Delhi: Rupa, September 2014.

30. 'Report No. 7 of 2012–13—Performance Audit of Allocation of Coal Blocks and Augmentation of Coal Production, Ministry of Coal'. Comptroller and Auditor General of India. Available at: http://cag.gov.in/content/report-no-7-2012-13 -%E2%80%93-performance-audit-allocation-coal-blocks-and-augmentation-coal (Accessed on 30 December 2016).

31. 'Report of the Committee on Allocation of Natural Resources'. Cabinet Secretariat. Available at: http://www.cuts-ccier.org/pdf/Report_of_the_Committee_on_Allocation_of_Natural_Resources.pdf (Accessed on 30 December 2016).

32. The minutes of the 36th meeting of the screening committee. Available at: http://coal.nic.in/sites/upload_files/coal/files/coalupload/minutes040908.pdf (Accessed on 6 February 2017).

33. *The Hindu*. 'CBI Registers 39th Case in Coal Scam'. *The Hindu*, 19 March 2015. Available at: http://www.thehindu.com/news/national/cbi-registers-39th-case-in-coal-scam/article7011391.ece (Accessed on 30 December 2016).

34. *The Times of India*. 'Coal Scam: ED Attaches Assets Worth Rs 186cr of Hyderabad Firm'. *The Times of India*, 23 July 2014. Available at: http://timesofindia.indiatimes.com/india/Coal-scam-ED-attaches-assets-worth-Rs-186cr-of-Hyderabad-firm/articleshow/38921446.cms (Accessed on 30 December 2016).

35. Milan Vaishnav and Saksham Khosla. 'The Indian Administrative Service Meets Big Data'. *Carnegie Endowment for International Peace*, 1 September 2016. Available at: http://carnegieendowment.org/2016/09/01/indian-administrative-service-meets-big-data-pub-64457 (Accessed on 21 February 2017).

Chapter 6

1. 'Partha S Bhattacharya'. Bio. Available at: http://www.dpemou.nic.in/ MOUFiles/TFBiodata2013-14/TF%20Power13-14%5CP%20S%20Bhattacharya. pdf (Accessed on 30 December 2016).
2. Coal India Limited. 'Co-creating Value for the Nation'. Annual Report & Accounts 2013–14. Available at: https://www.coalindia.in/DesktopModules/ DocumentList/documents/Coal_India_AR_2013_-_14_Deluxe_final_23092014. pdf (Accessed on 2 January 2017).
3. Mihir Sharma. *Restart: The Last Chance for the Indian Economy*. New Delhi: Random House, 2015.
4. 'Tara Prasad Singh Etc. Etc vs Union of India & Others on 7 May 1980'. Supreme Court of India. Available at: https://indiankanoon.org/doc/1628280/ (Accessed on 6 February 2017).
5. Pratim Ranjan Bose. 'Coal India will Switch to New Pricing Mechanism from Jan'. *The Hindu*, 25 December 2010. Available at: http://www.thehindubusinessline.com/companies/coal-india-will-switch-to-new-pricing-mechanism-from-jan/article2747188.ece (Accessed on 30 December 2016).
6. *The Times of India*. 'CIL Chief Suspended on Graft Charges'. *The Times of India*, 6 June 2003. Available at: http://timesofindia.indiatimes.com/city/kolkata/CIL-chief-suspended-on-graft-charges/articleshow/8825.cms (Accessed on 30 December 2016).
7. *India Today Online*. 'Coal Scam: Former Coal India Chairman Shashi Kumar Backs Parakh, Says Coal Mafia Does Exist in Ministry'. *India Today Online*, New Delhi, 28 October 2013. Available at: http://indiatoday.intoday.in/story/ coal-scam-coal-mafia-does-exist-coal-india-chairman-shashi-kumar/1/320657. html (Accessed on 30 December 2016).
8. Singh, Sudheer Pal. 'CIL Inflated Productivity, Says Draft CAG Report'. *Business Standard*, 11 April 2012. Available at: http://www.business-standard. com/article/economy-policy/cil-inflated-productivity-says-draft-cag-report-112041102013_1.html (Accessed on 30 December 2016).
9. Sukhtankar Sandip and Milan Vaishnav. 'Corruption in India: Bridging Research Evidence and Policy Options'. In *India Policy Forum*, vol. 11. New Delhi: SAGE Publications, 2014.
10. Jaithirth (Jerry) Rao. *Notes from an Indian Conservative*, 244. New Delhi: Rupa, 2010.
11. Ninan, TN. *The Turn of the Tortoise: The Challenge and Promise of India's Future*. New Delhi: Penguin, October 2015.
12. Saurabh Chaturved. 'U.K. Fund Exits Coal India'. *The Wall Street Journal* (15 October 2014). Available at: http://www.wsj.com/articles/childrens-investment-fund-management-sells-coal-india-stake-1413382522 (Accessed on 30 December 2016).
13. *Business Standard*. 'Model Pact for Developing CIL Mines under PPP in Final Stage'. *Business Standard*, 12 September 2014. Available at: http://www.business-standard.com/article/pti-stories/model-pact-for-developing-cil-mines-under-ppp-in-final-stage-114091201061_1.html (Accessed on 30 December 2016).
14. Money Control. 'Coal India Workers' Strike on Sept 2 Seen to have Limited Impact'. Money Control, 26 August 2016. Available at: http://www.moneycontrol.com/news/business/coal-india-workers-strikesept-2-seen-to-have-limited-impact_7346821.html (Accessed on 30 December 2016).

15. Krishna N Das. 'India's Coal Efficiency Drive Risks Ire of Powerful Unions'. Reuters, 3 May 2016. Available at: http://reut.rs/1TsDnN7 (Accessed on 30 December 2016).
16. The World Bank Group. 'Implementation Completion Report (ICR) Review—Coal Sector Rehabilitation Project'. 2012. Available at: http://projects.worldbank.org/ P009979/coal-sector-rehabilitation-project?lang=en (Accessed on 6 February 2017).
17. A M Shah, and *Cornerstone*. 'Navigating India's Coal Maze'. World Coal Association, 1 April 2015. (Originally published in *Cornerstone* 3, no. 1). Available at: http://www. worldcoal.org/navigating-indias-coal-maze (Accessed on 30 December 2016).

Chapter 7

1. Nitin Sethi. 'Green Nod to be Transferred to Allottees in Coal Block Auction'. *Business Standard*, New Delhi, 29 October 2014. Available at: http://www.business-standard.com/article/economy-policy/green-nod-to-be-transferred-to-allottees-in-coal-block-auction-114102900011_1.html (Accessed on 2 January 2017).
2. Subhomoy Bhattacharjee. 'Lehman and the Fear of Buying'. In *Surviving the Storm: India and the Global Financial Crisis*, edited by Dhiraj Nayyar, 116. New Delhi: Portfolio Penguin, 2010. [Also published in *The Indian Express*.]
3. Sanjay Dutta. 'We Got Honest Value of Coal through Auctions, Says Piyush Goyal'. *The Times of India*, 18 May 2015. Available at: http://timesofindia. indiatimes.com/ business/india-business/We-got-honest-value-of-coal-through-auctions-says-Piyush-Goyal/articleshow/47322786.cms (Accessed on 2 January 2017).
4. 'Re-Allotment of 67 Coal Mines through Auction & Allotment; Estimated Revenue of Rs 3,35,370 Crore Likely to be Generated'. Press Information Bureau. Available at: http://pib.nic.in/newsite/erelease.aspx?relid=118567 (Accessed on 2 January 2017).
5. 'State-wise Details of 29 Coal Mines Auctioned so far Along-with Specified End-uses and Estimated Revenue Which Would Accrue to Coal Bearing State During the Life of Mine/Lease Period'. Press Information Bureau. Available at: http:// pib.nic.in/newsite/erelease.aspx?relid=118566 (Accessed on 2 January 2017).
6. 'CIL Achieves 435.84 MTs Coal Production During 2011–12, Targets 470 MTs for 2012'. Press Information Bureau. Available at: http://pib.nic.in/newsite/ erelease.aspx?relid=82067 (Accessed on 2 January 2017).
7. Bombay Stock Exchange. 'The Numbers that Shook the Market—Jaypee Results'. Available at: http://www.bseindia.com/corporates/anndet_new. aspx?newsid=f7784467-af3f-44c6-96f5-04a9bffc6d10 (Accessed on 2 January 2017).
8. *The Economic Times*. 'IDBI Bank Transfers Dabhol NPA to SASF'. *The Economic Times*, 1 October 2004. Available at: http://articles.economictimes.indiatimes. com/2004-10-01/news/27375728_1_idbi-bank-npas-india-ltd (Accessed on 2 January 2017).
9. 'S H Khan—Soft Voice, Hard Talk'. The World of Urdu, 15 January 2016. Available at: http://urdufigures.blogspot.in/2016/01/s-h-khan-soft-voice-hard-talk.html (Accessed on 2 January 2017).
10. Swaminathan S. Anklesaria Aiyar. 'You Could Not Take India for a Ride, Rebecca Mark.' Swaminomics by Swaminathan S Anklesaria Aiyar, 16 February

2002. Available at: http://swaminomics.org/you-could-not-take-india-for-a-ride-rebecca-mark/ (Accessed on 2 January 2017).

11. Carleen Hawn. 'The Women of Enron: A Separate Peace'. Fast Company, 1 September 2003. Available at: http://www.fastcompany.com/47280/women-enron-separate-peace (Accessed on 2 January 2017).

12. Yashwant Sinha. *Confessions of a Swadeshi Reformer: My Years as Finance Minister*, 45. New Delhi: Penguin, 2007.

13. 'Montek Singh Ahluwalia as FS', Signposts. *India Today*, 15 April 1993. Available at: http://indiatoday.intoday.in/story/montek-singh-ahluwalia-appointed-as-finance-secretary/1/302049.html (Accessed on 2 January 2017).

14. Suresh Prabhu. 'From Investor's Darling, the Power Sector has Again Become a Pariah'. *The Economic Times*, 13 August 2013. Available at: http://articles.economictimes.indiatimes.com/2013-08-13/news/41375214_1_power-sector-distribution-sector-power-generation (Accessed on 2 January 2017).

15. 'Budget 1994–95 Speech of Shri Manmohan Singh', para 26. Ministry of Finance. 28 February 1994. Available at: http://indiabudget.nic.in/bspeech/bs199495.pdf (Accessed on 2 January 2017).

16. Gur Kirpal Singh Ashk. 'PSEB "Over-burdened" with 15,000 Employees'. *The Times of India*, 27 May 2003. Available at: http://timesofindia.indiatimes.com/city/chandigarh/PSEB-over-burdened-with-15000-employees/articleshow/47600253.cms (Accessed on 2 January 2017).

17. Mohua Mukherjee. *See Private Participation in the Indian Power Sector: Lessons from Two Decades of Experience*. World Bank Publications, October 2014.

18. *The Hindu*. IDFC to Increase Provisioning for Exposures'. *The Hindu*, 4 May 2015. Available at: http://www.thehindu.com/business/Industry/idfc-to-increase-provisioning-for-exposures/article7170694.ece (Accessed on 2 January 2017).

19. Sanjay Jog. 'It's Time to Look Up after Three Years of Nightmare: Sushil Maroo'. Interview with Executive Vice-chairman, Essar Power. *Business Standard*, 26 April 2016. Available at: http://www.business-standard.com/article/companies/it-s-time-to-look-up-after-three-years-of-nightmare-sushil-maroo-116042500347_1.html (Accessed on 2 January 2017).

20. Arun S. 'To Check for Potential NPAs, RBI Orders Audit of Allahabad Bank'. *The Financial Express*, 13 December 2013. Available at: http://archive.financialexpress.com/news/to-check-for-potential-npas-rbi-orders-audit-of-allahabad-bank/1207010 (Accessed on 2 January 2017).

21. 'Land Acq. Under CBA Act 1957'. Ministry of Coal. Available at: http://coal.nic.in/content/land-acq-under-cba-act-1957 (Accessed on 2 January 2017).

22. Indira Rajaraman. *Economically Speaking*, 203. New Delhi: Academic Foundation, 2016.

23. Subhomoy Bhattacharjee, Rita Sinha and Kaushik Dutta. *Fair Pricing of Land and its Compensation in an Emerging Economy: Case for India*. Available at: http://tari.co.in/wp-content/uploads/2014/02/land-acquisition-web-pdf-final-printed-report.pdf (Accessed on 2 January 2017).

24. Amitendu Palit and Subhomoy Bhattacharjee. *SEZs in India*. New Delhi: Anthem Press, 2008.

25. Subhomoy Bhattacharjee. 'Singur Verdict not to Affect Acquisitions for Public Purposes'. *Business Standard*, 1 September 2016. Available at: http://www.business-standard.com/article/current-affairs/singur-verdict-not-to-affect-acquisitions-for-public-purposes-116090101524_1.html (Accessed on 2 January 2017).

26. ET Bureau. 'Bhushan Steel's Bengal Plant Lands in Acquisition Trouble'. *The Economic Times*, 3 January 2012. Available at: http://articles.economictimes. indiatimes.com/2012-01-03/news/30584828_1_greenfield-steel-plant-secondary-steel-products-nippon-steel (Accessed on 2 January 2017).

Chapter 8

1. 'Statement by Prime Minister at COP 21 Plenary Paris, 30 November 2015'. Press Information Bureau, 1 December 2015. Available at: http://www.pib.gov. in/newsite/PrintRelease.aspx?relid=132123 (Accessed on 2 January 2017).
2. Coral Davenport. 'Nations Approve Landmark Climate Accord in Paris'. *The New York Times*, 12 December 2015. Available at: http://www.nytimes. com/2015/12/13/world/europe/climate-change-accord-paris.html?_r=1 (Accessed on 2 January 2017).
3. G Ananthakrishnan. 'Kerry Finds India "Positive" at Paris Climate Conference'. *The Hindu*, 9 December 2015. Available at: http://www.thehindu.com/sci-tech/ energy-and-environment/cop21-kerry-finds-india-positive-at-paris-climate-conference/article7962418.ece (Accessed on 2 January 2017).
4. *Business Standard*. 'Heat's Here to Stay'. *Business Standard* Editorial Comment, 8 June 2015. Available at: http://www.business-standard.com/article/opinion/ heat-s-here-to-stay-115060801243_1.html (Accessed on 2 January 2017).
5. Greenpeace Campaigner Demands explanation on Alleged "Lookout Circular" Against Her, letter dated 12 January 2015 to MHA.
6. TN Ninan. *The Turn of the Tortoise: The Challenge and Promise of India's Future*. New Delhi: Penguin, October 2015.
7. India Energy Outlook http://www.worldenergyoutlook.org/media/weowebsite/2015/IndiaEnergyOutlook_WEO2015.pdf
8. Nick Cunningham. 'The Decline of the Coal Industry is "Long-term" and "Irreversible"'. OilPrice.com, 18 February 2016. Available at: http://oilprice. com/Energy/Coal/The-Decline-Of-The-Coal-Industry-Is-Long-Term-And-Irreversible.html (Accessed on 2 January 2017).
9. Mikael Holter. 'Norway's $860 Billion Fund Drops 52 Companies Linked to Coal'. Bloomberg, 14 April 2016. Available at: http://www.bloomberg.com/ news/articles/2016-04-14/norway-s-860-billion-fund-drops-52-companies-linked-to-coal (Accessed on 2 January 2017).
10. Kaavya Chandrasekaran. 'US to Help India Meet Climate Goals with Coal: Elizabeth Sherwood-Randall'. *The Economic Times*, 1 September 2016. Available at: http://economictimes.indiatimes.com/articleshow/53953913.cms?utm_ source=contentofinterest&utm_medium=text&utm_campaign=cppst (Accessed on 2 January 2017).
11. Rahul Tongia. 'Report: Brookings India Roundtable on "Future of Coal—2020"'. Brookings India, 24 February 2016. Available at: http://www.brookings.in/ report-brookings-india-roundtable-on-future-of-coal-2020-11-02-2016/ (Accessed on 2 January 2017).
12. 'Nehru on Oil'. *The Economic Weekly*, 15 June 1957. Available at: http://www.epw. in/system/files/pdf/1957_9/24/nehru_on_oil.pdf (Accessed on 2 January 2017).

13. Sam Witte. *Gamal Abdel Nasser*, 44. The Rosen Publishing Group, 2004.
14. Fog of War: The Second World War and the Civil Rights Movement; Kevin M Kruse, Stephen Tuck, Oxford University Press, March 2011.
15. Constantino Xavier. 'India's Strategic Advantage over China in Africa'. IDSA Comment, 30 June 2010. Available at: http://www.idsa.in/idsacomments/ IndiasstrategicadvantageoverChinainAfrica_cxavier_300610#footnoteref15_0 qn8of9 (Accessed on 2 January 2017).
16. Sachin Chaturvedi. *The Logic of Sharing: Indian Approach to South–South Cooperation*. New Delhi: Cambridge University Press, 2016.
17. 'Mozambique: No Money for Moatize–Macuse Railway'. All Africa, 17 April 2015. Available at: http://allafrica.com/stories/201504180073.html (Accessed on 2 January 2017).
18. Ravi Velloor. *India Rising*. New Delhi: Konark Publishers, 2016.
19. Bibek Debroy, Ashley J Tellis and Reece Trevor. *Getting India Back on Track: An Action Agenda for Reform*. New Delhi: Random House India, June 2014.
20. Dennis Rumley and Sanjay Chaturvedi. *Energy Security and the Indian Ocean Region*. New Delhi: Routledge, July 2015.
21. *Hindustan Times*. 'China Spy Ship "Shadows" Indian, US, Japanese Naval Drill: 5 Things to Know'. *Hindustan Times*, Tokyo, 15 June 2016. Available at: http:// www.hindustantimes.com/world-news/china-spy-ship-shadows-indian-us-japanese-naval-drill-5-things-to-know/story-p3wLgshsNyZSAfaz2EDmFK. html?google_editors_picks=true (Accessed on 2 January 2017).
22. Yang Dali and Zhao Hong. 'The Rise of India: China's Perspectives and Response'. In *Socio-political and Economic Challenges in South Asia*, edited by Tan Tai Yong. New Delhi: SAGE Publications, 2009.
23. C Raja Mohan and Lydia Powell. 'Energy Rivalry Between India and China: Less than Meets the Eye?' in *The New Politics of Strategic Resources: Energy and Food Security Challenges in the 21st Century*, edited by David Steven, Emily O'Brien, and Bruce D. Jones. Washington, DC: Brookings Institution Press, November 2014.
24. Pramit Pal Chaudhuri. 'Making Waves in Indian Ocean: Modi Building Bridges to Island States'. *Hindustan Times*, 15 March 2015. Available at: http://www.hindustan-times.com/india/making-waves-in-indian-ocean-modi-building-bridges-to-island-states/story-kPGjODlHJO2vlwgaaGhEdL.html (Accessed on 2 January 2017).
25. Shyam Saran. 'A Lopsided Strategic Partnership'. *Business Standard*, 14 April 2016. Available at: http://www.business-standard.com/article/opinion/shyam-saran-a-lopsided-strategic-partnership-116041400917_1.html (Accessed on 2 January 2017).
26. Daniel Yergin. *The Prize*. London: Simon & Shuster, 1991.
27. Sandeep Unnithan. 'While Beijing Builds in South China Sea, India Dithers over its Own'. DailyO, 7 July 2016. Available at: http://www.dailyo.in/politics/south-china-sea-india-neglecting-island-territories-andaman-navy-lakshadweep-malacca/story/1/11910.html (Accessed on 2 January 2017).
28. Anita Inder Singh. 'Modi Trips Mark Sea Change in India's Foreign Policy'. *Nikkei Asian Review*, 30 March 2015. Available at: http://asia.nikkei.com/ Viewpoints/Perspectives/Modi-trips-mark-sea-change-in-India-s-foreign-policy (Accessed on 2 January 2017).
29. *The Times of India*. 'India Seeks to be Maritime, International Trade Power: President Pranab Mukherjee'. *The Times of India*, 27 February 2016. Available at: http://timesofindia.indiatimes.com/india/India-seeks-to-be-maritime-international-trade-power-President-Pranab-Mukherjee/articleshow/51166610. cms?from=mdr (Accessed on 2 January 2017).

30. 'Remarks by Prime Minister at Chabahar Connectivity Event (May 23, 2016)'. Press Information Bureau. Available at: http://pib.nic.in/newsite/PrintRelease. aspx?relid=145573 (Accessed on 2 January 2017).
31. Abu Bakar Siddique. 'Chinese-backed Power Plant Endangers Hilsa Sanctuary in Bangladesh'. The Quint, 30 August 2016. Available at: https://www.thequint. com/environment/2016/08/30/chinese-backed-power-plant-endangers-hilsa-sanctuary-in-bangladesh (Accessed on 2 January 2017).

Chapter 9

1. International Monetary Fund. 'Commodity Special Feature from World Economic Outlook'. April 2016. Available at: http://www.imf.org/external/ pubs/ft/weo/2016/01/pdf/SF_Commod.pdf (Accessed on 2 January 2017).
2. Qi Ye and Jiaqi Lu. 'The End of Coal-fired Growth in China'. Brookings, 4 August 2016. Available at: https://www.brookings.edu/blog/up-front/2016/08/04/the-end-of-coal-fired-growth-in-china/ (Accessed on 2 January 2017).
3. Rajiv Kumar. 'The Environment: Optimise Utilisation of Coal Reserves'. *Business Today*, 17 January 2016. Available at: http://www.businesstoday.in/ magazine/cover-story/the-environment-optimise-utilisation-of-coal-reserves/ story/227526.html (Accessed on 2 January 2017).
4. 'Renewable Energy and Jobs: Annual Review 2016'. International Renewable Energy Agency. Available at: http://www.se4all.org/sites/default/files/IRENA_ RE_Jobs_Annual_Review_2016.pdf (Accessed on 2 January 2017).
5. '*Rozgaar Mele ke Naam par Berozgaron se Thuggi* [Looting the Unemployed by Offers of Employment].' *Rajasthan Patrika*, 26 August 2011. Available at: http:// www.patrika.com/news/singrauli/employment-fair-of-the-unemployed-in-the-name-of-swindle-1373400/ (Accessed on 2 January 2017).
6. Amrit Amirapu and Arvind Subramanian. 'Manufacturing Futures: For India, Reversing the Process of De-industrialisation will be Hard'. *Business Standard*, 9 May 2014. Available at: http://www.business-standard.com/article/opinion/ amrit-amirapu-arvind-subramanian-manufacturing-futures-114050901478_1. html (Accessed on 2 January 2017).
7. Subhomoy Bhattacharjee. 'Cargo Supremacy: Jury Still out on Roads vs Railways'. *Business Standard*, 6 September 2016. Available at: http://www. business-standard.com/article/economy-policy/cargo-supremacy-jury-still-out-on-roads-vs-railways-116090600023_1.html (Accessed on 2 January 2017).
8. Ian Urbina. 'Piles of Dirty Secrets behind a Model "Clean Coal" Project'. *The New York Times*, 5 July 2016. Available at: http://www.nytimes.com/2016/07/05/science/ kemper-coal-mississippi.html?smid=tw-share&_r=0 (Accessed on 2 January 2017).
9. Chisaki Watanabe. 'Want to Burn Coal and Save the Planet? Japan Touts a Solution'. Bloomberg, 10 November 2015. Available at: http://www.bloomberg. com/news/articles/2015-11-10/want-to-burn-coal-and-save-the-planet-japan-touts-a-solution (Accessed on 2 January 2017).
10. Piyush Goyal. 'Coal to Remain Important Mainstay Fuel for India and Japan's Energy Plans'. Sector Update, Confederation of Indian Industry, 29 April 2015.

Index

About the Author

Subhomoy Bhattacharjee, with twenty-two years of experience in journalism, is a Consulting Editor for *Business Standard*. His areas of interest include public policy, especially regulatory issues, finance and urban development.

He is the author of *Special Economic Zones (SEZ) in India: Myths and Realities*. He has authored a study on the Land Acquisition Act, a project on comparative land prices in India's selected districts and its relation with industrialisation, commissioned by GIZ, India, and TARI. He has previously contributed to other books, including *Media at Work in China and India: Discovering and Dissecting* (SAGE, 2015).

Subhomoy studied economics at Shri Ram College of Commerce and at Delhi School of Economics, both affiliated to the University of Delhi. He began his career as a civil servant, joining the Indian Information Service through the civil services exam. He has subsequently worked with *The Economic Times* and was until recently the deputy editor at *The Indian Express* while writing for *The Financial Express* too.

Presently, he is also a consultant with Research and Information Systems for Developing Countries (RIS). He frequently appears on television and radio on economic news programmes and has lectured in several universities in India and abroad, on public policy.